MV

THE RISING TIDE

THE

Volume Six of a Series
on the Historic Birthplace of California

THE HISTORY OF SAN DIEGO

RISING TIDE

Written by
RICHARD F. POURADE

EDITOR EMERITUS, THE SAN DIEGO UNION

Commissioned By
JAMES S. COPLEY

CHAIRMAN OF THE CORPORATION, THE COPLEY PRESS, INC.

PUBLISHED BY THE UNION-TRIBUNE PUBLISHING COMPANY

PREVIOUS BOOKS

The Explorers, 1960
Time of the Bells, 1961
The Silver Dons, 1963
The Glory Years, 1964
Gold in the Sun, 1965

CONTENTS

PAINTINGS

Water symbols adapted from the sculpturing of Donal Hord

DEDICATION

In contemplation of a title for this, the sixth volume in the History of San Diego, it would seem appropriate that we summarize the twenty years, 1920 to 1940, that were the threshold to metropolitan greatness.

How appropriate then to look to Shakespeare, who wrote for all peoples for all times, to find the quotation from Brutus in the play *Julius Caesar* . . . *"There is a tide in the affairs of men, which, taken at the flood, leads on to fortune."*

And so we have seen *The Rising Tide* for San Diego. Now it is up to the present generation and those to come to sail with the tide that "leads on to fortune."

JAMES S. COPLEY

The California poet Joaquin Miller once exclaimed, "Arid America, we have
watered it with our tears."
Even in semi-arid coastal Southern California the early settlers soon learned
there was not enough available water. Its rivers were short, and the water
collected by a thousand tiny streams, from light and infrequent rainfall, quickly
ran down the mountain canyons, and spreading out through broad valley flood
plains, was soon lost into the sea.
Even if all the water could be captured and stored, there still would not be
enough water for all the people who wanted to live in Southern California.
How Southern California reached across the mountains to assure the survival
of its agriculture and its towns, is a story sometimes watered with tears
and other times enriched with foresight and enterprise.

INTRODUCTION

Flying across the country at great height unfolds in a few hours the westward movement of a century and a half.

This story of unparalleled migration, and of Spanish discovery and exploration which preceded it, has been told in a series of books of which this is the sixth, from the perspective of one area and one city.

Eight years have gone into research, and all that has been written comes to mind as the plane follows the sun across the continent.

In view below is the Missouri River. To the Mountain Men who first opened the West, God held no man accountable after he crossed the Missouri.

Over Oklahoma, to the right, is the Cimarron River where the great trail blazer Jedediah Smith, who walked into the Spanish-Mexican settlement of San Diego in the 1820's, finally was lanced to death by the Comanches.

Over New Mexico you can see the town of Santa Fe. The story of the Southwest begins here. It was from Santa Fe that the fur-trapping Patties, father and son, left on a journey that led down the Gila River in Arizona and into Lower California, and thence up to San Diego. The father lies buried under the grass somewhere on Presidio Hill.

Not long after a caravan trade route was opened from New Mexico to Southern California. This was the Old Spanish Trail.

From the sky the eye can follow it only dimly across the American Desert.

After the traders came the Army of the West and the Mormon Battalion. They made a wagon road of sections of the Gila Trail first followed by the Patties. California became part of the United States, and the tide of migration began to flow.

Coming into view now is the Colorado River. To the south is the site of Fort Yuma where the Butterfield Overland stages made the crossing and linked the East and the West with a transportation system.

On the horizon are the mountains and the railroad passes which decided whether one city in Southern California was to be greater than another.

It was the Colorado River, though, that decided whether many of these cities were to live. The lifting of its water over the mountains to the coastal plain is an epic of the conquest of nature.

Beyond the Coastal Mountains the towns of the West Coast begin to appear in the haze of the late California afternoon. They lived because of water from the Colorado River, or from other sources equally distant.

The rush of settlers to Southern California in the 1920's quickly exhausted many local sources of water; the approach of World War II made it a race to bring the supply of water in balance with the continuing rise in the tide of population.

This book, then, primarily must be a story of water, and of a city that almost didn't live. It did survive. How it surmounted its own indecisions to become a metropolitan center is a chapter in a story, however, that must be left suspended in time, as Southern California's change is constant and dramatic.

Richard F. Pourade

CHAPTER ONE

*Life was easy in coastal Southern California at the beginning of the 1920's.
Ocean tides exposed miles of inviting beaches or dashed against scenic cliffs
of a softly curving coastline.
Towns still were trying to make up their minds whether they wanted factories
or recreation. As many of their residents were retired people, existing on
pensions or limited investments, or who had fled from congested cities and
cold climates, appeals for industrial growth met with resistance.
Many of those who had come early saw no virtue in encouraging the rising tide
of eager immigrants.*

ENVY OF CITIES

In the days of the great cattle ranches Los Angeles County had been referred to derisively by northern Californians as the queen of the "cow counties." By 1920, however, the City of Los Angeles had surpassed San Francisco as the most populous city in California.

From the lordly hills on its narrow peninsula, San Francisco had watched with unconcern the successful efforts of Los Angeles to obtain the industry, shipping, railroads and highways that would bring the people to buy the land which stretched level and inviting for miles in all directions.

This had not been so with the City of San Diego, still a branch line town lying between the mountains and the sea near the southern end of the state. Many if its citizens had persisted in challenging the economic domination of its rival 135 miles to the north, even though they long since had lost the race to become the principal Southern California terminus of the transcontinental railroads. They were not sure how it had happened, but they were not ready yet to concede the greater glory of Los Angeles.

When the results of the federal census of 1920 were announced, *The San Diego Union* in an editorial consoled its readers as follows:

The citizens of Los Angeles have been waiting and scheming many years for this triumph. They have lain awake nights devising methods for the accomplishment of their object. Now that they achieved their goal, their exaltations will echo in a paean of joy to be heard around the world.

The San Diego Union was certain that San Francisco would dismiss Los Angeles as a sprawling aggregation of immigrants from other states who could not make good in the northern city. San Diego had "other fish to fry in the Los Angeles pan" and the editorial reflected the confidence of the city in the possibilities of its harbor:

> In the meantime we are building a great seaport with which Los Angeles will have no rivalry, because it is utterly impossible for Los Angeles to have any kind of a seaport . . . Los Angeles cannot beat San Diego by annexing the lagoon port of San Pedro.

San Diego had one of the world's finest landlocked harbors and it was the first port of call on the Pacific Coast of the United States for steamers northbound from the Panama Canal. One of its most energetic citizens, and one of California's wealthiest men, John D. Spreckels, almost single-handed had driven a railroad line across a mountain barrier to tie into the Southern Pacific's main line running from New Orleans to Los Angeles. Hopefully, it would provide access to the great railroad junction at El Paso.

Other citizens had carved out a road down the steep and dry side of the same barrier to meet or tap transcontinental highways then in a state of planning and development.

They had been told they lived in one of the most favored spots of the earth. It was never too hot in summer and never too cold in winter, with a fresh wind blowing off the sea during the day and a soft breeze blowing off the land at night. The federal government had recognized the unique geographical and climatic position of San Diego and was converting its bay front lands into military establishments where training on the sea and land, and in the air, could be undertaken the year around.

Most of the nation had been made aware of San Diego by the Panama-California Exposition of 1915 and 1916 which, though on a much smaller scale than the international fair in San Francisco which celebrated the completion of the Panama Canal, had been a thing of beauty and charm that even the most casual visitor never forgot.

Real estate promoters had no doubt but that there was enough land, fronting on the bright bay, and on the high, broad mesas and in the warmer interior valleys, to support at the very least a million persons. Before full advantage could be realized from the favorable publicity resulting from the exposition, World War I had intervened. By 1920 the memory of the war was fading fast and a nation was being put on wheels and on the move.

By the 1920's San Diego had lost out to Los Angeles in a competition to become
the trading and commercial center of Southern California.
But as long as San Diego had its natural harbor, one of the world's finest, its
business leaders and real estate developers never gave up hope.
This photograph shows San Diego's Broadway, as it was to appear until the
town was caught in the Boom of the Twenties, which dramatically changed
all of Southern California.

*When this photograph was taken Los Angeles had overtaken and passed
San Francisco as the most populous city in California.
The scene is at Broadway and Seventh Street, looking south. The decorations
were for a Shrine Convention.
At this time Los Angeles, an inland city open to railroad passes, was
developing its own harbor and reaching also for the ocean traffic that had
made San Francisco for so long the queen of the Pacific Coast.*

Though more people still lived in northern California than in Southern California, a trend had set in that never was to be reversed. In ten years from 1910 to 1920, the population of Los Angeles had increased from about 319,000 to 576,000. Los Angeles advertised itself as the "City of Destiny."

San Diego had shared in the disproportionate growth of Southern California, more than doubling its population in ten years. The actual figures, however, told a different story. In a century and a half since its founding, as the birthplace of Christian civilization on the Pacific Coast, it had been left a city of only 74,683. In the decade that saw Los Angeles surpass San Francisco, San Diego had added just 35,105 new residents.

All of the people residing in San Diego did not share the enthusiasm for growth. Many of them had fled congested eastern cities and the rigors of the Midwest to seek retirement in a mild climate or to obtain work which would not interfere too much with the enjoyment of sun and water. They grew geraniums and oranges and lemons and were content. They could stroll down Broadway and meet somebody they knew in every block. If they wanted to climb mountains or see snow once again, they had only to travel sixty miles to reach an elevation of 5000 feet. If they wanted heat, there were the interior valleys and the desert.

People lived longer in San Diego, too, though there were those unkind enough to say that it just seemed longer. The death rate per 100,000 was 11.5 in San Diego, 13.7 in New York, 16.4 in Kansas City, and 19.9 in New Orleans. In the rival Pacific Coast cities, the rate was 15.2 in San Francisco and 12.5 in Los Angeles.

It was true with San Diego, however, as with other Western towns, that much of their swelling populations had come not as settlers but as promoters and speculators in the quest of quick wealth. The fever that had risen in Southern California in the late 1880's persisted through depression and war.

Whether industry followed population, or people followed industry, had never been answered satisfactorily. It was not clear, either, just what San Diego expected in the way of industrial development. The end of the war had brought economic dislocations, in part because of the closing of two large plants which processed kelp for potash to be used in the manufacturing of explosives. After the war, efforts to develop kelp by-products had not been too successful and the kelp industry had faded away. A federally subsidized shipyard had turned out two concrete ships. A munitions plant barely survived the war and a struggling tire company, which had been established by Arthur W. Savage in 1912, was taken over by John D .Spreckels.

A thriving packing industry, in agricultural as well as fish products, which reflected the semi-tropical nature of the land and the rich possibilities of the sea, was almost ignored in the economic calculations for the future. In 1919 local canneries packed 60,000 cases of olives, 10,000 cases of olive oil, 250,000 cases of tuna, 150,000 cases of sardines, 15,000 cases of turtle meat, 70,000 cases of fruits and vegetables and 26,000 cases of tomatoes.

In the county there were almost a million bearing trees with products valued at more than $3,000,000 a year. The annual lemon crop alone was valued at nearly $2,000,000. Almost all fruits grew well, and avocado production was getting a start. However, cattle, which once had been the only source of wealth in San Diego County as well as most of Southern California, had been driven into mountain ranges and no longer were considered an important source of income.

Though four coastal steamship lines called regularly at San Diego, as well as many tramp steamers, trade was largely in local products. The goods of the world were not moving back and forth across the town's waterfront, as they had for so many decades through San Francisco and now were doing through Los Angeles. If its commercial potentials had not been fully realized as yet, the port certainly was becoming important to the entire country. Federal investments in military establishments on the bay were ap-

Fishing was a principal industry in a San Diego that had lived by the sea for a century and a half.
Here fishing boats cluster around a pier near the foot of Elm Street. As can be seen, some of the smaller fishing boats still had sails instead of gasoline engines. Canned white meat of the albacore tuna had become popular and each summer fishermen could depend on an albacore run occuring along the coast within easy cruising range.
The albacore, however, in time suddenly were to change their habits.

proaching $13,000,000, and the port was "home" to the light forces of the Navy's Pacific squadrons.

If San Diego couldn't attract industry and commerce, without first having more population or developing more possibilities for trade, it was convinced it had the assets to attract people. And people bought land, which was still the basic source of wealth in the West. How land could be made to produce, not crops, but cash, occupied the attention of its business leaders. In this they were not any different from the others in Southern California who already were experiencing and profiting by the first impact of a new migration unparalleled in the country's history.

The San Diego-California Club, the first of the nation's booster organizations, had been formed in 1919. It was a matter of debate for awhile whether San Diego should appeal directly to people residing in the Midwest, who had prospered during the war, or concentrate at a lower cost on trying to lure to San Diego new residents who already had been attracted to Los Angeles. San Diego decided that at the time it was no match for Los Angeles, with its economic opportunities, and instead, was to place most of its community advertising in the states east of the Rocky Mountains. Oscar W. Cotton, secretary of the San Diego-California Club, stated the case for San Diego at a public meeting:

Shall we invite laborers? Shall we tell carpenters and plumbers and other skilled artisans we have jobs for them?

Shall we urge businessmen who want a start to come and open more grocery stores, drugstores, clothing stores, meat markets, automobile tire stores, or fifteen-cent stories?

Do we want more hotel men to build more hotels?

Yes, when we can truthfully tell them that a need for their services exists here.

To create that need, what we want first is more families to patronize the stores and hotels we now have. We want to build up a permanent, stable population of people who are going to locate somewhere, just to live, and who might just as well come here.

The big outstanding opportunity that San Diego has to offer today is the opportunity to the man who has earned his pleasure and ease. To him we offer, at minimum cost, the greatest abundance of riches, the most charming place to live of any city in the United States.

We can be honest with him, and in locating him in San Diego we are performing a service to him as great as to ourselves.

By September the San Diego-California Club reported that $150,000 had been subscribed for its campaign and by Spring of 1920 more than 30,000 replies to the advertising program had been received and 200 new families had arrived. For the summer it was decided to extend the advertising campaign into the Southwest

Plenty of Rooms — at Reasonable Rates

Almost too good to be true!

But it is more than true,—these modern and spacious quarters, at moderate rentals, in the hotels at San Diego, Southern California's beautiful seaside city,—just a little distance from Los Angeles.

We'd tell you here of the wonderfully alluring beauties and attractions that make each day at San Diego a bewilderment of happiness,—but these can wait. You will find them on every hand.

What you want to know is,—how you are going to be made comfortable,—and that is the easiest thing of all!

Through orange groves and by the sea,—a fascinating afternoon by rail, or over splendid roads—and you're at San Diego, with comfort waiting for you close to blue bay and ocean, in any of two score up-to-date and well managed apartment houses and hotels.

Remember—rates are reasonable. Get rid of all your worries and enjoy the matchless winter months at

San Diego California

This booklet tells more about it. Sign the coupon and get it free by return mail.

SAN DIEGO-CALIFORNIA CLUB,
Spreckels Building, San Diego, California.
Gentlemen:
Please send me your free booklet about San Diego, California.

Name

Address

If industry wouldn't come, maybe tourists would.
The San Diego-California Club was the first community advertising venture in the United States.
Advertisements on the attractions of San Diego and the surrounding country were placed first in publications in the Midwest and East, to lure settlers, and later in Los Angeles publications, to lure winter tourists.
Shown is a typical advertisement of 1920-1921. It was designed to show how easy it was to reach San Diego from Los Angeles, and what to see enroute.

"hot belt," Imperial Valley, Arizona, New Mexico, Nevada and Utah, to attract tourists.

A survey of real estate values was made and Cotton found them still below those of the peak of the boom of 1912, when construction work was under way for the exposition and Spreckels was erecting or preparing to erect his three large buildings on Lower Broadway. He reported:

Oscar W. Cotton

> We now have our direct eastern railroad, which makes possible the development of commercial enterprises here, manufacturing and harbor development heretofore impracticable. The city has been organized into a unit for the purpose of advertising our advantages and bringing people here from every part of the United States to share with us the delights of the most wonderful place in all outdoors in which to live and work . . .
>
> Just how long it will be before the awakening to real estate opportunities comes and the market price makes a jump to catch up and again pass the real value line, it is impossible to say. Of one thing we can be sure. Those who take advantage of the present situation, and make their investments while the prices are at low ebb, will reap deserved and noteworthy reward from their foresight.

At the close of the year, 46,151 inquiries had been received and of these 3604 families had stated they definitely were coming to San Diego. Many of them did. A housing shortage developed, the sale price of houses doubled and land values began to rise once again.

At long last John D. Spreckels saw the possibility of realizing some return on the millions of dollars of the family fortune which had been built by his father in San Francisco, in shipping and sugar, and which the son had poured into the development of San Diego.

Spreckels dominated the political and financial life of the city. His holdings included two of the city's three daily newspapers, the street car system and the San Diego and Coronado ferry company, a mercantile supply company, ranch properties, three of the largest business buildings on the town's main thoroughfare, and control of one of the principal banks.

Construction of the San Diego & Arizona Railway, in fulfillment of his convictions that San Diego was certain to become the natural trading center of the Southwest and northern Mexico, had plunged him into financial difficulties from which he had been rescued by the Southern Pacific Railroad.

His faith in San Diego, however, never wavered. Impatient at times, generous and appreciative at others, he exercised a power common to American cities before the professionalization of municipal government and the ascendancy of public policy over individual interests. He did not differ greatly from the adventurous

11

pioneers and financial plungers who a generation before him had laid the railroads across the Sierra Nevada and opened the mines and lands of California.

When pressed for money, he had sold to the city the water system on which it was so dependent and offered to rent for use as a city hall the Spreckels building which housed the ornate theater of which he was so proud. The Planning Commission rejected the offer, because, in the words of its chairman, Julius Wangenheim, as expressed in his memoirs, Spreckels already was too powerful without owning the City Hall. The mayor responded by firing the commission. The proposal, however, was forgotten.

The mayor, Louis J. Wilde, impulsive yet able politically, was a banker who had been elected on a platform of industrial development. He favored, as it were, smokestacks over geraniums. He once

In 1920 the heir to the throne of the British Empire visited San Diego
while on a goodwill tour.
He was Edward, Prince of Wales, who later was to surrender the crown
in order to marry an American divorcee.
He is shown here at Hotel del Coronado. On the right is Governor William D.
Stephens of California. On the left are Mayor and Mrs. Louis J. Wilde of
San Diego.
In the area at the same time was Wallis Warfield. She was the wife of a
junior naval officer. She and the Prince did not meet. Years later, however,
they were to be married.

walked up to a councilman in a hotel lobby and punched him on the jaw.

He looked after his own. In 1920, the Prince of Wales, who later was to abdicate the throne of the British Empire, arrived at San Diego aboard the British battleship *Renown* on a two-day goodwill visit. On April 7, he addressed a crowd of 25,000 in the city stadium and in the evening attended a ball at Hotel del Coronado. Though he was official host to the prince, the mayor presented the ball as a coming-out party for his daughter, Lucille. There were few debutantes that season who could point to such an array of guests. They included a royal prince, the governor of California and most of the high-ranking officers of the United States Pacific Fleet.

San Diego prospered during Wilde's regime, coincident perhaps with the success of the community advertising program and the general rising economic conditions throughout the state. Politically, it was the retirement from Congress of William Kettner that posed a serious problem to the city's future. Kettner had exerted considerable influence on the executive and legislative decisions in Washington, D.C., which were converting San Diego into one of the world's leading military centers. After eight years in Congress, Kettner, a conservative Democrat who also had received the support of Republicans, was tired and his insurance business had suffered by his long absence from San Diego.

The 11th congressional district which he represented embraced seven counties. Though its voice thus was a minority one, San Diego had been adroit in the manipulation of political power. From time to time Orange, Riverside and San Bernardino counties had tried to break San Diego's hold on the congressional seat. At a meeting of representatives from the three counties to choose a candidate to oppose anyone from San Diego, the delegation from Orange County in a surprise move threw its support to Phil D. Swing, of Imperial County.

Swing, a former district attorney and general counsel for the Imperial Valley Irrigation District, and a superior court judge, already had made a reputation lobbying in Washington for federal legislation on control of the Colorado River. He had learned, though, that a project of such a size, even though it might be supported by federal agencies, needed a champion within Congress.

A dam on the Colorado River was imperative for the protection of Imperial Valley, where for two decades farmers had lived under the constant threat of floods. Just as important was a new canal, to replace one that delivered Colorado River water to valley lands through Mexican territory, where it was subject to large diversions

13

*Baja California, no less than its neighboring states to the north, saw
its future in the terms of opportunity.
In this illustration for a promotional publication the key to the commerce and
development of Baja California was indicated to be San Diego, the first
port to its north.
It also showed the region near the delta of the Colorado River being opened
to agriculture, mostly with money from across the border.
This development and its need for delivered water would pit one country
against another in a struggle over the Colorado River.*

14

and the whims of foreign officials. What was needed, Swing had told any congressman who would listen, was an All-American Canal.

When Swing went on to win the support of all three of the northern counties for the Republican nomination, leaders in San Diego promptly announced the candidacy of Ed P. Sample, the state senator who had been a district attorney in Kansas before coming to San Diego in 1913. Swing was undaunted and carried his campaign to the heart of the opposition.

Business houses in Imperial Valley closed their doors while their proprietors participated in an auto caravan to San Diego to tell its people why the nomination and election of Swing, and the development of dependable sources of water, were so important not only to Imperial Valley but to all of the district.

Enthusiastic articles in the *San Diego Sun* reported that 5000 persons had driven 125 miles and the caravan passed through streets before a "cheering Swing-mad crowd, eager to do homage to San Diego's congressman." The *San Diego Sun*, owned by E. W. Scripps, the newspaper tycoon who had settled at nearby Miramar, customarily supported anything opposed by Spreckels, and the candidates it backed ranged from liberal to socialist. *The San Diego Union's* version of the Swing caravan was somewhat different. It reported the parade was a political fizzle, with 119 machines and only fifty of them from Imperial Valley.

After visiting stores in the business area, and carrying the message of Swing's candidacy, his supporters held a rally at which Swing spoke. In his memoirs, he recalls:

> I referred to the Spreckels-controlled papers, which in their efforts to minimize the popular impact of this show of strength by my supporters, said the auto-invasion was made up mostly of Fords. I told my hearers I would be happy with the support of Ford owners, and let my opponent seek the votes of the . . . Cadillac owners.

Spreckels, though dominant in the Republican organization in San Diego County, was publicly cautious in his handling of the Swing-Sample election fight. The railroad which he had sponsored at such great personal expense, the San Diego & Arizona, was the lifeline of Imperial County and it was with this line on which Spreckels had banked so much of his own future as well as that of San Diego County.

The heavy opposition to Swing came from Los Angeles, which was not even in the same congressional district. Harry Chandler's *Los Angeles Times* accused Swing of not being a true Republican

Hiram Johnson

Phil D. Swing

but a Progressive and a follower of Hiram Johnson. Chandler was a co-owner of 900,000 acres in Lower California, and Swing in his memoirs, wrote that the *Times* was bitterly opposed to the suggestion of an All-American Canal since it would deprive Chandler's lands of a guaranteed water supply to be furnished at the expense of the people of Imperial Valley.

The nomination, however, did not turn on the water issue but on the question of service in World War I. In the closing days of the war Swing had waived exemption as a public official in order to enlist. Sample, a popular legislator, had no military record and quietly retired form the campaign.

Though a substitute candidate was put forth, and court action undertaken to force his name onto the ballot, it was too late. Swing won the nomination unopposed and in the general election easily disposed of the Democratic nominee. *The San Diego Union*, in endorsing the straight Republican ticket, gave its support to Swing:

> Judge Swing is a citizen of Imperial County. San Diego and Imperial are more closely related, commercially, industrially, politically and geographically than any other two sections in the state. They are virtually one community with diverse interests, interdependent and mutually necessary to the prosperity of each county. Judge Swing would represent these interests as a single factor in all phases of their congressional requirement.

Upon taking his seat in Congress, Swing introduced legislation for construction of a dam and storage reservoir on the Colorado and an All-American Canal, and went to see Senator Hiram Johnson, the former Progressive Republican governor of California. His memoirs suggest he didn't find Johnson enthusiastic:

> When I took him a copy of my bill ... for him to introduce in the Senate, he put his arm around me in a fatherly manner and said, "Phil, you go ahead and put it through the House and when it comes over here, I will put it through the Senate."

At the driving of the golden spike marking the completion of the San Diego & Arizona Railroad in 1919, Spreckels had remarked that it was well that men could not foresee all the obstacles and difficulties lying ahead in the undertaking of great enterprises. It was just as well, too, that Swing could not foresee the long struggle ahead of him, and all the personal attacks which he would have to endure, in reaching the goal that he had set for himself, the conquest of the Colorado River.

The railroad on which Spreckels had so counted for the development of San Diego as a trading center for the Southwest, so far had proved disappointing. A winter of hard rains had caused landslides in Carrizo Gorge which resulted in a shutdown in operations for eight months. Service was resumed in November of 1920, but perishable products from the Imperial Valley were moving directly into eastern markets, by way of the Southern Pacific mainline, or for distribution markets in Los Angeles.

Regardless of the success of the community advertising, which was bringing to San Diego a flood of newcomers, the old idea that industrialization was a more certain road to prosperity did not easily die.

If industry did come, where would it settle? In 1921 the Chamber of Commerce organized a campaign to purchase 650 acres of waterfront land fronting on National City and Chula Vista. This land had been part of the holdings of a company organized by officials of the Santa Fe Railroad, when San Diego had been tentatively selected as the terminus of their transcontinental operations. San Diego had given way to Los Angeles. The land was purchased for $75,000 and deeded to the Chamber of Commerce, with subscribers to be reimbursed by future sale.

The speculative fever of the previous booms carried over into the 1920's. In Los Angeles the development of the oil industry was helping to put the nation on wheels and enticing the unwary investor. In San Diego, Mayor Wilde organized a company for another of a long series of fruitless drilling ventures that yielded nothing. Wilde's term drew to an end, and he announced he would not seek re-election. He was succeeded as mayor in 1921 by John L. Bacon.

John L. Bacon

Then pioneer atmosphere was gone. No longer did single developments determine the fate of cities or areas as had happened so often in the past. Many factors were entering into the business and industrial growth of Southern California. Most important was the westward movement of the American people. They were creating new markets and building homes and schools and shops and plants.

Though the "flivver" had replaced the covered wagon, and there were many thousands more of them, the newcomers arrived much as had those of another generation before them, with their possessions and their children and their hopes.

A number of transcontinental highways, made up more of designated local segments than developed routes, converged at El Paso. The Bankhead Highway originated in Washington, D. C., and passed through Roanoke, Virginia; Nashville, Tennessee; Little Rock, Arkansas; and Dallas, Texas. At Kent, Texas, it joined the

In the early 1920's the bay of San Diego presented a tranquil scene. *Morning on the Bay was* painted by *Alfred Mitchell from his residence overlooking the red brick tower of St. Joseph's Church. In the background is North Island, with its scattered naval structures, and the almost empty slopes of the lee side of Point Loma. The commercial shipping which had been expected with the opening of the Panama Canal really had never come.*

Booklets "sold"
a romantic past

Who could
resist this one?

Old Spanish Trail to El Paso. The Old Spanish Trail originated at Jacksonville, Florida, and went by way of Mobile, Alabama, and across the Mississippi River to Houston, San Antonio and El Paso, Texas.

It was at El Paso where the new settlers or the tourists could decide as to their ultimate destinations. After that point they could be diverted and lost to rival Los Angeles. At El Paso, the southern traffic could feed into a stream moving west toward San Diego over what was designated as the Borderland Highway. From El Paso it generally followed the international border to Deming, New Mexico, and through Arizona by way of Douglas, Bisbee, Tucson and Phoenix, where it swung southward to Yuma.

Phoenix and Yuma also were points of possible diversion. Roads also led from there directly to Los Angeles. At Yuma, California was entered by crossing a bridge over the Colorado River. The Borderland Highway then dropped below sea level on its route through Imperial Valley.

The routes followed in part the historic paths of migration, paths trod by Indians and rutted by carettas and stage coaches. Yuma had been the last post before the crossing of the deep desert which had taken its toll in suffering, from the days of Juan Bautista de Anza and the colony from Mexico that had founded San Francisco, to the time of Stephen Watts Kearny who led his Army of the West toward the conquest of California.

A pamphlet published in 1923 by the San Diego-California Club in cooperation with the County Board of Supervisors, read:

From El Centro, the route goes over the last range of mountains, where the highest elevation is less than 3300 feet. On the last lap of the journey the motorist passes swiftly through the foothills and valleys and finally glimpses San Diego, spread before him in a wonderous panorama that includes mountains, harbor and ocean.

In the first three years of the decade it was estimated that the population of San Diego rose from 74,683 to more than 116,000. With the adjoining communities of East San Diego, Coronado and National City, the metropolitan population was more than 142,000.

Over the years, ever since the earliest pioneering days, the city's margin of survival had been a narrow one. With the average rainfall only about ten inches a year, it soon became evident that pumping of underground water was not enough and runoff of wet years had to be impounded to assure domestic supplies over relatively long periods of time.

In times of drought there was support for spending more money for water development. When the rains arrived and filled the reservoirs, public interest would lag.

In the winter of 1921-1922 raging flood torrents washed out railroad tracks and the highway bridge at Sorrento Valley, and sent two feet of water into the Union Station at the foot of Broadway. Seven billions of gallons of water swelled the city's reservoirs. How best to conserve the water that at the same time always wasted into the sea precipitated one political struggle after another.

Spreckels had sold his own Otay-Cottonwood storage and delivery system to the city and had been influential in the selection of Hiram N. Savage, formerly with the United States Department of Interior, as the city's hydraulic engineer. Early in 1923 the city's Water Commission brought in a report rejecting Savage's recommendations for development of the San Diego River. The two commissioners, Frederick M. White and Charles T. Chandler, opposed a reservoir site in Mission Gorge that had been selected by Savage. It also urged that the city not press its claim to all rights to the water of the San Diego River, and instead negotiate for purchase of the Cuyamaca system owned by the Ed Fletcher interests. Fletcher's previous efforts to sell the system to the city had been blocked by Spreckels.

Hiram N. Savage

Mayor Bacon promptly removed the commissioners from office for "promoting dissatisfaction, inefficiency and discord." Subsequently, a vote of the people abolished the commission.

But the great city that Spreckels thought he could command to rise on the edge of the bay and produce a commercial empire that would compare with the one built by his father at San Francisco, soon learned it no longer was so dependent on his economic and political leadership, as in the past. Power was being diffused.

The rapid increase in the number of automobiles resulted in paving of streets and the improvement of others. Spreckels' street car company, however, had ignored a provision of the City Charter which required it to maintain the roadbed between the tracks and two feet on each side of them. Some of the worst conditions existed on Adams Avenue, along the rim of Mission Valley. Public complaints caused the City Council to request that the company live up to its franchise. When the company pleaded poverty and asked for time, the Council was forced into an investigation of its books which disclosed that in twelve years profits had equaled the original investment of $4,000,000.

At the same time Spreckels was seeking another franchise for a line on Sixteenth Street, between Market Street and Broadway, and business leaders protested that it would divert business from the downtown area centering along Fifth Street.

The city operations manager, Fred A. Rhodes, was asked for a routine report on the company's request. To everyone's surprise he recommended that it be denied. The town split into two camps, those favoring Spreckels and those opposed to him. Petitions were circulated demanding that the franchise be granted or put up to a vote of the people. The Council was driven into an open break with Spreckels and an election was set for October.

The climax came when the City Council called for bids to pave Adams Avenue and notified the street car company it would have to take care of its own roadbed. Shortly after midnight of August 26, 1922, company work trains arrived at Adams Avenue and crews began tearing up the rails. Residents, awakened by the noise, thronged angrily into the street, some of them bearing arms. The mayor rushed to the scene with a force of policemen and arrested the company's foreman. The city appealed to the State Railroad Commission, and it ordered the company to maintain street car service on Adams Avenue. A compromise eventually was reached

National highways were just beginning to take shape in the 1920's.
The principal railroad terminals for Southern California were at Los Angeles, and San Diego began looking toward the highways for tourist and business traffic.
Two tentative transcontinental highways converged at El Paso: the Bankhead which originated in Washington, D.C., and the Old Spanish Trail which originated at Jacksonville, Florida.
From El Paso tourists could take the Borderland Highway to San Diego— if they were not diverted to Los Angeles at Phoenix or Yuma.

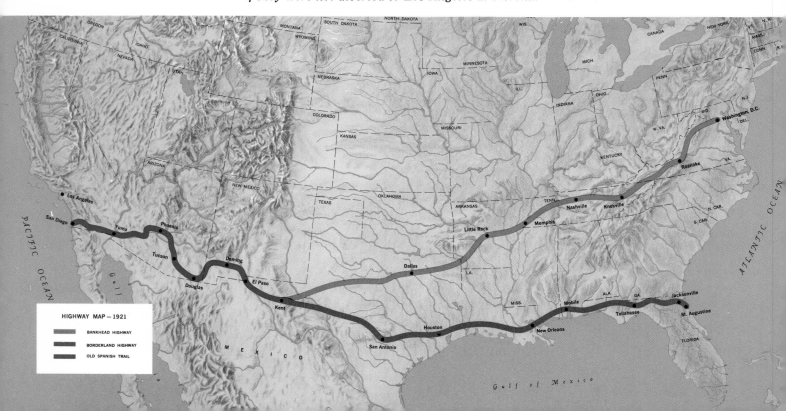

HIGHWAY MAP – 1921

BANKHEAD HIGHWAY

BORDERLAND HIGHWAY

OLD SPANISH TRAIL

on the matter of paving. Spreckels won a minor victory at the polls when the street car franchise for Sixteenth Street was approved by a seventy-one vote margin.

Nine months later, on May 19, 1923, Spreckels gave a dinner for a hundred or so San Diego business leaders, at his Hotel del Coronado, in the knowledge that while he had committed himself to many more projects, his active life was drawing to a close and his son must soon take over. From him poured out long pent-up feelings:

John D. Spreckles

> Some years ago, when some of our peanut politicians were warning San Diego not to fall for the crafty schemes of the foxy "Spreckels interests," a certain well-known wit and sage said that my name must be John Demented Spreckels because if I were not crazy I would not subject myself to this constant yelping of village curs, but would sell out my holdings, put all my money in government bonds, sail away on my yacht, and let San Diego go to hell—or look to the bunch of anti-Spreckels knockers to save the city, under the highminded leadership of the *San Diego Sun.*
>
> Gentlemen, he did not know me, or he would never have suggested a surrender on my part. Whatever else I may or may not be, I am not a quitter.

He was particularly bitter about the opposition of the *San Diego Sun* and its principal owner, E. W. Scripps. He continued:

> Of course, we all know the chief source of the malicious influence which, by fanning the flames of factional strife, prevents San Diego from outgrowing its smalltown traditions, a scurrilous, unscrupulous and hypocritical newspaper whose life depends on stirring up discontent . . . it is one of a numerous string of similar sheets owned by a multi-millionaire who has publicly admitted that he made his millions by hounding other millionaires and by posing as the champion of the poor, downtrodden working man . . . What has he ever done for San Diego?

Scripps, though he still maintained his home at Miramar, was not particularly concerned with San Diego and its troubles and spent most of his time at sea on his yacht. Spreckels had staked everything on San Diego and he was convinced the reason it had not yet become the metropolis and seaport that its geography and unique advantages entitled it to be, was because of a lack of civic cooperation:

> I have had my say. I have spoken frankly in the hope that from now on a larger and more genuine spirit of cooperation may prevail. If the young red-blooded progressive business men of the city will only get together and stick together, nothing will be too big to expect for San Diego.

In his bitterness Spreckels perhaps forgot how San Diegans in years past had combined resources in a vain effort to become a

23

national railroad terminus, had raised a million dollars for an exposition, and that the voters had agreed to city acquisition of some of his water system when he was in dire need of money.

As far as Scripps and his *San Diego Sun* were concerned, the speech was a "swan song" marking the decline of the influence of Spreckels:

> You've done too much in your full life to go out in a towering, thundering rage, singing your own praises at a banquet paid for by yourself, and damning all those who oppose you . . .
>
> An old man singing his swan song is not a pretty picture . . . passing along his crown to his son and seeking to pass along his prejudices and intolerances with his sceptre.

Claus Spreckels

Two weeks later 600 business men, including delegations from El Centro and Yuma, attended a "Spreckels appreciation" dinner in the ballroom of the U.S. Grant Hotel. In his response to many personal tributes, Spreckels referred to his remarks at Hotel del Coronado and said that "I know you have complied with the appeal that I then made to you for cooperation and teamwork."

The toastmaster was Ed Fletcher, a long-time opponent of Spreckels on many issues, and he told of a visit with Claus Spreckels in which both of them pledged cooperation in the future for the good of San Diego. In turn, Claus told the 600 San Diegans:

> You never heard anyone in Los Angeles say a word against Los Angeles . . . My father has promised you tonight that I will go through with the rest of the game and further build up what he has started—and he is not going to break that promise.

The warm pledges of cooperation for future progress were not long remembered. San Diego and Southern California were beginning to feel the full effect of a rising tide of change more powerful than the influence of any individual.

CHAPTER TWO

In the plans of John Nolen for a "city beautiful," certain streets running from the bay to Balboa Park were to be boulevards, or prados.
In his second plan, Cedar Street, at the waterfront, was to be the northern boundary of a grouping of public buildings in a "Cabrillo Portal."
In a slightly altered plan, Cedar Street was to become the principal avenue connecting the Civic Center and the park. In the 1920's Cedar Street was quiet, tree-lined and inviting; four decades later, all this was gone and it led only to a monument of civic indecision.

CHARTING A WAY

During the speculation of the early 1920's in the land and resources of California, the enthusiasm for civic planning which had come with the advent of the Twentieth Century for a time almost disappeared. Los Angeles was widening out in a sprawling mass of unregulated subdivisions. Only in a few residential areas, where the wealthy had settled, were community or aesthetic values protected.

Fifteen years had passed since San Diego's brief glimpse of the city it might have become. At the invitation of a group of citizens, the nationally known planner John Nolen had described the geographical, climatic and topographical advantages which would permit a civic development in the manner of the more beautiful seaside cities of Europe and Latin America.

Such a concept was far removed from a town barely out of its pioneering phase. A smokestack was a much more identifiable sign of progress, and at the first opportunity voters had overwhelmingly approved construction of a commercial pier at the foot of the city's principal thoroughfare and in an area which Nolen had recommended be reserved for civic, recreational and cultural purposes.

The beautiful Spanish-Colonial buildings of the 1915-1916 Panama-California Exposition, however, remained as silent but impressive witnesses to what could be accomplished. George W. Marston, for one, though aging and ill, had not given up. He had financed the now neglected study of John Nolen, and in 1921 he had been instrumental in the preparation of other plans by the former direct-

27

or of works for the exposition, Frank P. Allen. The architect of the exposition, Bertram G. Goodhue of New York, also was designer of the United States Marine Base and the Naval Training Station on the northern shores of the bay, and Marston hoped to achieve a harmonious development of the entire waterfront. Marston was quoted as saying:

At present the San Diego waterfront is being managed in a very haphazard way. It would be a tremendous task, beset with many difficulties, to correct present conditions, but I believe that $100,000 spent here now in correcting those conditions would be worth a million dollars later on. Whenever I have been discouraged in attempting to work out plans for the harbor's betterment I have thought of the condition of Balboa Park land before the exposition. What has been done on Balboa Park hill can be done on the shores of San Diego Bay.

Again community interest was lacking, and in 1922 construction was begun on a second pier, this one at the foot of B Street, and further commercial development proceeded north along the area

About 1908 the noted planner John Nolen described how San Diego could be developed in a manner to rival in beauty the great waterfront cities of the world.
Though nothing much was done about it, the concept persisted through the years. By 1922, however, it was almost dead.
At that time construction of a new commercial pier, shown to the north of the existing Broadway pier, was begun at the foot of B Street.
Almost immediately commercial development proceeded northward in an area which Nolen had suggested be set aside for extensions of parkways and for public buildings.

which had been envisioned as the extension of a prado lined with parkways and public buildings from the bay to Balboa Park.

The pier was begun at a time when tonnage through the harbor had declined. By 1923, however, it was rising enough to justify the expectations of the pier's supporters that by the time it was completed in 1925 San Diego would be an important port city. But the pier, with its accompanying waterfront industrial sites, brought a realization at last that with the rapid growth of the city there had to be some plan if there was to be any orderly development at all.

While across the country there were indications that the building boom might collapse, San Diego's growth was continuing steadily though not as spectacularly as that of Los Angeles. San Diegans assured themselves they really didn't want a boom. As *The San Diego Union* stated editorially:

George W. Marston

> Naturally, San Diego doesn't care for booms. They "bust." Old-timers here are familiar, to their sorrow, with that enduring truth. The present state of growth is far preferable to any more spectacular flurry.

However, experts from Los Angeles and San Francisco were summoned to San Diego and they told business leaders that what was needed was a definite program and community cooperation. At a meeting of the Chamber of Commerce, E. B. Gould Jr., its president, asked:

> Are we absolutely going to get behind these basic fundamentals, or are we going to sit back and let things develop, as they may, without our combined efforts?

Two bankers, G. Aubrey Davidson and Frank Belcher Jr., argued for industrial development. Davidson commented:

> Employment is one of the most serious things we are up against. People need something to do after we get them to come here and that means more industries are required.

G. Aubrey Davidson

As a result the Chamber of Commerce, though supporting a search for compatible industry, recommended adoption of a plan which would take into consideration the necessities of commercial, residential and aesthetic requirements, and prominent in this would be a Civic Center. To avoid the mistakes of other cities, the Chamber urged proper zoning, supervised guidance of subdivisions and further development of Balboa Park.

Mayor Bacon was more receptive than the former mayor to the arguments of the "geranium growers" who insisted that civic beautification need not be sacrificed in commercial and industrial

This is how the San Diego Zoo began. Wild animal cages line a section of Park Boulevard in the north central area of the park.
Across the street was the Indian Village created for the 1915-1916 Panama California Exposition.
The village also was a feature of the 1935-1936 California Pacific International Exposition and was known as the Indian pueblo.
By that time the San Diego Zoological Society had relocated its exhibits in the park proper and had begun building a zoo that became known around the world.

growth. Though Spreckels had supported Marston for mayor in the "geraniums vs. smokestacks" campaign of 1917, his influence was not always exerted on the side of community-wide planning. He had many development projects of his own.

Interest in civic planning revived. Rehabilitation of exposition buildings gave the community a center of cultural and recreational interest. The Art Association, which for years had concerned itself with landscaping, also began to talk of an art gallery, certainly a necessary asset for a town which all knew for sure soon would take its place among the great cities of the Pacific Coast.

The promise of a gallery came from Mr. and Mrs. Appleton S. Bridges. Bridges had married the daughter of H. H. Timken Sr., and was president of the Timken Investment Company. The Timken fortune came from the invention of the roller bearing. Timken, son of the inventor, had brought his family to San Diego County in the 1890's and the family still owned considerable downtown property. Bridges estimated the cost of a gallery at $40,000. It would cost $400,000.

The little zoo that had been started through the enthusiasm of Dr. Harry M. Wegeforth was moved from its location on Park Boulevard to undeveloped acreage within Balboa Park. Ellen Browning Scripps, the sister of the newspaper publisher, donated fencing to make possible the collection of entrance fees.

An urbanization was under way. In 1922 Ocean Heights was annexed to the city and in the following year, East San Diego, an area of nearly nine square miles. The Spreckels companies began laying a street car line to Mission Beach and La Jolla. Spreckels soon would spend more millions of dollars in creating a resort at Mission Beach to rival his Coronado and Tent City.

Marston again got in touch with the planner Nolen, and said he was hoping that soon there would be a concerted movement in cooperation with the City Planning Commission for a comprehensive development. "The time is not ripe yet but it is approaching," he wrote.

While San Diegans tried to out-maneuver Los Angeles on highways and industry, and at the same time bring about some order in the city's growth, the Army and Navy were irrevocably shaping the area's future. There were only a few persons, however, who understood the significance of all that was taking place.

In 1922, the Navy dedicated a Naval Hospital in Balboa Park, and commissioned the first permanent building of a Naval Supply Depot on the tidelands. A year later on June 1, the Naval Training Station was put in commission and soon after the first Marine recruits arrived for training at the new Marine Corps Base.

There were now ten major Navy and Marine installations being built or authorized. Nearly $4,000,000 was being spent in developing the Naval Air Station on North Island and its auxiliary Ream

Even sand as well as soil could be converted into dollars.
John D. Spreckels owned Hotel del Coronado and its famed Tent City,
but in the early 1920's he began laying a street car line to Mission Beach
and La Jolla.
This shows Mission Beach and, presumably, eager prospective buyers of
speculative building sites in what at that time was San Diego's newest resort area.
The tourist possibilties in the lure of the seashore were just beginning to be
fully appreciated.

*Lieutenant
Frank W. Seifert*

Lieutenant Oakley Kelly

Lieutenant John Macready

Field on the south bay. The Marine barracks were costing nearly $3,000,000 and the Naval Training Station more than $2,000,000. Other important installations were a Fuel Depot, Radio Station, Destroyer Base, Submarine Base, and administrative offices for the 11th Naval District.

In an interview aboard the cruiser *Seattle*, published on August 3, 1923, Rear Admiral George W. Williams, chief of staff to Admiral Hilary Jones, commander-in-chief of the United States Fleet, said that in the space of a few short years San Diego had become the greatest naval port in America, and its strategic and administrative importance was second only to that of Washington. But, he continued:

> San Diego missed a golden opportunity of getting the Battle Fleet when it failed to erect a small breakwater on the sea side of Coronado, and connect this breakwater with Coronado's street car system to accommodate the thousands of bluejackets landed daily from the capital ships, and otherwise prepared to take full advantage of the fact that San Pedro soon is to lose the Battle Fleet.

He did say, however, that within the next twelve months San Diego would become the operating base for twenty of the largest submarines afloat, and their tenders, and that expansion of the Destroyer Repair Base was a necessity. The Navy's eyes were on the Pacific. Williams said that plans for a first-class naval base at Pearl Harbor should be carried out to accommodate the large number of warships to be stationed in Hawaiian waters. On the following day, command of the United States Fleet was transferred at San Diego for the first time. Admiral Jones was relieved by Admiral Robert Coontz in a ceremony on the *Seattle*.

In 1925 a total of 120 battleships, scout cruisers, destroyers, submarines and auxiliary ships of the combined fleets of the Navy completed maneuvers off Lower California and steamed for San Diego. It required five hours for the massed fleet to reach their moorings in the harbor and in the Coronado Roads. The date was March 12. The fifteen commanding admirals and their subordinate officers were entertained at numerous civic and social functions. The city's identity as a "Navy town" was firmly established.

The Navy shared North Island with the Army Air Service. Army and Navy pilots were rapidly expanding the potential of aviation. In 1922 Army Air Service Lieutenants Oakley Kelly and John Macready set a sustained flight record by remaining in the air for thirty-five hours and eighteen minutes, and Lieutenant James H. Doolittle set a coast-to-coast record from Jacksonville, Florida, to San Diego, of twenty-one hours and nineteen minutes.

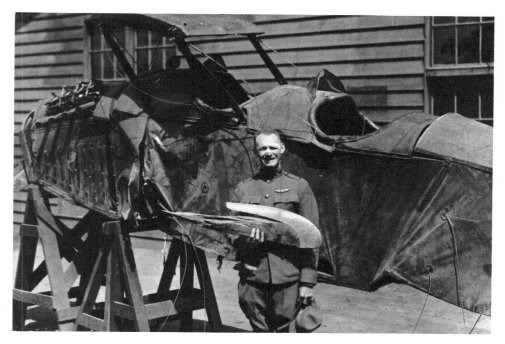

The Army Air Service was breaking flight aviation barriers from Rockwell Field on North Island.
Planes may not have been fast but they were hazardous. Here, a young pilot shows what was left after an accident. As long as you could walk away from it, no accident was to be taken too seriously.
Many great fliers who later led American air forces over Japan and Germany in World War II had their early training at Rockwell Field.

In the following year, Navy photographers from North Island took the first aerial picture of a solar eclipse, while flying over San Diego at an altitude of 20,000 feet. Lieutenants Kelly and Macready this time flew from Mitchell Field, New York, to San Diego on the first non-stop transcontinental flight. The flying time was twenty-six hours and fifty minutes. Refueling in flight became a reality. Over San Diego Harbor, Lieutenants Frank Seifert and Virgil Hine lowered a hose to Lieutenant John Paul Richter who successfully inserted it into the fuel tank of his plane piloted by Captain Lowell Smith. In 1924 the Navy brought its big dirigible, the *Shenandoah,* to North Island, to end the first transcontinental flight by a lighter-than-air ship.

Another young Army pilot named T. Claude Ryan, a graduate of the primary cadet school at March Field, Riverside, in 1921 and Mather Field, Sacramento, in 1922, was flying on a volunteer forest fire patrol in northern California. By the end of the year he decided there could be a future for him in commercial aviation. Unfortunately, he couldn't find anyone who agreed with him. He worked for a time in an auto supply company and then took his savings

An airplane was refueled in the air for the first time in 1923.
On June 27, a biplane received gasoline by a hose dangled form a second plane and remained aloft over San Diego for six hours and thirty-nine minutes. Subsequently there were two other endurance flights, one of more than twenty-three hours and another of more than thirty-seven hours. Food, warm clothing and messages were lowered in a weighted basket.
Later the same crew refueled the first border-to-border flight, from Canada to Mexico.
In another plane as an observer was Major H. H. Arnold, later commander of United States Air Forces in World War II.

and went to Rockwell Field, the Army's part of North Island, where he could at least get in some more flying on his reserve commission.

Commercial flying was limited to barnstorming, sightseeing, instruction and smuggling. There was a small dirt landing strip on the tidelands at the foot of Broadway, and its principal occupant had been a flier who had been convicted of smuggling Chinese from Mexico. Ryan induced the harbor master of the city of San Diego, Joseph Brennen, to let him use the field. Now all he needed was an airplane. Major H. H. Arnold, the commanding officer at Rockwell Field and who later as a five-star general was to command the United States Air Forces in World War II, advised him to bid on one of the war-surplus biplanes at the field. He bought one for $400 and went into the flying business.

Income was slow in developing. A visiting carnival provided some customers and Ryan went with it to the next town. The result was disappointing and Ryan returned to San Diego and for a time took a job as pilot with a barnstorming expedition in northwestern Mexico. This provided enough cash to purchase some ancient standard biplanes from the government and he moved his operation to an area known as Dutch Flats, opposite the Marine Corps Base.

With the aid of some mechanics he converted the planes into cabin transports, and in 1925 with a new partner, B. Franklin Mahoney, a local sportsman who provided some much needed capital, Ryan organized Ryan Airlines and inaugurated an air service between San Diego and Los Angeles, the first regularly scheduled year-round passenger airline in the United States. One of the early passengers was J.H.N. Adams, a contributor to the Chamber of Commerce magazine, *San Diego Business*, who wrote:

Those who saw the superb film classic, *The Thief of Bagdad*, will recall with a pleasurable thrill the brilliant spectacle of the Thief and Princess soaring through the air on the Flying Carpet. It is with a similar feeling that I recount a recent experience.

T. Claude Ryan, with the support of B. Franklin Mahoney, a sportsman and amateur pilot, inaugurated the first regularly scheduled air service in the United States.
This was between San Diego and Los Angeles. The date was March 1, 1925. The front open cockpit on this Ryan "Standard" biplane was covered over. With his passengers peering out the window, Ryan piloted them northward on their great adventure.
A writer of the times described his experience on a flight as being on a "magic carpet."

Adventure anyone?

T. Claude Ryan

Fifteen minutes after leaving San Diego we were over picturesque Del Mar, and passing swiftly over Cardiff, Encinitas, Carlsbad, Oceanside, Las Flores, San Onofre ... We soon saw the quaint old Mission at San Juan Capistrano, in less than one hour since our take-off. Ninety miles an hour—and yet no sensation of hurtling through the air.

At four o'clock I had been in San Diego—at five-thirty I was seated in a friend's automobile and was being whisked a few blocks away to his home in Los Angeles ... If you would emulate Douglas Fairbanks, phone Main 4688.

Across the continent in Buffalo, New York, in 1924 Reuben H. Fleet was keeping a promise he made to himself during World War I while stationed with the Army Air Service at Rockwell Field. He had successfully entered the business of building airplanes. He had seen many young fliers go to their deaths in unstable planes and he was turning out military trainers which he felt were dependable and safe. The name of his firm was Consolidated Aircraft.

Though Ryan was demonstrating the practicality of commercial aviation, and San Diego, along with many other cities, realized it would soon need a community airport, primary interest as far as transportation was concerned was in highways. The fear of remaining isolated in the southwestern corner of the United States had persisted since the first transcontinental railroad surveys of the 1850's. In the period from 1920 to 1925 traffic on state highways increased ninety-three percent. In San Diego County the number of autos and trucks increased from 18,000 in 1920 to 30,000 in 1923.

The highway from San Diego to Los Angeles was paved all the way, but twenty-three miles of the inland highway to Los Angeles, all of it in San Diego County, remained to be paved. Eastward, the highway had been paved only as far as The Willows, thirty-three miles inland at an elevation of 2300 feet. Beyond, there were passes at 4000 feet, and more than ninety miles from San Diego there was Mountain Springs grade, still a winding, occasionally precarious dirt road leading in and out of the desert. In the Imperial Valley sections of the road between El Centro and Yuma had not yet been improved as to assure regular passage. Southward from San Diego the highway to Tijuana was paved by way of Chula Vista and Highland.

The flood of immigrants into Los Angeles had at last forced the San Diego-California Club to recognize the advantage of advertising there about the attractions of the city to the south. The city's hopes of effectively tapping the main westward traffic had not materialized.The advertisements appeared in 1923 and conceded that those who had remained in Los Angeles, and invested wisely, had become rich. In San Diego, however, there was the prospect of happiness as well as riches. The advertisements, in part, stated:

36

Twenty years ago Los Angeles had a population of 175,000. Today it has probably 850,000—an increase of nearly 500 percent. The business men who began with small establishments in Los Angeles in 1903 have large business houses today. Those then in the larger establishments today have colossal buildings to house their institutions. The men who owned even a lot or two near the business district twenty years ago today are rich.

One hundred and thirty-five miles south of Los Angeles is Southern California's second city, San Diego, which twenty years ago had a population of 20,000. Today the population numbers 125,000—an increase of more than 500 percent. Pioneer businessmen in San Diego in 1903 are the heads of strong business institutions in that city today. Bankers, merchants, real estate owners, and professional men have profited in proportion to the steady growth and development that has taken place in San Diego.

To these men and their families life has been sweet because they have lived ... on the shores of a beautiful harbor, with every advantage of Southern California's most delightful year-round climate, scenic beauty, outdoor sports and recreations.

The event that San Diego was certain would change all of its prospects and make the mountain route instead of the coast highway the principal gateway to the county, took place on November 17, 1923. President Calvin Coolidge pressed an electric button in Washington and rang a gong in the Plaza in downtown San Die-

The first true southern transcontinental highway was dedicated in 1923.
The Lee Highway originated in the nation's capital and terminated at San Diego.
San Diego was sure that the development of highways would put the town on the map and make up in large part for the loss of the direct railroad connections to the East.
While the Lee Highway formally terminated at Washington, it provided access to New York and New England markets. More important, it was an all-weather route for tourists and the new settlers Southern California expected with the beginning of the auto age.

HIGHWAY MAP — 1923

LEE HIGHWAY

go. At that signal, Ed Fletcher unveiled a marble milestone which marked the Pacific terminus of the Lee Transcontinental Highway, which had its beginning in the nation's capitol. It was the first true southern all-weather transcontinental route.

At the dedication, Fletcher, a vice president of the Lee Highway Association, said:

> For fifteen years San Diego has made strenuous efforts, and at last succeeded, after the expenditure of millions of state and county money, in building a direct highway through almost impassable mountains, and across the great Colorado desert to the Arizona line at Yuma.
>
> We are indeed happy to know that within the next six weeks a contract will be let to construct the missing link between Yuma and El Centro which, when completed next year, will give us an up-to-date graded, graveled or paved highway the entire distance from San Diego to El Paso. Within the next two or three years every foot of our highways across the continent will be built.

The Lee Highway provided access to New York, by way of Washington, and westward it ran through Chattanooga and Memphis, Tennessee; to Little Rock, Arkansas; Lawton, Oklahoma; through northern Texas, southeastern New Mexico to El Paso; and from there to San Diego.

Though the owners of the city's three newspapers only had a few years to live, their influence was still deeply felt. John D. Spreckels, with the city for which he had worked beginning to come into view, was embarking relentlessly on his final work. Though E. W. Scripps spent most of his time at sea, his *San Diego Sun* was curiously detached from the community and sounded a strident voice of opposition, swinging first one way and then another, always interesting but often disturbing.

The business community wanted its own voice, and a group of its leaders established the *Independent* as a weekly newspaper. Among the founders were George W. Marston; Ed Fletcher; Appleton S. Bridges, the philanthropist; W. Templeton Johnson, the architect; Judge W. A. Sloane, who served on the Supreme Court of California; and, among others, Ellen Browning Scripps. The *Independent's* first edition was published in May of 1924.

The rising confidence in the city's future, and the revival of interest in planning, led Marston to ask the City Council to reconsider the Nolen Plan of 1908. The Council appropriated $10,000 and Nolen's advice was sought by the city's three principal commissions, Planning, Park and Harbor. By late 1925 Nolen had evolved a new plan of development, the second Nolen Plan, and he wrote:

Without doubt San Diego should be a more distinctive city in its physical development. Its topography, its climate, and its purposes are all different from the average American city. Not to be distinctive is an advantage lost, and some things in San Diego cannot be changed. The question is, what can be done to recover lost ground and lead the city toward a more distinctive San Diego for the future?

The plan differed from the one he had presented in 1908. He did not suggest this time that the future appearance of San Diego could be made to rival the great seaport cities of Europe and Latin America. However, he did envision a "city beautiful" fronting on the bay and preserving its own historic values. He wrote:

The history of the settlement of San Diego is one of unusual interest, and while much has been done to preserve places of historical association, much still remains to be done. For example, the site of the San Diego Mission, the complete planning and development of Old Town under an appropriate and consistent scheme, and making the most, under public ownership and control, of these and other spots, like Ramona's Marriage Place, should be given attention by the city authorities or by a representative and well-supported organization.

Nolen argued that comprehensive planning of the waterfront for commerce and recreation was the chief contribution that city planning could make to the prosperity of San Diego:

The main feature in making the waterfront available for the variety of uses which it must serve is the proposed Harbor Drive, 200 feet in width which we recommend should run from the southern city boundary of San Diego to the U.S. Naval Reservation at Point Loma.

Thus, the principal scenic avenue would not be a main prado, lined with beautiful buildings, which he had originally envisioned for Date Street from the bay to Balboa Park, but the wide drive following the curve of the bay and ending with a sweeping view of the city from the tip of Point Loma.

He moved the proposed Civic Center from the center of town, where he had originally placed it, to a waterfront location:

San Diego has needed a Civic Center for a quarter of a century or more, and should begin building it now. Such action would not merely give the city the buildings necessary for its municipal life, but would transform the civic spirit of the citizens and attract favorably the attention of visitors.

Nolen commented that an open plaza at India and A streets, with a grouping of public buildings around the plaza and an impressive approach from the waterfront portal would be an ideal location but too expensive:

In view of the high cost of land now on account of San Diego's failure to act earlier, and the heavy indebtedness of the city ... the best practical solution can be found in using the tidelands between Altantic (Pacific) Avenue and Harbor Drive as the Civic Center for San Diego.

For some time San Diegans had realized the potential attractiveness of a drive around the bay, and Nolen detailed how it could be zoned and developed to protect necessary commerce as well as the aesthetic values he considered equally important. His plan embraced only the eleven miles of bayfront from the city's southern boundary to the tip of Point Loma. In his opinion San Diego was making a mistake in expanding northward instead of logically southward along the southern edge of the bay.

San Diego hoped to avoid the early mistakes of Los Angeles and plan its growth to prevent urban sprawl.
The noted planner John Nolen drew this concept of a city centered on the bay, with the allocation of specified waterfront areas for shipping, commerce, recreation and civic buildings.
It was his idea that San Diego should place an airport on the tidelands.
Central to the plan was a drive circling the eastern and northern shores of the bay. Civic buildings would be grouped at what he named the Cabrillo Portal Entrance.

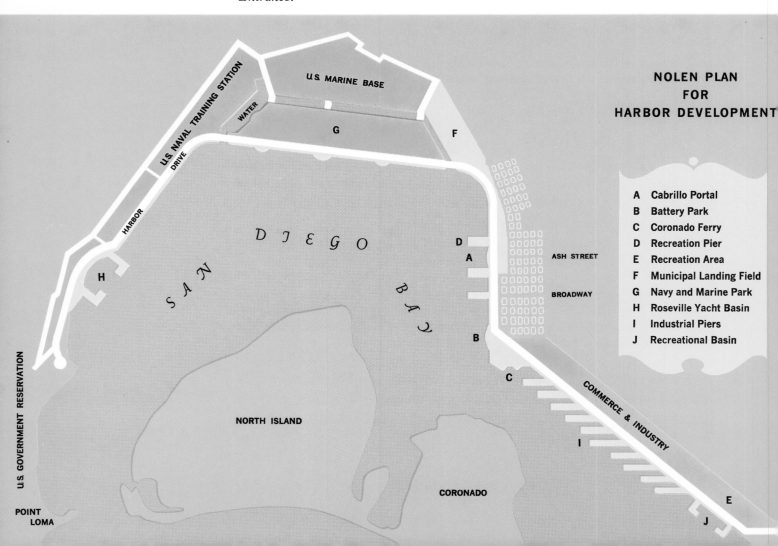

NOLEN PLAN
FOR
HARBOR DEVELOPMENT

A Cabrillo Portal
B Battery Park
C Coronado Ferry
D Recreation Pier
E Recreation Area
F Municipal Landing Field
G Navy and Marine Park
H Roseville Yacht Basin
I Industrial Piers
J Recreational Basin

For the area from the southern city boundary to Market Street, he endorsed the policy adopted by the Harbor Commission, that it be developed as the future industrial and commercial outlet of San Diego. Because of its great length of more than three and a half miles, Nolen recommended that it include recreational features at the foot of Twenty-eighth Street for the industrial workers who would be living near the area:

Market Street should mark the north boundary of industry for San Diego. At this point also exists the connecting point by ferry to Coronado. It is especially fitting that such an important focal point have recognition in the city plan. It is therefore recommended that Battery Park be created on the waterfront to mark this important focal point and to serve as a waterfront development for suitable recreation and park purposes, and also have adequate traffic thoroughfares.

There could be located here a Marine Aquarium, a suitable ferry house, open space to be enjoyed by city workers at their noon hour, and a lasting civic monument, distinctive in its openness and suitable surroundings.

The area from Market Street, where the bay turned abruptly northward, to the new municipal Pier No. 1 at the foot of B street, and seven blocks long, he said would now always have to be in effect a portal entrance to the business section of San Diego. In his original plan he had suggested that commercial development be contained below E Street. This time he recommended that no more piers for commercial use be built north of the new one and that the zone should be a barrier to any commercial activity to the north. From this pier to Cedar Street, a distance of four blocks, he said that San Diego had a fine opportunity to create one of the most outstanding and distinctive civic features ever attempted:

It is recommended: 1) that in this zone be established the Civic Center and Portal Entrance of San Diego. 2) That a recreation pier be built to balance Pier No. 1, and that thereby a basin be created of sufficient depth to serve pleasure boats and yachts; that the recreation pier be made to serve as a place for concessions such as dining, dancing, fishing clubs, city club and other semi-public associations. 3) That the land immediately back of this portal basin be developed as a Civic Center for City, County, State and Government buildings; that an archway be the center of the scheme, with a street running through it to the retail business section over a viaduct, eliminating the railroad grade crossing. 4) That this area be called the Cabrillo Portal Entrance, in honor of the discoverer of San Diego Bay.

From Cedar Street to Laurel Street, an undeveloped area of eight blocks to be created by fill from the dredging of the harbor, he suggested recreational uses that might be related to Balboa Park, in a way that could have great potential for the attraction of tourists:

It is also recommended that this section of the city be looked upon as capable of intensive residential expansion, creating an apartment house district, that hotels be encouraged to select sites along Atlantic Avenue, facing the waterfront, and that the architecture of these waterfront buildings be restricted by height, setback and other legal arrangements so that unity may result.

The area between Laurel Street and the Marine Base, he said, offered excellent advantages for a close-in airport, for both land and seaplanes, that few cities could match.

Even the military cooperated in the idea of creating a city beautiful on the bay. The accompanying photograph shows the United States Marine Recruit Depot at San Diego as it appeared about 1923. The Marine Corps had retained the chief architect of the 1915-1916 exposition to design its buildings in harmony with the Spanish-Colonial atmosphere of Balboa Park.
The city planner John Nolen suggested that a bay area fronting the Marine Base should be an "island" devoted to recreational purposes for all of San Diego.

Both the Marine Corps Base and the Naval Training Station, because of their location, the architecture of their buildings, and the proposed landscaping, were to be integral sections of the "city beautiful" on the bay. From the suggested airport to the southwest boundary of the U.S. Naval Training Station, he recommended that an island be created off Harbor Drive which could be used for recreational purposes and as a parade ground for marines and sailors.

The area from the Naval Training Station to the Naval Reservation, which followed the curve of the bay around and along the base of Point Loma, he planned as a recreational outlet for residents of Point Loma and La Playa. From the Naval Reservation to the tip of Point Loma, was another matter:

This area is occupied entirely by reservations of the U. S. Government, a small section by the U. S. Navy and the major portion by the U. S. Army. It comprises an unspoiled tract of great natural beauty, and the main roads are open to the public under government regulation. The outlook from the plaza at the end of the drive commands one of the most remarkable views in the accessible world.

Nolen recalled the description of the view from Point Loma, written by the author Charles Dudley Warner:

The general features are the great ocean, blue, flecked with sparkling, breaking wavelets, and the wide, curving coastline, fusing into mesas, foothills, ranges on ranges of mountains, the faintly seen snow peaks of San Bernardino and San Jacinto to the Cuyamaca and the flat top of Table Mountain in Mexico. Directly under us on one side are the fields of kelp, where the whales come to feed in winter; and on the other is a point of sand on Coronado Beach, where a flock of Pelicans have assembled after their day's fishing, in which occupation they are the rivals of the Portuguese.

The perfect crescent of the ocean beach is seen, the singular formation of North and South Coronado Beach, the entrance to the harbor along Point Loma, and the spacious inner bay, on which lie San Diego and National City, with low lands and heights outside, sprinkled with houses, gardens, orchards, and vineyards. The near Hills about this harbor are varied in form and poetic in color, one of them, the conical San Miguel, constantly recalling Vesuvius. Indeed, the near view, in color, vegetation, and form of hills, and extent of arable land, suggests that of Naples, though on analysis it does not resemble it. If San Diego had half a million people, it would be more like it, but the Naples view is limited, while this stretches away to the great mountains that overlook the Colorado Desert. It is certainly one of the loveliest prospects in the world, and worth long travel to see.

Among other recommendations, Nolen urged that further encroachments on Balboa Park be prevented and that there be a system of parks based on the area's strong natural features, such as its bays, Point Loma, the San Diego River and Mission Valley, Mount Soledad, Chollas Valley and Torrey Pines. Though he had abandoned the idea of a prado, he did suggest that there could be a number of parkway connections between Balboa Park and the waterfront.

Other principal recommendations were the improving of the highway entrance to San Diego; extension of Sixth Street from University Avenue across Mission Valley to Camp Kearny Highway; a new thoroughfare across Dutch Flats to connect with Mission Beach Boulevard; an outer circuit parkway, out by way of Mission Valley, across East San Diego and back by way of Chollas Valley; a Mission Bay parkway; and park reservations in other canyons.

The Nolen Plan was presented to the City Council in February 1926 and was explained at a public meeting. One of the speakers was Hugh R. Pomeroy, regional planner for Los Angeles County. He told a thousand San Diegans:

We have learned to our sorrow in Los Angeles County that the opportunities which you fail to take advantage of today are a perpetual mortgage on the future.

The age was a sentimental one.
Cities had their own booster songs by which romance and nostaglia could be
fired up on appropriate occassions.
The cover of In San Diego depicted the graceful charm of the Cabrillo bridge
and the California tower of the exposition.
It was in the early 1920's that a determination was made to rehabilitate and
save as many as possible of the original exposition buildings.
These buildings were the San Diego that so many visitors had remembered
and the reason why so many returned to make their home there.

The plan was praised by the Chamber of Commerce Civic Committee, and Julius Wangenheim was named to head a subcommittee to investigate the possibilities of the suggested bayfront Civic Center. The San Diego *Independent* published Marston's comments that he hoped San Diego would rise to its opportunities. After a pause of several days, *The San Diego Union* followed with an editorial:

> A city plan, of course, is in danger of becoming merely everybody's business, and no matter how enthusiastically we may adopt the Nolen Plan, we shall certainly find individuals coming forward in the future to seek special privileges and modifications of the plan in their own interest. If the plan is allowed to lapse into a hazy commonplace, some of these requests will be granted; and sooner or later somebody will put a fish cannery in the park, or a brewery . . . on the esplanada.

Nothing had come of the first Nolen Plan. The second was adopted by the City Council, not as a plan but as a guide.

There was a realization, too, that something would have to be done about the park itself and its heritage of stately Spanish-Colonial buildings. The temporary structures were showing signs of weathering and deterioration. The original Southern California Counties Building at the east gateway to the park, on the north side of the Prado, had been used for a number of years as a Civic Auditorium. On the evening of November 25, 1925, while the building was being readied for the annual Fireman's Ball, it caught fire from a faulty oil heater. By the time the first fire engine arrived the building was a total loss, so swiftly did it burn. An hour later it would have been crowded with revelers.

Even though the pressures of the rising boom were writing their own drastic changes on the face of Southern California, during the next few years some of the recommendations of the Nolen Plan were to be carried out.

CHAPTER THREE

*It required a decade of argument and court action to decide who owned the
water in this river.*
*At this point the San Diego River flows through Mission Gorge, a chasm
it carved through the last hilly barrier between the high mountains and the sea.
The city of San Diego claimed rights to all the water, because the river flowed
through the boundaries of the original Spanish pueblo.*
*Private interests, however, claimed rights to water that had come down
through the purchase of lands once owned by the Mission of San Diego. Who
was right and who was wrong divided the town for years and delayed vital
development projects.*

WATER IS KING

Nature had been kind to Southern California except in one gift,
water. In the 1880's Theodore S. Van Dyke wrote that "rain was
the sweetest music to the California ear."

The Southern California that most of its residents knew, and the
site of all its large cities, is a lowland strip of 200 miles formed by
two coastal mountain groups. Most of it is open to the sea, and
invading cool marine air maintains relatively temperate conditions.

The two mountain groups are the Transverse Ranges and the
Peninsular Ranges. The Transverse Ranges stretch inland from
Point Arguello while the Peninsular Ranges extend northward
from Mexico. The little moisture that comes with the marine air is
left on the western slopes of the mountains. Even if all of it could
be trapped and stored, it was all too obvious that there never would
be enough.

Beyond the mountains lie what are known as the "rain-shadow"
deserts which are so peculiar to the Pacific coastal regions of the
North American continent. North of the Transverse Ranges is the
Mojave Desert; to the east of the Peninsular Ranges, the Salton
Sink. In the coastal area strip ten to fifteen miles wide, rainfall
varies from ten to thirteen inches annually. In the foothill areas,
the average rainfall is about seventeen inches, and in the higher
mountains, it might be as much as forty-five inches a year.

However, there is no constant relationship between rainfall and
runoff, as much depends upon the intensity and duration of storms

and the amount of moisture aleady in the ground. A normal annual rainfall near the coast of about ten inches might come in one or two storms and produce heavy runoff. Another season of fifteen inches of rain might result from a number of small storms producing little or no runoff.

As early as 1908 Los Angeles had begun to reach northward across the Transverse Ranges and the Mojave Desert toward the Owens Valley to catch the melting snow of the eastern slopes of California Sierra Nevada Mountains and provide water for the thousands of settlers entering its coastal plain.

San Diego, with even less rainfall than Los Angeles, several times in its history had been near disaster because of a lack of water. Periods of three years without any runoff had been recorded, and San Diegans had learned that to develop streams for stable supplies of water required expensive storage works and long transmission lines.

Exploration of its water resources largely had been by private companies, though there was an awareness that there had to be sufficient storage for domestic and irrigation uses to carry over for a period of at least seven years, the calculated length of possible periods of drought when there might be little or no runoff. But development always seemed to lag behind demand.

By the 1920's San Diego's margin of survival was no more than four years. Where would its future lie? Would its growth be forever dominated by the extent of its own meager resources, or could it, too, turn to a source far beyond its own borders?

The Owens Valley was 240 miles from Los Angeles, at the foot of the eastern slopes of the Sierra Nevada. The Colorado River was 200 miles from San Diego. None of the water in the Colorado rose in California. Instead, the river collected the runoff of the Rockies and carried it along part of the California border and into the Gulf of California.

Between San Diego and the river were 100 miles of desert and sixty miles of mountainous country of the Peninsular Ranges with rocky peaks over 6000 feet and rugged, broken ridges and valleys gradually falling off toward the sea. In the early 1920's John R. Freeman, an eastern consulting engineer retained by the city to advise it on developing its water resources, told the City Council that for the people of San Deiego to hope to take water from the Colorado River was like hoping to find the pot of gold at the end of the rainbow.

The efforts of Representative Phil Swing, to obtain congressional approval for construction of the All-American Canal in Imperial

The early rapid growth of Los Angeles soon caused a water crisis.
Los Angeles was the first Southern California city to reach over the mountains for a domestic water supply.
This is a construction scene of the Jawbone Siphon of the Los Angeles-Owens River Aqueduct, completed in March of 1913.
The aqueduct tapped the runoff of the eastern slopes of the Sierra Neveda and carried it 240 miles to Los Angeles.
A few years later Southern Californians began to look toward the Colorado River as the "last waterhole" of the West.

Valley and a necessary storage reservoir on the river at Boulder Canyon, brought into contention the question of the rights of all states of the Colorado Basin.

In the semi-arid West the prevailing doctrine on water was "first in time, first in right." This had been applied in assigning priorities between users in states. But the question of the rights of states had

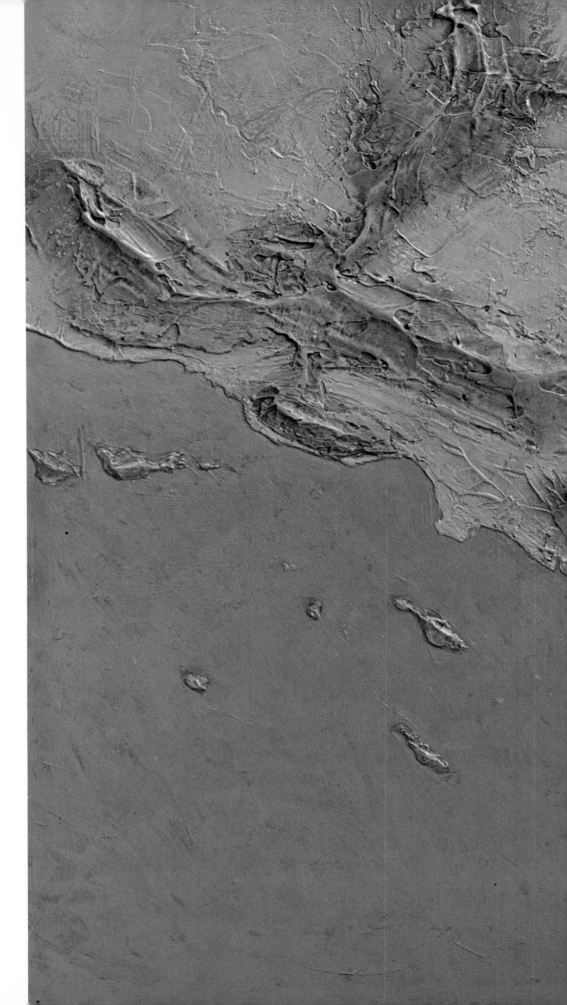

This relief map shows how Southern California would appear from a great height, yet it reveals many things. The Southern California of the tourist advertisements is in reality a narrow strip of coast.

It is formed by two mountain groups, the Transverse Ranges running inland from above Santa Barbara and the Peninsular Ranges running north from Baja California.

Toward the north at Palos Verdes Point, the Los Angeles metropolitan area spreads out in the sheltered basin between the sea and the mountains.

Toward the south is San Diego and its landlocked bay. Below San Diego the coastal strip runs into Lower California. Behind the ranges are "rain shadow" deserts and the Colorado River. Extensions of the coastal lowland form the San Fernando Valley and the more interior Perris-Hemet Valley.

The amount of cool sea air penetrating into the valleys is less than that which influences life on the coastal strip.

The relief map also makes clear why Los Angeles instead of San Diego became the transportation center of Southern California.

The two principal passes through the mountains lead to Los Angeles, One, approachable from a northerly direction, is at a low point between two mountain groups of the Transverse Ranges. The other, approachable from a more southerly direction, leads by way of Salton Sea through the junction of the two great ranges.

Fred Heilbron

Fred A. Rhodes

not been settled. It became known, though, that the Secretary of the Interior, A. B. Fall, would affirm federal interest in the river and that the government intended to seek congressional authority to construct the projected dam, and that revenue from the sale of hydroelectric power would be used to defray costs of construction. In self-protection private power companies hurried to make filings on the river.

At a meeting of the City Council in San Diego in July of 1921, Fred Heilbron, a member of the Council who was in business as a plumbing and heating contractor, suggested that as a precaution the city of San Diego also file a claim to water, before all of its flow could be allocated. Los Angeles had gone several hundred miles to obtain water, and Heilbron, who had arrived in San Diego in 1888 at the age of eleven, had never forgotten the drought that began with the winter of 1895-1896 and persisted into the new century. He recalled in later years:

> There wasn't a lawn in the city. But some people went without baths so they could water their pet shrubs. Everybody with money left town. Those of us who remained became water experts.

A short time later, in the heat of mid-summer, and as instructed by the City Council, the city manager of operations, Fred Rhodes, and a deputy city attorney drove to the Colorado River to the site of the Laguna Dam. It was a low dam of rock, with control gates at each end, thrown across the river where it begins to narrow into the dry hills a dozen miles above Yuma. The Reclamation Service had completed the dam in 1909, to divert water to the Yuma Valley Project in Arizona, and considered it a model project for the development it envisioned for much of the West.

The site was selected because it was near the point where the Imperial Irrigation District hoped to divert water into the projected All-American Canal. Instead of being passed through Mexico, the water would be driven through the sand hills, carried across the harsh East Mesa and dropped into a vast farming area largely lying below the level of the sea.

On the west bank of the river, on the California side, in the tradition of mining claims, Rhodes erected a small monument of rocks and inside it placed a can containing a legal claim to power as well as water, on behalf of the people of San Diego. A stick with a little flag was left to mark the spot.

At a Southwestern Water Conference held at San Diego on December 12, 1921, A. P. Davis, director of the U.S. Bureau of Reclamation, presented the government's plan and it was endorsed by nearly all who attended, including Mayor Bacon of San Diego. The early support of San Diego was more in the interests of Imperial Valley than in anticipation of its own future demands for water, and in the exciting possibilities of irrigating more vast empty desert areas.

This was the land which Spreckels had tried to penetrate with the San Diego & Arizona Eastern Railway, and he expected that some day products for and from all of the Southwest would move over his tracks and across the docks of the port of San Diego. As *The San Diego Union* stated editorially regarding the Fall and Davis program:

> There is epic inspiration in its vision of what this gigantic enterprise will induce . . . it will be the foundation for a new nation within the confines of a vast arid region that for nearly a century has lain waste for lack of water with which to develop its limitless possibilities of soil and climate. What the possibilities are is apparent in the development of the Imperial Valley from the source of wealth which lies in the Colorado River.

By 1923, six of the seven states in the Colorado Basin, including California, ratified a compact dividing the river's water between the upper and lower basins. At the last moment Arizona failed to do so, bringing proposed developments to a halt, and thus a long and bitter struggle was opened and waged in and out of Congress for years. In May representatives from Imperial and Coachella valleys, Los Angeles, the San Diego City Council, and other counties of Southern California met at Fullerton and formed the Boulder Dam Association. Their leaders were Mayor Bacon of San Diego and Mayor S. C. Evans of Riverside. Opposed to them were the private power companies, who were facing a challenge from public power advocates, and the Chandler interests with their huge acreages below the border in Lower California who saw a threat to their water supply by the All-American Canal.

A year had gone by and Swing had been unable to get the House Committee on Irrigation and Arid Lands to vote on his bill for Boulder Dam and the All-American Canal. He reintroduced the measure in 1923, and again hearings dragged on through another year, without any action. Senator Johnson introduced a companion measure in the Senate and the Boulder Dam legislation became known as the Swing-Johnson bill.

A drought in 1924 brought Los Angeles to a suspicion that the Colorado River might be "the last waterhole in the West." As with San Diego its original interest had been concerned more with the possibilities of electric power and the irrigation of desert lands than in water for its residents. Los Angeles now filed on the river for water for domestic uses, thus precipitating a new round of argument and opposition in other basin states.

While the arguments raged, the fiercely independent settlers of Imperial Valley uneasily watched the swift increase in the use of Colorado River water by the land owners of northern Lower California, both American and Mexican. From 1908 to 1925 land under cultivation increased from 7000 acres to nearly 217,000 acres. The longer the dam and the canal were delayed, the less water there might be for the farms of Imperial Valley.

Mexico had insisted on the right to appropriate half the water that the Imperial Irrigation District was able to divert through Mexican territory. But the large acreages being put into cultivation suggested a possibility that Mexico, through prior use, might establish rights to even more water.

There was one thing the Imperial pioneers of a desert empire wanted, and that was control of an assured water supply. They had managed to take over the former private irrigation systems serving the valley and proposed to repay the federal government for the cost of the All-American Canal.

No one could foresee when the dam and canal would be built, and in San Diego there was an insistence that the county's available water resources should be fully developed before there was any thought of trying to tie the city's future to the distant Colorado River. But as Heilbron had commented, droughts had made everybody a water expert and all suggestions or plans were met with controversy.

San Diego County forms a rectangle, and its dimensions are about sixty miles from north to south and seventy miles from east to west. The Peninsular Ranges which traverse the county from the northwest to the southeast are made up of the Agua Tibia, Palomar, Hot Springs, Volcan, Cuyamaca and Laguna ranges. Approximately two-thirds of the county lies west of the divide, and the waters of the western slope drain into the Pacific Ocean. The runoff of the precipitous eastern slope, or what little there is, drains into the Salton Sea which is the lowest level of the Imperial Valley basin and once the site of ancient Lake Cahuilla.

These are the rivers of San Diego County. The longest entirely within the county drops 5000 feet in only sixty-five miles.
The little rain and snow that falls on the sides of the mountains can run swiftly into the sea and be lost to man forever.
San Diegans soon learned that if they were going to depend on the rivers, and be on the safe side, enough water had to be stored to last for seven years.
However, nobody ever seemed to agree on when and where dams should be built.

56

There are seven principal streams which collect the runoff of rainfall and mountain snows and carry it down the western slope to the Pacific Ocean. They are, from north to south, the Santa Margarita, San Luis Rey, San Dieguito, San Diego, Sweetwater, Otay and the Cottonwood-Tia Juana rivers. From a vantage point on Volcan Mountain at 5500 feet above sea level, it might be possible to see the headwaters of all the major streams of San Diego County, with the exception of Santa Margarita River.

These were not the same type of rivers which the early settlers of Southern California had known in their homelands in the Midwest and East. The longest river in San Diego County was only sixty-five miles in length, but in that distance it dropped 5000 feet. The rivers generally had running water only in certain seasons but could spring from trickles to floods almost overnight.

The Spaniards who first explored California were never able to follow all of the rivers to their sources. After the American conquest United States railroad engineers had traced the courses of rivers in San Diego County in disappointing searches for usable passes through the mountains.

The Santa Margarita begins as Temecula Creek, on the northern slopes of Palomar Mountain, and flows in a northwesterly direction, crossing into Riverside County and passing through Aguanga Valley. It then swings westward to a point south of Temecula, where it enters the narrow gorge known as Temecula Canyon. From there it emerges in San Diego County as the Santa Margarita River and empties into the Pacific Ocean north of Oceanside, forty-five miles north of San Diego.

Water from the southern slope of Palomar helps to enrich the San Luis Rey River. Upper San Luis Rey has two forks, one coming down from Palomar and the other from the Hot Spring Mountains. They come together in San Jose Valley near Warner's Hot Springs and flow as one, northwesterly, plunging down through rocky canyons which United States railroad engineers had once described as impassable even for mules. But by the time it reaches the San Luis Rey Valley it has become a full river. In the California pattern, however, it can dry up in summer, yet in exceptionally wet years roll toward the sea with devastating fury. It also reaches the ocean north of Oceanside.

The first of the rivers to flow in a southwesterly direction is the San Dieguito which begins as Santa Ysabel Creek, collecting the runoff and melting snow of the west slope of Volcan Mountain with its great stands of giant cedar and pine trees. It passes gently by the site of a little Spanish *asistencia* mission in Santa Ysabel

Valley and then winds through several deep canyons and enters San Pasqual Valley. Here the creek becomes the San Dieguito River, which in very wet winters gathers up a tremendous volume of water and spreads it through the wide San Dieguito Valley and into the ocean north of Del Mar.

The huge bulk known as Volcan Mountain also furnishes the first of the water for the San Diego River. This river begins on the south side of the mountain and only a short distance from the San Dieguito. At a point below Julian and just above the settlement of Santa Ysabel, it leaves the pine and oak country of the Julian area and begins a mountainous journey, plunging south through an inaccessible canyon. From its walls the stream that is to become the San Diego River can barely be seen a thousand feet below. In the shadows of the depths the green of heavy underbrush becomes a hazy blue. Eventually the river emerges from the mountain country and rounds El Cajon Mountain, which stands above the water as a guardian of the wealth that it promises to all who can hoard and use it. From there it begins to spread out, crossing the north side upper section of El Cajon Valley and sweeping past Lakeside and Santee.

At the edge of the valley it penetrates the last of its hilly barriers, Mission Gorge. Over vast periods of time the river cut its way through six miles of almost solid rock in order to reach its flood plain in Mission Valley. Thousands of years ago before the onset of drier ages, the San Diego River gouged a canyon 500 feet deep in the San Diego mesa. This mesa originally was one mass, but was cut in two by the river, with the San Diego mesa to the south and the Linda Vista mesa to the north.

As a raging torrent in ancient times the river ran rapidly to the coast and fell into the ocean. As the continental ice caps melted, over thousands of years, the ocean slowly rose 100 feet to its present level. As it rose, the river silted up its own bed to the level of the ocean. The same silt alternately threatened to destroy both the San Diego and Mission bays, until in modern times the river was channeled directly into the ocean.

In the 1920's the San Diego River was the only one that passed through the city of San Diego. It also was the river that had given life to the first Franciscan mission and to the first Spanish presidio of California. Though dry for much of its length for most of the year, the power of its periodic floods was demonstrated in 1916, when highway and railroad bridges were smashed and the town almost isolated.

The Cuyamaca Mountains to the south of Volcan are the source

Even when dams were built in the early days, the task of getting the water from a reservoir down to a town was not always a simple one.

This shows the flume which in the 1960's still carried water from Barrett Reservoir down to other storage basins. From there the water entered the city's distribution system.

It is a wooden structure that first came into use in the 1890's, to carry runoff from upper watersheds to the Lower Otay Reservoir. Sections virtually were tacked to the sides of rock mountains.

of the Sweetwater River. This river flows in a southwesterly direction for forty-five miles and empties into San Diego Bay between National City and Chula Vista. Its watershed is not a large one, compared to that of the San Luis Rey and the San Diego rivers. The smallest of the rivers is the Otay, with a length of only twenty-five miles. It actually is made up of the flows of a number of creeks of the lower mountains. It also ends its limited journey at the southern edge of the bay.

It was the Tia Juana River which was causing San Diegans some concern in the early 1920's. This river begins as Cottonwood Creek, high upon the 5000-foot slopes of the Laguna Mountains, and was one of the earliest sources of developed water. After flowing south for a considerable distance, Cottonwood Creek turns westward, with two tight canyons providing ideal sites for dams and reservoirs, and then heads south through another canyon toward the Mexican border.

To this point the river has traveled fifty-two miles. In Lower California it flows through a large valley which is five miles below the boundary. It becomes the Rio Tecate and flows to the southwest until it merges with the Tia Juana River coming up from the south. As the Tia Juana, it flows northward past the town of Tijuana and crosses the United States border to empty into the Pacific Ocean just above the international line.

Less than thirty percent of the drainage basin of the Tia Juana River system is within the United States, but that thirty percent contributes most of the water. As it is an international stream, it soon became involved in the Colorado River controversy. Mexico was becoming concerned over United States appropriations of water from the Tia Juana-Cottonwood system and the Rio Grande in Texas, as well as from the Colorado.

The Chandler interests were suggesting that they might want water from the Tia Juana River for their lands in Lower California, if their claims to Colorado River water were reduced. Negotiators in both countries also heard suggestions that water from one river could be "traded" for water from another river.

Representative Swing warned San Diego that it should establish rights to as much water as it could develop from the Tia Juana River as well as Cottonwood Creek, before any agreements for division of the water of the three rivers were entered into between the United States and Mexico.

More than any single individual Ed Fletcher had realized the potential value of sites on the rivers for storage reservoirs, and over the years he had walked and ridden through river canyons in

What type of dams were to be built, as well as where they were to be built, caused endless arguments.
This is Barrett Dam at its dedication in 1922. It is a massive gravity arch type, the only kind the city's hydraulic engineer ever wanted to build.
It is on the Cottonwood Creek in the south central part of the county and above the Otay watershed where a dam had been washed out in the storms of 1916, and then rebuilt by the city.
During construction the lake behind the unfinished dam began to rise with the heavy rain of the Spring of 1922. It became a race to keep the dam going up faster than the water.

search of the narrow gorges and rock hillsides where dams could be anchored. The city of San Diego itself had neglected more available sources and reached into the southern part of the county to acquire the transmission system and reservoirs of the Spreckels interests on the Otay River and on Cottonwood Creek. Purchased were the Upper Otay, Lower Otay and Morena dams. A fourth, Barrett Dam, also on Cottonwood Creek, was completed by the city in 1922. The city also had a pumping capacity in the San Diego River of 4,000,000 gallons daily from underground supplies.

The Sweetwater River system was supplying water for National City and Chula Vista. In the north county the Santa Fe Railroad had financed construction of the Hodges Reservoir on the San Dieguito River, and it was the primary source of water for the creation of irrigation districts which were opening frost-free coastal areas to settlement and development. It was in this area in 1922 that the tropical avocado from Mexico and Central America was first planted in large experimental acreages.

The figure behind the Santa Fe Railroad's interest in the San Dieguito River watershed and the development of Rancho Santa Fe lands which it owned was Fletcher. In 1920 the city had contracted with Fletcher and William G. Henshaw for water from Hodges reservoir to supply the La Jolla area. Henshaw was owner of Warner's Ranch, an original Spanish land grant, and became involved with Fletcher and the Santa Fe Railroad in acquiring dam sites and water rights in San Diego County.

Among water rights obtained by Fletcher and Henshaw were ones on the San Luis Rey River, and they had tried on a number of occasions to interest the city in a plan to develop water on War- ner's Ranch and transport it by gravity flow to the Linda Vista mesa north of the city. They were met with rebuffs. Henshaw formed the San Diego County Water Company and took over the water rights, though Fletcher remained as a director, and began building a dam on Warner's Ranch by which he intended to supply water to the inland agricultural areas of Escondido and Vista.

Ed Fletcher

More important was the fact that Fletcher and the Cuyamaca Water Company stood astride the San Diego River. As early as 1889 the privately-owned Cuyamaca Water Company had deliv- ered water to San Diego from Cuyamaca Lake on Boulder Creek, a tributary of the San Diego River, through a wooden flume thirty-five miles long. The system was purchased by J. A. Murray, a Montana capitalist, at the instigation of Fletcher, and Murray Dam was built as a storage reservoir on another tributary of the river.

In 1922 the system, improved over the years with storage reser- voirs, was still serving East San Diego, La Mesa, El Cajon, Spring Valley, Lemon Grove, Grossmont and the El Cajon Valley as far as Lakeside. The newly organized La Mesa, Lemon Grove and Spring Valley Irrigation District expected to obtain its water from the same source or to acquire the Cuyamaca system.

Upstream filings for water had been made under state law; downstream the city was pumping in the sands of the same river. Whether the city or the Cuyamaca Water Company had the superior right to the water of the river divided the town for years, reduced friends to enemies, delayed necessary improvements and involved the courts in deciding between conflicting rights and decrees originating in Spain and Mexico.

Twice in the past the Fletcher interests had offered to sell the Cuyamaca system to an uninterested city. At one time the city

could have acquired all of its water rights, as well as the original flume system, for $300,000, and later, when Murray Dam had been built, for $745,000.

When the city finally turned its attention to the San Diego River watershed it selected a tentative site for a reservoir and obtained federal approval to flood some of the lands of the El Capitan Indian Reservation. Fletcher withdrew opposition on assurance the city was concerned only with impounding excess flood waters and would not interfere with his diversions in the upper river or challenge his claim to legal ownership of all the flow he could impound.

It soon became apparent to engineers that the El Capitan site at El Cajon Mountain, which was owned by the Cuyamaca Company, was the key to the entire river watershed. The city attorney, Shelley Higgins, fell back on a decade-old opinion written by a predecessor, T. B. Cosgrove, which concluded it could be established that, by virtue of Spanish colonial law, the city actually was lawfully entitled to all water of the river and all of its tributaries. Rights granted under the laws of Spain, he stated, had passed successively from Spain to Mexico to California, and hence to the United States by the treaty which ended the war with Mexico.

T. B. Cosgrove

As it long had threatened to do, the city brought suit to establish its paramount rights and decided to proceed with construction of El Capitan reservoir and the necessary pipelines. After a conference which brought together two old antagonists, Fletcher and Spreckels, the Cuyamaca system was offered to the city for $1,400,000, which would have ended the dispute over rights and averted long and costly legal proceedings.

The sale was blocked by members of the City Council majority which told Fletcher, and a group of prominent citizens who appeared with him, that he and Murray had nothing of value to sell except a broken-down flume system without any water; that the city owned all the waters of the river and the Council was not going to buy something that already belonged to the people of San Diego.

Whether to proceed with El Capitan Dam, as recommended by

This is the creek which kept a city alive—for a time.
A dam was constructed in 1887. Water was released to a diversion structure from where it was turned into a wooden flume and sent to San Diego.
Boulder Creek is one of the principal contributors to the San Diego River. In the center background is Cuyamaca peak.
On the coast the annual rainfall averages about ten inches; in the Cuyamaca Mountains, almost forty inches. But Cuyamaca Dam and flume were not able to catch, store and deliver that much rainfall. This was a vein that soon ran too thin.

the city attorney and the city manager of operations, Fred A. Rhodes, soon embroiled the town in controversy. A City Council majority supported the city attorney and Rhodes and brought about the dismissal of the city's hydraulic engineer, Hiram Savage. Savage favored an alternate site in Mission Gorge on the same river but below El Capitan. The private consulting engineer retained by the city, John Freeman, did not believe the city could afford a costly dam at El Capitan and recommended that its construction be postponed for perhaps twenty years.

Voters at a special election were asked to decide whether they wanted to go ahead with an alternate dam in Mission Gorge. Mayor Bacon, the Citizens' Water Committee and the Chamber of Commerce favored Mission Gorge. They were supported by Scripps' *San Diego Sun*. Spreckels' truce with Fletcher was at an end and he set his newspapers against the mayor and with the Council majority which favored building El Capitan. The community cooperation, for which Spreckels had pleaded in his talk before business leaders the year before, was forgotten. As regards El Capitan, Bacon said:

> It may be a better dam site for Spreckels, Heilbron or others that will have a chance to sell the city the material for the million-dollar pipe line, but the voters will know better than to take the advice of "engineer" Rhodes instead of that of such men as Freeman and Savage.

The voters, however, on September 10, 1924, heavily rejected a bond issue to construct a dam in Mission Gorge.

The City Council rejected another offer to settle the river dispute in 1925. Soon afterward, the County Grand Jury indicted a councilman on charges of asking for and agreeing to accept bribes from Fletcher and Charles F. Stearn. Fletcher's partner, Murray, had died and his interests had been purchased by Stearn, a resident of Los Angeles.

The indictment was based on incidents alleged to have taken place two years before. Fletcher and Stearn claimed that councilman Harry K. Weitzel had asked $100,000 to use his influence to have the Council buy the Cuyamaca system and $4000 for his influence in helping to bring about the annexation of East San Diego.

No money had been paid though the conversation had been recorded by Fletcher. Weitzel raised the question of why Fletcher and Stearn had waited two years to bring the matter to public attention, and until after the collapse of the final negotiations over the purchase of their system. However, he was convicted and sentenced to ten years in prison. The verdict later was set aside by the State Supreme Court on the grounds that the state laws on bribing public officials did not embrace legislative officers.

Realizing that they now faced a protracted legal struggle over the site of the proposed dam and the rights of the Cuyamaca Water Company, Fletcher and Stearn turned about and agreed to sell the system to the La Mesa, Lemon Grove and Spring Valley Irrigation District for $1,201,980. Included in the sale was the site favored by the city for its proposed El Capitan Dam.

Mat F. Heller

Conditions now had changed, and the city's opponents were not private interests but neighboring communities in the metropolitan area which were as dependent as the residents of San Diego on the river and its water. Spreckels found himself opposed by the most influential and prominent citizens, who over the years had been in the forefront of civic planning and beautification. Among them were George W. Marston, S. M. Bingham, Melville Klauber, O. E. Darnall, Hugo Klauber, L. A. Wright, Milton Heller, Albert E. Scott, Alfred Haines, A. H. Frost, J. W. Sefton Jr., Mat F. Heller, G. Aubrey Davidson, A. S. Bridges and M. T. Gilmore, all of whom favored a compromise settlement.

Though he insisted he no longer had any financial interest in the outcome of the dispute, Fletcher urged his fellow citizens to reject any bonds for El Capitan Dam and accept the compromise settlement with the irrigation district:

> The compromise plan of the district is that they shall have an equitable supply of water from the San Diego River, which has been allocated to the district by the State of California. This will leave 15,000,000 gallons daily for San Diego City when the San Diego River is completely developed—certainly an equitable adjustment.
>
> The district now owns El Capitan reservoir site—not the city. Neither can the city condemn said site as against the district. Whoever thought of borrowing money to build a house on another fellow's lot which he can't buy and can't condemn? Vote "no" . . . and help to keep the city from making itself ridiculous.

Under the influence of Spreckels the city attorney, the city manager, and a City Council majority, who argued that the failure to proceed might impair the city's claims to paramount rights, the people rejected all suggestions of a compromise and on November 18, 1924, approved by a three-to-one margin a $4,500,000 bond issue for El Capitan Dam. But ten years would go by, and many billions of gallons of water would waste into the sea, before the dam finally would be built.

In preparation for a court trial, early settlers were questioned as to diversions and uses of river water. The history of Spain in America was studied and old archives searched. San Diego's position was founded primarily on a prior California Supreme Court determination that Los Angeles City held paramount rights to waters within its boundaries as successor to the original Spanish pueblo, or town. Whether the Spaniards expected San Diego to remain a presidio, or military garrison, and not be raised to the status of a pueblo was the question at issue.

Attorneys for Fletcher and the irrigation district produced a document they had located in the Bancroft Library of the University of California at Berkeley. It was addressed to Fr. Junípero Serra, founder of the Franciscan Missions in California, and signed by Julio Ramon Mendoza, second secretary to the Spanish Viceroy of Mexico, Antonio María Bucareli y Ursúa, and approved by him on December 17, 1773. It authorized removal of the original San Diego Mission from Presidio Hill to a new site in Mission Valley and construction on the San Diego River of a dam and irrigation system. In the body of the document, it was stated:

Last page of letter to
Fr. Serra on water rights

"Referring to the specific purpose of this letter, and for the better understanding of Your Reverence, His Grace reposes herein a sacred trust in your integrity, and that of the Reverend Mission Fathers, to acquire and administer, by means of this Royal Concession and Privilege, the waters of aforesaid stream, for the common benefit of all the people, both Gentiles and converts, who now reside, or in the future may reside within the jurisdiction of Mission San Diego de Alcala. This concession, and the benefits thereof, is to be held for their sons, and the sons of their sons, and successors, for all time, forever.

In carrying out their grant, and assuring a steady supply of water for the mission and its lands, the padres went up the river into Mission Gorge and near its head built a dam 224 feet long and thirteen feet high, which was to withstand the storms and floods of a century. A tiled aqueduct carried the stored water down the gorge for six miles.

The document from the viceroy took note of the existence of the presidio near the mouth of the river, but said this could not prejudice the water rights of the mission as there would always be sufficient water for the army. For the military's lands and herds there was another river to the south where the King's, or National Ranch, was located. This is now known as the Sweetwater River.

The "gentiles" to whom the document referred were pagan Indians. The assignment of water rights to them and to converted Indians was in the spirit of Spanish intentions that mission lands were being held in trust for the natives, and that when they were civilized, missions would be converted into self-governing pueblos.

Midwesterners migrated to California in response to advertisements which
described not only the climate but how they could have their own orchards
and pick lemons, oranges, and yes, even tropical avocados right off their
own trees.
This is a view of El Cajon Valley, looking west toward Mount Helix in the left
foreground, Grossmont in the center and Fletcher Hills in the right background.
By 1929, however, the city of San Diego was claiming it owned all of the water
on which this valley depended, and its existence was threatened.

Charles C. Crouch

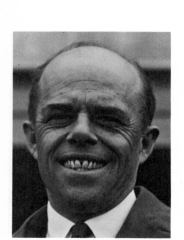

Shelley J. Higgins

Mission San Diego administered more than 58,000 acres, all west of the presidio and a great proportion of it straddling the San Diego River.

It was the contention of Charles C. Crouch, attorney for Fletcher, that the water rights in the San Diego River had been formally withheld from the settlement at San Diego, and with the secularization or confiscation of the mission by the Mexican government, they had passed to land owners and to those who had filed for water under the laws of the State of California.

It was necessary for the city to remove all doubts about the settlement of San Diego, as to whether it was to be a pueblo or a presidio. Its own investigators produced a copy of the Plan of Pitic, which was an order describing the manner in which the pueblo of Pitic in the New World province of Sonora was to be established, and that the plan was to be extended to all other new pueblos. It provided that its boundaries should be marked out and, as translated by city attorney Higgins, it stated:

... its pastures, woods, water privileges, hunting, fishery, quarries, fruit trees and other privileges shall be for the common benefit of the Spaniards and Indians residing therein, and its suburb or village ... the residents and natives shall enjoy equally the woods, pastures, water privileges and other advantages of the royal and vacant lands that may be outside of the land assigned to the new settlement.

The city contended that it was clear from the instructions given to Serra and to Captain Gaspar de Portola, leader of the Royal Expedition, that San Diego was to become a pueblo in the general plan for the colonization of California. However, a pueblo was not formally organized until the Mexican period when the old presidio had crumbled away and residents were living in Old Town at the foot of the hill. This was on December 21, 1834. The boundaries of the pueblo were vague but generally in keeping with Spanish regulations. These boundaries were officially accepted by the United States, after the defeat of Mexico, as being the lands of the City of San Diego. A large proportion of the original pueblo lands were still being held by the people at the time of the trial.

From old local histories, written memoirs and the direct testimony of early settlers, a pattern of continual use of water from the river was established as the means of survival of the settlement, from the time of the original presidio through the life of the pueblo. It could be argued that any water rights conveyed to the mission were intended to be held only in public trust, and died with the mission.

After many court maneuvers, a decision was handed down on December 7, 1926, by Superior Judge M. W. Conkling, of Imperial County, who had been designated by the governor to hear the case. Conkling held that the City of San Diego was the owner of the prior and paramount rights to the use of all the water. However, while denying that any of the city's rights had been "lost or extinguished or forfeited" by a failure to challenge upper river diversions, he attempted to apportion the water by allotting water to the Cuyamaca Water Company on the basis of established use and because other communities and users had become dependent upon the water. This decision satisfied no one, and the case was carried to the California Supreme Court. Three more years would go by.

The rising boom of the Twenties, and the threat of another period of drought, emphasized the necessity of not only ending disputes over water rights but of assuring adequate supplies. Some of the personal power which a tiring Spreckels had exercised was passing to his son, Claus. The San Diego business leaders, including Fletcher and George Marston, who had felt his opposition, converted their weekly newspaper, the *Independent,* into a daily and sought to assert a new leadership.

With little prospect of constructing El Capitan in the foreseeable future, the city in 1925 adopted a recommendation of its manager of operations, Rhodes, that another private river storage and delivery system be acquired. This was the San Dieguito system from

Dams were never built fast enough, or high enough, to conserve all of the water that might come rushing down from mountain watersheds during wet winters.

Hodges Dam was erected by a subsidiary of the Santa Fe Railroad and subsequently was purchased by the city of San Diego.

The dam consists of twenty-three arches. This was the type of dam favored by Ed Fletcher, who had represented the railroad in its development.

One city hydraulic engineer insisted such dams were not safe and refused to build them. It was still standing in 1967.

which the city already was getting water for La Jolla. It also had been privately developed by Fletcher for the Santa Fe Railroad but had passed into possession of the San Diego County Water Company controlled by the Henshaw interests. The city agreed to acquire Hodges and San Dieguito dams and reservoir lands and pipelines, and in addition the Pamo and Sutherland dam sites. The city also assumed the company's previous commitments to the San Dieguito, Rancho Santa Fe and Del Mar areas. A year later voters approved a $2,000,000 bond issue to construct a dam at the Sutherland site and a diverting dam at San Vicente.

Even the drought of the Twenties failed to move Congress into action on the Swing-Johnson bill for construction of Boulder Dam and the All-American Canal. The farmers in Imperial Valley watched crops wither while for three years they drained a diminishing flow of the Colorado River. In 1925 a new six-state compact was submitted to the basin states, but a provision by the California Legislature that its ratification was subject to federal construction of a high dam, which meant one capable of producing hydroelectric power, threw the entire matter into dispute once more.

Water was becoming more valuable with the arrival of each new settler. In 1926 San Diego, acting on the claim it had filed five years previously and at the urging of Congressman Swing, formally applied to the State Division of Water Resources for a right to 112,000 acre feet annually from the Colorado River. There was no mention of right to power. At that time no determination had been made as to how water from the Colorado River would be delivered 200 miles to San Diego.

San Diego's claim had been filed at the same point where the All-American Canal was expected to divert its water and carry it across the desert floor to the base of the mountains. There, San Diego's share perhaps could be lifted and passed through tunnels and finally dropped into reservoirs of the streams of the western slopes. There were two other possibilities: the building of a separate conduit all the way to the river, or joining with Los Angeles in a metropolitan district with a common aqueduct which could be tapped where convenient.

The financial cost of such an undertaking might have seemed far beyond the reach of a town of barely 130,000 population, and Fletcher and many others insisted that San Diego should go ahead with developing all of its local sources. But the rain on which San Diego depended, and which Theodore Van Dyke said was the sweetest music to the ears of Southern California, would always be an unfinished symphony.

CHAPTER FOUR

KEEP OUT
OF THE WATER

He did!
OFFICIAL PHOTO
BY ERICKSON.

An event that thrilled the world began in San Diego. In 1927 Charles A. Lindbergh flew the San Diego-built Spirit of St. Louis *across the United States and then across the Atlantic Ocean to Paris.*

An unfinished Ryan-designed monoplane was adapted to Lindbergh's specifications. Crews of a little airplane plant in a converted fish cannery worked night and day to meet a sixty-day deadline.

They did. And before his historic flight, a smiling and confident Lindbergh posed before the Spirit of St. Louis *and a placard advising him to "keep out of the water." Later, after his successful flight, someone scribbled on the photograph, "He did!"*

THE FLUSH YEARS

The Roaring Twenties were approaching their height and the tide of movement was ever westward. The year was 1926 and the nation was enjoying an unprecedented prosperity. In California banks were being merged and giant financial institutions created. In Los Angeles more than 2,000,000 persons clustered in and around the city.

In San Diego Spreckels was erecting the massive structure that was to dominate the main business street of the city over which he had exerted so much influence for nearly forty years. He named it the John D. Spreckels Building.

The "geraniums vs. smokestacks" argument seemed to be largely academic. Prosperity was rising with a tourist business and the arrival of retired people who wanted to live out their days in warm comfort and of persons with regular incomes who merely wanted to enjoy themselves.

Only a year before Spreckels had opened his new resort at Mission Beach. A $4,000,000 amusement center was dedicated in May during celebrations of the 75th anniversary of California's admission to the Union. There was a large bathhouse and dancing casino, and along the ocean front was an esplanade and seawall 1600 feet long.

The amusement center was to be just the beginning, and there were plans for a hotel, a stadium for water sports, an auditorium for conventions and theatrical productions and an ice skating rink. It

The Boom of the Twenties was reaching its climax in 1926.
It seemed as if the flow of people to Southern California would never slow down.
For their amusement, and for the sale of real estate, resorts were springing
up everywhere.
This is a 1926 air view of the Mission Beach amusement center, one of John
D. Spreckels' last major development projects. The buildings shown here were
only to be a beginning in the creation of a combined tourist and convention
center.

was considered certain that Mission Beach would strengthen San Diego's ambition to be the recreational capital of the West.

The Spreckels companies also had completed the extension of their electric street car line from Ocean Beach through Mission Beach to La Jolla and almost overnight opened up a scenic marine area for promotional developments which followed almost immediately. If perhaps San Diegans were misreading the signs of the times, and what they might mean to them, they were no different from the businessmen and land salesmen in any other section of the country.

After the death of his brother, Adolph B. Spreckels, in San Francisco in 1924, John D. Spreckels had spent more of his time with the financial affairs of the J. D. & A. B. Spreckels Securities Company, which controlled much of the family fortune, and left some of his interests in San Diego in charge of his son, Claus.

In a curiously impersonal letter dated June 11, 1925, the father suggested that his son surrender all of his connections with these companies and assume the chairmanship of an advisory committee to coordinate all of the expanding San Diego operations. William

Clayton, who had been Spreckels principal manager in San Diego, assumed direct charge of the twelve companies.

While this was being carried out, word was received in San Diego of the death of E. W. Scripps aboard his yacht off the coast of Liberia, North Africa, on March 12, 1926. He was seventy-one years of age. For thirty-four years he had maintained a home at Miramar. Through his newspaper, the *San Diego Sun*, he had dabbled in San Diego politics, sometimes seriously and helpfully and at other times whimsically, but in the main he had spoken for the opposition to the plans of Spreckels. In his later years he had removed himself from the burdens of the operations of his newspapers and from the ambitions of politicians and statesmen, and died virtually alone and was buried at sea.

Spreckels became ill the same Spring. A brother, Rudolph, of San Francisco, with whom he had been estranged for many years, was refused permission to see him, according to notes in a family scrapbook. Death came on June 7, 1926. His son, Claus, was at his bedside. The great building, or monument, he was erecting on Broadway between Sixth and Seventh streets was only half finished.

In issuing a proclamation asking that public buildings and business houses be closed during funeral services, Mayor Bacon said that "this is little enough tribute at the passing of a great San Diegan." Memorial services were held in Balboa Park in the Organ Pavilion which he had built and donated to the city for the Panama-California Exposition in 1915 and 1916. George Burnham, chairman, said:

San Diego has no greater name than John D. Spreckels ... he was the heart and life and nerve ... of the city he loved and helped to build.

His will disposed of shares valued at nearly $15,000,000 in the J. D. and A. B. Spreckels Securities Company. Most of it went to his son, two daughters, and the children of a deceased son. The largest bequest, for $300,000, went to Mercy Hospital. In a little more than one month Claus Spreckels announced he was resigning from the advisory board of the Spreckels interests, and later formed three companies of his own. He stated:

I wasn't much more than an office boy, and I felt that I did not need to work under such conditions. I believe my services will be more valuable to me elsewhere—where what I have to do or say will amount to something.

In the two decades the two Spreckels brothers, John and Adolph, had doubled the $25,000,000 inherited from their father,

*A building that was intended to be a personal monument was rising on
Broadway between Sixth and Seventh streets in San Diego.*
It was named the John D. Spreckels Building.
*Before it was completed, Spreckels died. For nearly forty years he had
dominated a community that he had decided must become one of the great
cities of the Pacific Coast.*
*After his death, the Spreckels empire in San Diego was broken up. One of
the first properties to be sold was the John D. Spreckels Building.*

Claus Spreckels, despite having had losses in San Diego. In addition to the holdings in San Diego, the company properties included half-interest in the Spreckels Sugar Company, full ownership of the gigantic Western Sugar Refinery, downtown San Francisco real estate, the Oceanic Steamship Company Line, and properties, plantations and business holdings at Coos Bay, Oregon, the Hawaiian Islands and the Philippines.

The death of John D. Spreckels also marked the last time that any Spreckels sat on the board of directors of the sugar companies. The Spreckels brothers were succeeded in the company management, not by sons but by in-laws. The securities company was changed from a partnership to a corporation and the estate of Adolph Spreckels was held in a trust which permitted the exercise of control. The investments in San Diego had never been popular with the other San Francisco members of the family.

The breakup of the large Spreckels holdings in San Diego was near at hand. When John D. Spreckels first saw San Diego it was a town of about 35,000. When the boom of the 1880's ended, the population dropped to 16,000. Before his death he had seen it climb to at least 140,000. The final five years had been the most significant and could have produced the rewards for which Spreckels had spent so much and worked so long.

Much of the freight along the coast moved by ship in the Twenties. And so did people.
This photograph shows one of two famed white sister ships, the Yale *and* Harvard, *which plied the Pacific Coast and gave passengers cosmopolitan treatment, with bands and buffets.*
With the boom, the value of cargo in ocean shipping at San Diego jumped in five years from nineteen million to more than thirty-five million annually. In one day five ships arrived with two million feet of lumber.

For three years San Diego had been a "white spot" on the nation's business map. Between 1920 and 1926, the number of building permits issued annually increased from 2609, valued at $3,537,107, to 8320, valued at $18,198,200. The city building inspector, Oscar G. Knecht, said that just to keep pace with growth in the next year San Diego would have to have $3,500,000 in new homes and $6,500,000 in new hotels, schools, churches and business buildings.

The value of ocean shipping increased in five years from $19,000,000 to more than $35,000,000 annually. Five steamships arrived in a single day, bringing more than 2,000,000 feet of lumber. Congress appropriated $250,000 to begin work on a $1,000,000 naval pier and bids were opened for further federal dredging of the harbor. The ornate Commonwealth Building and its theater at Fifth and B streets opened a new world of entertainment. The Medico-Dental Arts announced a thirteen-story professional building would be erected at the corner of Second and A streets. Charles Holzwasser, who had opened a department store at Broadway and Fifth Street in 1920, announced plans for an adjoining fourteen-story structure. The membership campaign of the newly organized San Diego Athletic Club passed its goal and a $550,000 club building was to be erected at Sixth and A streets.

John P. Mills

The tourist business for the winter of 1925-1926 was considered to be the best on record, and the Chamber of Commerce magazine reported that apartment houses had been filled:

As a result of the rush the housing bureau of the San Diego-California Club has proved a friend in time of need to a number of winter visitors. Every day the services of the bureau have been called upon to solve a housing problem for people from other sections of the United States who have come to San Diego to dodge winter climate which prevails in their home towns.

Alexander Pantages

From Hollywood came the Talmadge sisters, the actresses Constance, Norma and Natalie, to open a subdivision they called Talmadge Park. Beach lots at La Jolla Shores were selling at prices from $4000 to $10,000. The newly organized Club La Jolla de la Playa was selling memberships for its club on La Jolla's "whispering sands." A real estate and oil lands speculator in Los Angeles, who had run a stake of $400 into $6,000,000 in four years, came to San Diego to look over the opportunities, at the suggestion of a local banker, Jesse Shreve. He was John P. Mills. Together, they walked through the sage brush on the ocean side of Point Loma and decided to subdivide it. Shortly afterward they were joined in

All undeveloped coastal lands were subject to speculation in the Great Boom. In the days before high income taxes Hollywood money flowed in all directions. One of San Diego's more exclusive residential areas of the day was developed by the Talmadge sisters, of the films.
They are shown at the opening of sales for lots in Talmadge Park.
There were so many people coming to Southern California and San Diego, that many of them had to be quartered in private homes until more houses could be built.

the project by Alexander Pantages, the theater chain owner. In a statement Mills said:

All great authorities agree that Southern California is, without doubt, to become the most densely populated center in the United States within a very short time. The reason, of course, primarily, is climatic conditions; San Diego has something that no other city in the United States has—that is, the most equable climate in all of this great country.

The question was asked: what is the population of California going to be? The *Los Angeles Examiner* compared the size of the state with England and Italy. Great Britain had a population of more than 42,000,000 persons in an area of less than 90,000 square miles, and Italy a population of perhaps 39,000,000 in 118,000 square miles. In contrast, California with 158,000 square miles, in 1926 had a population of only 5,000,000.

Los Angeles had become one of the most important manufacturing centers of the country. In searching for reasons why San Diego had not kept relative pace, the managing secretary of the Chamber of Commerce, Orville McPherson, said he had become convinced the city had to determine what one big product it was best suited to manufature and then concentrate on it. He suggested aviation:

Commercial aviation is entering on an era of development that will equal the automobile industry and perhaps surpass it some day ... San Diego is fortunate in having a very promising nucleus already in the Ryan monoplane factory.

The airline that T. Claude Ryan had inaugurated between San Diego and Los Angeles had grown to fifteen airplanes, the largest a "twelve passenger air bus." He became dissatisfied with the type of planes available and designed a high-wing monoplane. An article in *Air Transportation* magazine of 1928 recalled the pioneering period:

B. Franklin Mahoney

> Three men were gathered around a table covered with papers and drawings late one night in November, 1925. The place was San Diego, California, and the men were B. F. Mahoney, Hawley Bowlus and T. C. Ryan. The rough drawings of Bowlus showed three views of an unusual parasol type monoplane. The monoplane type was singular enough in those days for Fokker was the only manufacturer at that time who was using this design commercially in this country.
>
> None of those present was sufficiently schooled in engineering to figure a stress analysis of the new model, and consequently the services of Wm. Waterhouse, a Los Angeles engineer, were called in to complete this important detail.

The new airplane was designated the M-1 and the first one was produced in a shed on Dutch Flats in less than ninety days and was tested on February 1, 1926. The M-1 made aviation history up and down the coast. It flew from Vancouver Field, Washington, to Los Angeles, more than 1100 miles, in nine hours and fifty minutes, non-stop. As a result the Pacific Air Transport Company, a forerunner of United Air Lines, was drawn to the sturdy little ship and ordered seven of them.

In September the increased production of the M-1 and of an improved model known as the M-2, required an expansion and operations were moved to an unused cannery on the waterfront at the foot of Juniper Street. About twenty-three M-1s and M-2s were turned out the first year of production.

When he started manufacturing planes, Ryan discontinued the San Diego-Los Angeles air service, after about a year of operation. It had carried passengers and some express but no airmail. By the end of 1926, Ryan disposed of his interest in the company to his partner and financial backer, B. Franklin Mahoney, although he remained as general manager.

The recommendation of the planner John Nolen that San Diego should have a major airport and that it should be on waterfront tidelands, was taken up by the aviation committee of the Chamber of Commerce. The site was within ten to fifteen minutes of the business district, the post office and all other transportation terminals. Major T. C. Macaulay, a former pioneer Army flier, was chairman of the aviation committee, and he urged a bond issue for its construction in the near future. He said:

San Diego will occupy the unique position of being one of the few cities in the world, if not the only city, where the municipal airport allows both types of aircraft, one operating from the land, the other from the water.

Major T. C. Macaulay

By resolution the Nolen Plan was the official development plan for San Diego, but there were many in the city who remembered how the original city plan submitted by Nolen in 1908 had been violated almost immediately and quickly buried. A test of the new Nolen Plan came in its first year in 1926. A new site was sought for San Diego State College, which had outgrown its buildings at Normal Street and Park Boulevard. It was proposed that it be placed in Balboa Park east of Park Boulevard, which would have absorbed all of the remaining undeveloped land in the park.

The park as well as the waterfront were central to Nolen's conception of the kind of a city San Diego should become. In a re-study of the park he recommended appropriate landscaping, the location of new roads and that the disputed area be devoted to recreation. Nolen warned that the encroachments upon the park were serious, probably more so than in any other major American city, and urged San Diegans to preserve what remained of the park's integrity. George Marston, who had recovered his health and again was active in civic affairs, Ellen Browning Scripps, and Lane D. Webber, president of the Chamber of Commerce, led the fight against a park site. The proposal was defeated by a two-to-one margin at a city election November 23, 1926.

Lane D. Webber

The 18th amendment to the Constitution, which prohibited the sale of liquor, and the flow of tourists brought a simultaneous boom to Tijuana, the Mexican town across the border. It had been a tourist attraction since the inauguration of horse racing with betting, which was illegal in California, in 1916. By 1926 it had somewhere around seventy-five bars, with all of the accompaniments of sin and trouble. On February 6, a Mr. and Mrs. Thomas M. Peteet and their nineteen-year-old daughter were found dead in their small home in San Diego. Another daughter, twenty-six, was in a dying condition. Removed to a hospital, she succumbed three days later. The house had been closed tight and the gas turned on.

Their story soon came out. They had been to Tijuana, and the girls drugged and subjected to abuse. The parents evidently pre-

Tijuana was enjoying its first tourist boom in 1926.
This is a street scene, taken a few years before the boom began to reach its height.
The suicide of a family after a visit to Tijuana brought about the arrest of a number of Mexican officials and a cleanup campaign that made Tijuana safe for tourists.
The frontier days were over, at one of the last outposts of Pacific Coast settlement.

ferred death for all to disgrace for their daughters. The deaths caused a furore in two nations and the United States government ordered the international border closed each evening at 6 o'clock until 8:00 the next morning. In Baja California, Governor Abelardo Rodríguez closed fifty-two saloons, permitted only five restaurants to remain open, and drove undesirables out of town. The chief of police was among seven persons indicted for complicity in what had happened to the Peteets in Tijuana. The seven were eventually tried, but no convictions ever resulted. But slowly Tijuana began to assume an air of respectability that would make it one of the continent's major tourist attractions in the number of annual visitors.

In the Julian mountain country of San Diego County gold again was being mined. Gold was discovered in 1870, but after several millions of dollars in metal had been taken out, the thin veins went too deep for practical recovery at that time.

The cultural side of a booming area was not to be neglected. The Fine Arts Gallery, the gift of Mr. and Mrs. Appleton S. Bridges, was dedicated in Balboa Park on February 27, 1926. One of the exposition's most ornate buildings, on the north side of the central plaza, had been torn down to make way for the gallery. It was designed by William Templeton Johnson in keeping with the Spanish-Colonial period which had characterized the exposition. George Marston retained an associate of John Nolen to plan a park on land he owned around the old Spanish presidio above Old Town.

Though Ellen Browning Scripps was ninety years of age, her life

*The mountains always had been an obstacle in the path of the civic greatness
San Diegans always expected.*
*There were no passes comparable to those which led into Los Angeles. But
years of struggle were culminated by the paving of Mountain Springs grade
which led up from the desert floor.*
*This grade was the most difficult part of the southern transcontinental highways,
and even with its pavement, it was shunned by many tourists who took an
easier but longer route to Los Angeles.*

Ellen Browning Scripps

Friend W. Richardson

Clement C. Young

was not yet at an end. The Scripps College for Women, which she had endowed as one of a group of colleges at Claremont, opened its doors in September of 1927. This was the third of her major contributions. The others were the Scripps Institution for Biological Research, which became part of the University of California in 1912, and the Scripps Hospital and Metabolic Clinic. As a result of her interest and her gifts of land, the Torrey Pines Park Preserve was formally established by the City Council.

The era was one of a good feeling and general business expansion. Republican Calvin Coolidge was President and in California Republicans were well into their long domination of the state government. A conservative Republican governor, Friend W. Richardson, encouraged business and industry and kept a tight rein on government costs and expansion, except in highway development. His program, calling for a bond issue and additional motor vehicle taxes, was approved by the voters, and 300 miles of roads were paved in the state during his regime.

In San Diego County, two routes had been taken into the state system: the highway from San Diego to Los Angeles and the highway from San Diego to Imperial Valley and Yuma. In 1927 the state graded and laid a twenty-foot pavement from the top of Mountain Springs grade to the floor of the desert, a distance of about eighty miles. Even with this improvement, the road had sharp curves and a gradient of seven percent. Accidents were numerous, as by this time many heavy, slow-moving trucks with trailers were transporting farm products into San Diego from Imperial Valley in competition with the San Diego & Arizona Railway.

Richardson's successful highway program was not enough to save him from defeat. He lost his bid for renomination to Clement C. Young, who had the support of Senator Hiram Johnson and what was left of the progressive-liberal forces in the Republican Party, who resented Richardson's vetoes of many of their legislative proposals. Young's nomination was tantamount to election, and he took office in January of 1927. The radical novelist, Upton Sinclair, ran for governor on a Socialist ticket and received only a little more than 45,900 votes. But he was to be heard from again.

With water problems off his hands, Ed Fletcher convinced the Chamber of Commerce to back him in a cross-country auto trip on behalf of a proposed national highway between the Pacific and the Atlantic oceans, from Savannah, Georgia, to San Diego. The Lee Highway was the only national cross-country route designated as ending at San Diego. It drew traffic from New York into Washington, D.C., and along a southern, all-weather route. He was expected to finance the trip himself, and did. Only five percent of the roads between the two points had been paved. The race against time began on October 20, 1926. With his son, Ed Fletcher Jr. and two companions, he followed the Borderland Highway to Phoenix and Tucson. At Phoenix Fletcher was quoted on the value of a paved road between Yuma and Phoenix:

A golden stream of 10,000 people a month is the biggest asset you can get to help this town. It is worth your while to get cooperation on this national highway.

From Tucson, the route led through Bisbee and Douglas, Arizona, through Lordsburg and Deming, in New Mexico, to El Paso. East of El Paso they picked up what was known as the Dixie Overland Highway and crossed Texas by way of Fort Worth and Dallas, and then it was almost straight east through Shreveport, Louisiana; Vicksburg, Mississippi; and Montgomery, Albama. They entered Georgia near Columbus and terminated at Savannah on the coast. The trip of 2535 miles, with few stops, was made in seventy-one hours and fifteen minutes, breaking the transcontinental auto record by eleven hours and fifty-six minutes, and exceeding the best train time by twenty-eight hours. The trip was publicized nationally and within two months the route from Savannah to San Diego was officially designated U.S. Highway 80.

Phoenix, however, proved to be a thorn in San Diego's tourist ambitions. At Phoenix auto traffic could be diverted onto Highway 60 and to Los Angeles. Business and political interests in Tucson, with the cooperation of San Diegans, laid out a bypass which made it easy to eliminate Phoenix in driving west over the southern route. This was the Casa Grande-Gila Bend cutoff. It left Highway 80 at Tucson and rejoined it west of Phoenix at Gila Bend, saving ninety miles on the route to San Diego.

There were only a few whitecaps in a sea of prosperity. In one of the strange occurrences of nature, albacore suddenly began to change their accustomed travels. Albacore, the "chicken of the sea," was the choicest of tuna and had become in great demand as a result of its substitution for meat during World War I. This was to bring about a drastic change in the operations of the California fishing fleet.

So little was known of the sea and its possibilities for the enrichment of man. In 1925 the name of the Scripps Institution for Biological Research, which had become a part of the University of California, was changed to the Scripps Institution of Oceanography and its program enlarged to embrace physical, chemical, geological and geophysical studies of the oceans, as well as biological studies.

At one time there had been eleven plants in Southern California for harvesting and processing kelp, but they had largely disappeared with the end of the war-time demand for potash for explosives and fertilizers. By 1927 interest in the by-products of kelp revived and two companies began large-scale harvesting. One of them was started by a can company to obtain algin to be used in sealing tin cans, and it became the Kelco Company. The company also began producing dried kelp meal as a vegetable-mineral supplement in animal feeds. Another firm harvested seaweed for use in health pills.

Some of the revenue from the state's leasing of kelp beds went to the Scripps Institution of Oceanography, to help in furthering research in the mysteries of the sea.

Sale of portions of the Spreckels empire, now controlled from San Francisco, was being discussed privately with prospective buyers. All that was known publicly, however, was that the J.D. & A.B. Spreckels Securities Company obtained authorization from the Board of Supervisors to build a low bridge between San Diego and Coronado, at a cost of $2,400,000, and would take the matter before Army engineers.

Most of the political influence of the Spreckels interests was gone, however, as a city election approached. The county assessor announced a sharp increase in assessed valuations and hence in taxes. Rumors spread that all was not going well with the water development program which had been sold to the public. A contract had been awarded for construction of a multiple arch type dam at the Sutherland site on the San Dieguito River system, but there were reports that costs were exceeding estimates and foundation difficulties were being encountered. No one seemed to know when, if ever, the city's rights on the San Diego River finally would be determined. The water development program, so important to a community in a semi-arid country, sank into more controversy and error.

Confidence in the city administration was beginning to wane and in the primary election in March of 1927 there was a scramble for the office of mayor when John Bacon announced he would not seek re-election.

It was at this election that the voters were asked to formally pass on the key point of the Nolen Plan, the grouping of public buildings on a tidelands site. The City Hall was on lower Fifth Street, no longer a principal business area, and the Courthouse on Broad-

Harry C. Clark

way had been in use for more than half a century. An alternative proposal to the tidelands site was for an easily-accessible combined city-county "skyscraper" on the Courthouse site in the center of the city. Proponents of the Nolen Plan argued that San Diego no longer was a "one-street" town and the tidelands site offered an opportunity to dramatize the city and to avoid the crowded conditions of ugly eastern cities.

The opposition, however, was subdued and mostly confined to exhortations to defeat the plans of "tax eaters" who would saddle homeowners with millions of dollars of unnecessary expenditures. A Civic Center on the tidelands was approved by a narrow margin, 15,617 to 14,006.

Don M. Stewart

The closeness of this vote perhaps reflected one of the costs of the advertising campaigns that had lured retired people and others of modest incomes to San Diego. They had little interest in the economic projects of the business community or the civic improvement programs of the politicians. A bigger city and higher taxes had no appeal for them.

Nominated at the primary to run-off for the office of mayor were a lawyer named Harry C. Clark and a businessman and mortician, Percy J. Benbough. A candidate for the City Council accused the existing Council of having made a "pork barrel" out of the need for water in its decision to build Sutherland Dam. He was S. P. McMullen, a former chief of police whom the *San Diego Sun* charged had been fired for permitting a wide open town.

As a result of the primary and general elections of 1927, Clark was elected mayor and a new Council majority went into office. Defeated were Fred Heilbron, who had led the effort to claim Colorado River water for the future, Don M. Stewart and John A. Held. Elected to the council were S. P. McMullen, Edward H. Dowell, a labor leader, and Frank W. Seifert, a materials dealer who as a pioneer Army flier had participated in the first aerial refueling.

Soon afterward, Fred Rhodes, who had directed the city's water program after the discharge of Hiram Savage, was fired as manager of city operations. An investigation disclosed that the part of the foundation for Sutherland Dam was not safe and geologists recommended that the site be abandoned and the dam moved upstream about a thousand feet. Cost of the structure was expected to double.

S. P. McMullen

Upon leaving office Bacon said that the dismissal of Savage had been a great mistake and had disrupted San Diego's logical and steady program of development of its local water resources. He

Southern California rivers are deceptive. Usually dry, they can become raging floods in a matter of hours.
This shows the San Diego River at flood stage in 1927. Runoff from a series of storms flooded Mission Valley, from one side to the other, and threatened to carry out the Santa Fe railroad bridge.
Engineers prepared to dynamite it to alleviate a backing up of flood waters. But the water subsided almost as quickly as it had risen.

warned though that the city should proceed quickly to protect its rights on the Colorado River:

Our future water supply must come from the Colorado River ... were every drop of water that falls in this part of California to be conserved, it is hard to see how San Diego can satisfy her ever-increasing water demands for more than twenty years in the future.

The winter of 1926-1927 brought almost disastrous storms and in February San Diego was isolated by the flooding of the San Diego River. The approaches to the highway bridge over the river were dynamited to ease the pressure of water that spread across the floor of the valley. With train service by the Santa Fe and San Diego & Arizona suspended for six days, mail was carried to and from Los Angeles in boats by the U.S. Naval Reserve.

In a single storm that lasted from February 13 to 17, six and a half inches of rain fell in the city and more than twenty-eight inches at Cuyamaca Lake. The city's five reservoirs were filled to overflowing, and though the city now had a five to seven-year supply of water, the greatest in its history, billions of gallons had been lost to the sea by the failure to construct the dams that had been argued about for a decade. Sites for storage reservoirs that might have contolled the San Diego River flood were tied up in the seemingly endless litigation over water rights.

Even if he knew of San Diego, its problems could have been of no concern to a young pilot who had volunteered for the first experimental flying of mail. His name was Charles A. Lindbergh and he was twenty-five years old. Aviation had developed to a point where it was possible to deliver a letter from New York to San Francisco in thirty-six hours, as compared with a train time of four days.

While on a lonely night flight between St. Louis and Chicago in the Fall of 1926, Lindbergh thought of the $25,000 that had been offered as a prize for the first non-stop trans-Atlantic airplane crossing.

Dirigibles had made the ocean crossing and two civilian pilots had flown from Newfoundland to Ireland and one Navy flying boat out of a flight of three had managed to cross from Newfoundland to Portugal. But the attempt to span the Atlantic between New York and Paris in heavier-than-air craft already had claimed four lives and seriously injured three others fliers. But for the first time the possibility occurred to Lindbergh that he might be able to make such a crossing. In his book, *We,* he wrote:

Several facts soon became outstanding. The foremost was that with the modern radial air-cooled motor, high lift airfoils, and lightened construction, it would not only be possible to reach Paris but, under normal conditions, to land with a large reserve of fuel and have a high factor of safety throughout the entire trip as well.

In St. Louis, Lindbergh obtained the financial backing of business men, but negotiations with two companies for an airplane of the requirements and capabilities he desired were disappointing. They did not take the young, unknown pilot very seriously.

It was then that he noticed the advertisements of a small company on the West Coast whose planes had been making good records in flying the mail in all kinds of weather. The advertisement of Ryan Airlines read:

Step into a parachute and take the Ryan M-1 to 10,000 feet. It will only take a few minutes—then try to turn it inside out.

Loop it, barrel roll it, dive it a thousand feet and pull back quick on the stick. Try to whip-stall it; try to spin it, wind it up in a tight spiral, full throttle, kick top rudder, give it everything; then float it down and look it over.

A biplane would probably need re-rigging. But the Ryan M-1 will be just as tight as the day it left the factory. Your little test ride will not even be a good work-out.

A LINDBERGH ALBUM

A wingless Spirit of St. Louis *is pulled by auto from the converted fish cannery where is was built. Charles A. Lindbergh looks backward protectively.*

The wing of the Spirit of St. Louis *was built separately in the loft of the Mahoney plant and lowered by crane to the street.*

This is the Ryan Field along Barnett Avenue as it appeared in 1927. It was here that Lindbergh's plane was put together.

*Test flights proved the plane's stability and load-carrying ability.
A final landing on Ryan Field, and all was ready.*

*The goodbyes were said. Lindbergh is shaking hands with Army flier Ira C. Eaker,
later one of America's air generals. At the extreme left is Donald A. Hall, the
company's engineer, and next to him, A. J. Edwards, with whom Lindbergh roomed.*

Charles Lindbergh "guns" the Spirit of St. Louis *before lifting off for North
Island, from where he began his flight East.*

The company was working at the time on an improved and larger version of the M-1 and M-2 which would become known as the Ryan Brougham. The first one was being specially built for a speed flier, Frank Hawks, and was referred to as the *Gold Bug*. After some figuring, Claude Ryan, who was still with the company as manager, and Donald A. Hall, the recently hired engineer, responded to Lindbergh's inquiry with an assurance that within sixty days and at a cost of only $6000, plus the engine and instruments, they could deliver a plane capable of making a nonstop flight from New York to Paris.

Lindbergh visited the small plant and inspected the uncompleted *Gold Bug*. It was not a sight that might have inspired the confidence of rival pilots who were readying planes for the trans-Atlantic flight that were costing $100,000. But Lindbergh quickly realized that the Ryan plane was something different. He talked with Ryan, who at age twenty-nine already was an established designer and manufacturer of airplanes; the company president, B. Franklin Mahoney, who was only a year older than Lindbergh himself; and the factory manager, William Hawley Bowlus, as well as Donald Hall, the engineer. It was decided that the *Gold Bug* being built for the speed flier could be adapted for the flight, and with the engine, the cost would be $10,580. Hawks agreed to let Lindbergh have the plane which he had ordered.

A contract was signed on February 28, 1927. Lindbergh told reporters confidentially, "I'll get to Paris with this airplane." This was important news in San Diego, and perhaps in St. Louis, but in New York, where other pilots with multiple-engine planes were preparing for the same flight in the hope of winning the race across the Atlantic, Lindbergh's name received little, if any, attention. Lindbergh roomed in San Diego with the company's sales manager, A. J. Edwards. In his own story he related:

The personnel of Ryan Airlines at once caught the spirit of the undertaking, and during two months of construction the organization labored as it never had before. Day and night, seven days a week, the structure grew from a few lengths of steel tubing to one of the most efficient planes that has ever taken the air. During this time it was not unusual for the men to work twenty-four hours without rest, and on one occasion, Donald Hall, the chief engineer, was over his drafting table for thirty-six hours.

Near the end of April the fuselage of the Ryan plane was rolled out of the hangar, and its forty-six foot wing, four feet longer than the projected version of the Ryan Brougham, was lifted by crane out of the loft. One of the plant foremen who watched the roll-out was Fred H. Rohr. The fuselage and wing were trucked to the

Ryan field north of Barnett Avenue, on Dutch Flats. Assembled, the plane stood nine feet, eight inches high and had an overall length of twenty-seven feet, eight inches. It had five fuel tanks and weighed 2150 pounds. Fully loaded and with its pilot it would weigh 5180 pounds.

The first test flight was set for April 28. The deadline of sixty days had been met. Painted on the tail of the plane was *Spirit of St. Louis*. With Lindbergh at the controls, the plane took to the air after a run of only 165 feet and though some stability had been sacrificed for range and load capacity, the first flight was considered highly successful. Load test flights were conducted from the parade ground of the Army's World War I camp on Kearny Mesa north of the city, where rocks were cleared from a surface that stretched for 12,000 feet. Speed tests were conducted on May 4 over the south bay on a course laid out by the Army Air Service.

When all of the scheduled tests had been completed, the *Spirit of St. Louis* had exceeded its theoretical design performance. It was determined that it could fly at economic speeds non-stop for 4210 miles, and thus could reach Paris, 3610 miles from New York by the Great Circle Route, in a little more than forty hours. With the completion of the tests came the end of Claude Ryan's association with the original company he had founded.

While Lindbergh was preparing to leave San Diego, two French fliers, who had hoped to be the first to span the Atlantic on a non-stop flight, disappeared at sea. Lindbergh's departure for St. Louis was delayed by a storm which blanketed the Southwest. On the afternoon of May 9, the chief of the U.S. Weather Bureau at San Diego, Dean Blake, predicted favorable flying conditions would begin on the following day. In the morning Lindbergh flew the *Spirit of St. Louis* across the bay to Rockwell Field on North Island, to take advantage of its long runway, and took off at 3:55 in the afternoon, escorted by two Army observation planes and a Ryan monoplane with Hall as a passenger. As Lindbergh told his own story:

The ship passed over the first ridge of mountains, about 4000 feet, very easily with reduced throttle. The escorting planes turned back at the mountains and I passed on over the desert and the Salton Sea alone. And at sunset I was over the deserts and mountains of western Arizona.

The moon was well above the horizon and with the exception of a short period before dawn I was able to distinguish the contour of the country the entire night. I flew a compass course, passing alternately over snow-capped ridges, deserts and fertile valleys. One of the mountain ranges was over 12,000 feet high and completely snow-covered. I cleared this range by about 500 feet and went over the plains beyond.

A medal for Lindbergh

He touched down on Lambert Field, St. Louis, at 8:20 in the morning, and at 8:13 o'clock the next morning, May 12, he left for New York, arriving at Curtiss Field on Long Island at 5:33 in the evening. Overnight the reticent figure in the small plane captured the imagination of the country. He was the "Lone Eagle." As soon as weather conditions were favorable, the plane was trucked to the adjoining Roosevelt Field and at 7:52 in the morning of May 20 he took off for Paris. Thirty-three hours and twenty-nine minutes later he saw the lights of Paris, circled the Eiffel Tower and landed at Le Bourget Field. Nothing since the end of World War I caused such reaction throughout the world. He had become a living legend of American youth.

At the moment of the triumph of the plane that was the product of his imagination and enterprise, Claude Ryan was returning to San Diego from New York where he had obtained a manufacturing license and distribution contract for the Siemens aircraft engines of Germany. These engines, known as Ryan-Siemens, became standard equipment on most makes of American private type aircraft.

In autographing the book of his flight, Lindbergh wrote, "To Claude Ryan, who built the company that built the *Spirit of St. Louis*." As with the pioneers of flight on Rockwell Field, who later became commanders of vast war fleets of the air, Ryan and Fred Rohr, who had worked as a foreman on the *Spirit of St. Louis*, would later help to guide an industry from hand work to assembly lines and then into the space age.

CHAPTER FIVE

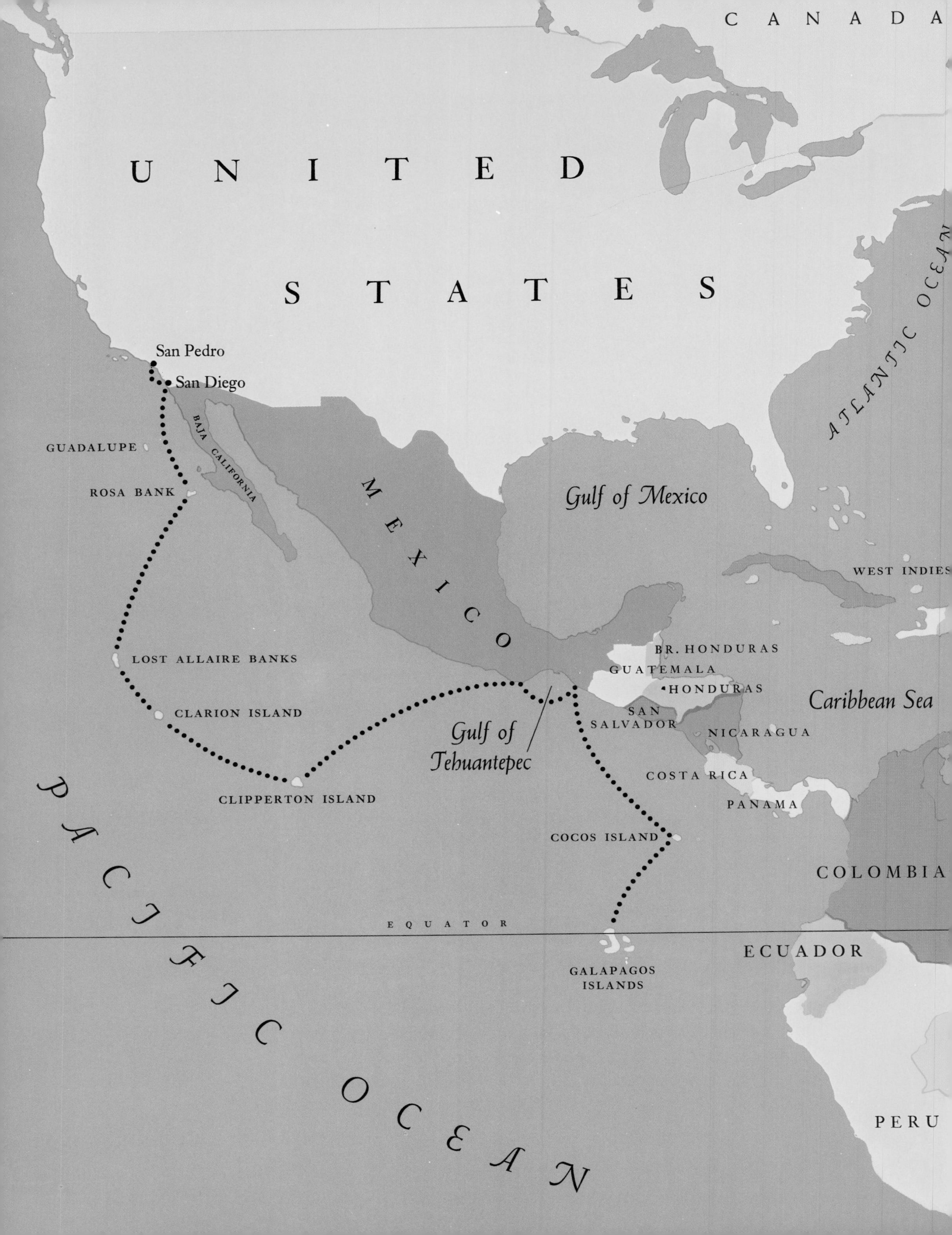

CANADA

UNITED
STATES

ATLANTIC OCEAN

San Pedro
San Diego

GUADALUPE

ROSA BANK

BAJA CALIFORNIA

MEXICO

Gulf of Mexico

WEST INDIES

LOST ALLAIRE BANKS

CLARION ISLAND

CLIPPERTON ISLAND

Gulf of
Tehuantepec

BR. HONDURAS

GUATEMALA

HONDURAS

Caribbean Sea

SAN
SALVADOR

NICARAGUA

COSTA RICA

PANAMA

COCOS ISLAND

COLOMBIA

PACIFIC

EQUATOR

ECUADOR

GALAPAGOS
ISLANDS

OCEAN

PERU

The pursuit of tuna is one of California's exciting stories.
In the early years of the fishing industry albacore was the favorite for canning,
and made tuna acceptable as a quality food all over the United States.
But then the albacore changed their habits and largely disappeared from the
Pacific Coast for a considerable length of time.
This map shows how the pursuit of the albacore began. The pursuit ended,
however, in the discovery of vast yellowfin grounds which revolutionized
the industry.

THE LONG CHASE

For all that anyone knew, it had always been that way. About the first of July of each year, sometimes earlier, sometimes later, albacore arrived at the Coronado Islands in Mexican waters just south of San Diego. In three weeks they worked their way up the California coast through the channel between San Pedro and Catalina Island. By August they were in the vicinity of Santa Cruz Island in the Santa Barbara channel.

By September they had worked their way back to the Coronados. When the skipjack appeared, the albacore disappeared, "like the blowing out of a light."

Albacore was the choicest of the tuna fish and a whole industry had grown up with a rising demand for its white, tasty meat. Three other varieties of tuna in California and Mexican waters were being taken and processed, yellowfin, bluefin and skipjack. The yellowfin always came in season first, with the beginning of the year, and the fishing lasted about sixty days, when the bluefin came and ran all summer.

The coastal area frequented by the albacore was found to be very small in extent. The southward limit of commercial possibilities was Descanso Point not far below the international border, though occasional specimens were found as far south as San Quintin Bay. The albacore seemed to travel some well-defined ocean highway that reached the coast near San Diego. Where it began or ended nobody knew.

In 1926 the albacore suddenly began shifting farther out to sea and some fishermen feared that they might disappear from the coast altogether. The cause of the change in their habits was not known. There was speculation it might have been due to a shift in the Japanese current, or to a faint contamination of the water from the oil of boats, or from sewers.

The albacore catch in 1925 was more than twenty-two million pounds. In 1926, albacore caught off the California coast had dwindled to a little less than two and a half million pounds. The total rose somewhat in 1927, but the following year was the poorest on record, with less than 300,000 pounds taken in coastal waters.

Summer arrived late in 1929. There really had been no Spring at all. Toward the last of June a few warm days occurred and immediately, as if bred by the sunshine, excited rumors were spread around of albacore landings—big landings—but always at some distant port. By the middle of July some landings were being made at San Diego and a few at San Pedro.

Fishermen were confident that the Long Fin, as they were known, were actually returning in numbers as they were appearing in groups or schools, instead of being dispersed over large areas of the sea. A boat either landed a good catch or none at all. By the end of August, however, it was estimated that the total catch had not exceeded sixty-five tons. In the *West Coast Fisheries* magazine of September of 1929, George Roger Chute wrote:

When the sun goes down at six o'clock, you may know that the albacore season is through. With the waning of the days, the Long Fin take their departure, for even the lingering heats of a late September fail to deter them from the instinctive trait of making their autumnal disappearance about the close of the month of August.

Therefore we know that the end is here. And a queer sort of end it is, for it seems almost like the conclusion of a thing that never had a beginning. Rather than the end of actual fishing, it is the end of our hopes, for all of us —as always—have hoped against hope that this year, this year, the fish would return at last.

The pursuit of albacore into warmer waters was disappointing. Boats cruised the 825-mile long coast of Lower California, waters they had known but whose fishing possibilities they had never fully developed. Crews became familiar with the isolated bays of the unfriendly peninsula. From San Quintin Bay, 160 miles south of San Diego, they pushed on to Cedros Island and Vizcaino Bay, 300 miles from home, and then visited Turtle Bay just below Vizcaino Bay. Magdalena Bay was 375 miles farther down the peninsula.

Then they turned the bows of their vessels around Cape San Lucas and into the Gulf of California. Eventually the search was carried westward as far as the Hawaiian Islands.

Fishermen learned from their fruitless chase of the albacore that the farther south they went the richer the fishing for yellowfin and skipjack, which were steadily growing in importance. An advertising campaign successfully stimulated the acceptability of "light-meat" instead of "white-meat" tuna. Fishermen discovered in their invasion of the southern seas they did not have to be tied to seasons in taking yellowfin and skipjack.

Tuna often were found with the porpoise and there seemed to be some symbolic relationship between them. Fantastic stories were circulated as to the size and abundance of warm water tuna. The slopes of underwater hills proved to be rich with fish hunting each other. Manuel G. Rosa, a Portuguese skipper who had been born on the island of Pico in the Azores, discovered a fishing bank southwest of Vizcaino Bay which became known as the "Rosa Bank." He later recalled:

Manuel G. Rosa

> The tuna were so thick that it looked as if one could have walked across the ocean on their backs. They were hungry, too, and it required very little time to fill our boat to capacity.

The year that the albacore disappeared the fleets caught more than 16,000,000 pounds of all varieties of tuna in Mexican waters. The total catch, in the waters above and below the international border, was more than 45,000,000 pounds. In another year this was doubled.

In a short time a wide-ranging, live-bait fishing fleet had been created, with a range of more than 5000 miles. It was Manuel O. Medina of San Diego who built the first of the great clippers and then set his eyes on the equator.

The fishing colony of Southern California was dominated by the Portuguese. Medina was born on the volcanic island of Pico in the Azores group 600 miles off the coast of Portugal, as had so many in the fishing fleet. Others had come from San Miguel in the Azores, or from the mainland, and later they were joined by Portuguese from the Madeiras and the Cape Verde Islands off the coast of North Africa. Long periods at sea were common to the Portuguese fishermen. The Lisbon fleets had been sailing regularly from the River Tagus in Portugal to the Grand Banks of Newfoundland, on voyages lasting six to eight months.

Manuel O. Medina

Other Portuguese had been picked up from their islands by the whaling fleets of New Bedford, Massachusetts. Before them, others

The Atlantic was the first of the real tuna clippers. It was built for long-range ocean fishing and the pursuit of tuna as far south as the Galapagos Islands 3000 miles from San Diego. It led the first tuna boats across the equator in 1929. More to be feared than mere distance were the storms, particularly the chubascos, which are born along the Mexico-Guatemala border and move in a northwest direction with fearful winds blowing up to 125 miles an hour.

San Diego

San Quintin
Bay

CEDROS
ISLAND

Vizcaino
Bay

Turtle
Bay
SAN ROQUE
ISLAND   ASCUNCION
San   ISLAND
Hipolito
Point

Magdalena Bay

Cape San Lucas

*Baja California
Points and Bays*

had migrated to America and had roamed the Pacific seas with the Boston fur ships. And even before them, a Portuguese in the service of Spain, Juan Rodriguez Cabrillo, had been the first to explore the northern Pacific Coast and sight the ports of California.

In San Diego they had clustered in the La Playa-Roseville area of Point Loma, from where they originally had pursued the gray whales on the annual migrations up and down the Pacific Coast from breeding grounds in the lagoons of Lower California. In competition with Chinese and Italians, the Portuguese, with their long love and respect of the sea, gradually came to control the off-shore fishing fleets as they spread out over a vast area almost two-thirds the size of the United States.

But when Medina started building the *Atlantic* many in the industry thought he was "crazy." The *Atlantic* was 112 feet long, the first tuna boat of more than 100 feet. It was equipped with refrigeration and a diesel engine. Even at that it probably was only forty-five to fifty feet longer than the *San Salvador*, the flagship of the tiny fleet with which his countryman, Cabrillo, almost 350 years before had explored the coast at the mercy of the winds.

While the fishermen who persisted in hoping that the albacore would return to Southern California still clung to protected waters, other captains had begun widening their cruises far out to sea. On the cruises which led them to Clarion Island they searched vainly for the Allaire Banks, reported discovered by a commercial ship which claimed it had been able to anchor easily 700 miles off the coast of Mexico.

The banks were thought to be a range of mountains rising from the ocean bed to within a few fathoms of the surface. Perhaps this was the spawning ground of the yellowfin. But the clippers never did find the banks. Neither did they know that this also was the spawning ground of severe storms.

Southeast of the lost banks was Clipperton Island, and far beyond the horizon to the east was the Isthmus of Panama.

In the Spring of 1929 the *Atlantic* with Medina as captain and Joe Marques as engineer, led four sister vessels past Cape San Lucas at the tip of Lower California, past Cocos Island off the coast of Central America, and drew up at the fabled Galapagos Islands, 500 miles off the coast of Ecuador in South America and more than 3000 miles from home. This was the grandest fishing grounds of them all.

All during 1930 the *Atlantic* was high ship. It brought in more full fares more times than any other ship, its total of landed fish was higher and the percentage of the catch which had to be discarded unusually small. For the first time the total catch of tuna exceeded 100 million pounds.

Even before the equator had been crossed at the Galapagos, and the richness of the southern waters proved, the lead of Medina had been quickly followed. In the summer of 1929 three even larger tuna boats were being readied for launching at the Campbell Machine Company at San Diego. The *San Joao*, the largest, 121 feet in length, was being built for Sabina Y. Inos, Medina Sabina and associates, and cost $95,000. The *Invader*, being built for Joe C. Monise and Mathew Monise, was 117 feet long. The *Navigator*, 120 feet in length, was being built for Manuel H. Freitas.

The success of larger boats ended attempts to conduct tender fishing, that is, with a "mother" ship and a flock of smaller craft, and discouraged plans for canneries in Lower California which might shorten the distance a clipper would have to travel to unload and return to the banks. In a short time at least fifteen larger clippers were under construction, ranging in size from eighty-five to 120 feet and with capacities of seventy to 200 tons of iced fish.

A description of one of the early cruises to these distant waters in 1930 was carried in *West Coast Fisheries* of 1931. Edgar E. Crane, of Kalamazoo, Michigan, signed aboard the *Navigator* with a companion named Ralph Upjohn. He wrote:

> We boarded her at the La Playa anchorage under the lee of Point Loma ... together with the captain (Manuel Freitas), the cook and a crew of twelve Portuguese. Among these there was a preponderance of "Joes," of which there were five; "Tonys" ran a close second, there being three; two "Franks"; one each "Tiago" and "Chico"; fine fellows all.

After stopping at Cape San Lucas for additional supplies, the *Navigator* stood out to sea once again, followed by the diesel clipper *Atlantic*, with Captain M. O. Medina, which boasted a wireless transmitter and an operator, a source of great comfort to the apprentice seamen Crane and Upjohn.

The most northern of the Galapagos group was sighted at 4:45 in the morning, April 12. They circled it before proceeding south to Wenman, sighting no fish although large schools had been reported in the area. However, on reaching Redondo Rock, at the north end of the great Isabela, also known as Albermarle Island, and astride the equator, fishing began in earnest, as Crane wrote:

> A few hours of strenuous work rewarded us with fourteen tons of three-pole tuna. Groups of three men, each individual having in his hands a strong bamboo pole, the one-fathom lines from which converged at a single hook, did the work. The barbless hooks were baited with a large sardine; when a

Joe C. Monise

Mathew C. Monise

Manuel H. Freitas

tuna struck, all three men lunged backward simultaneously, catapulting the great fish out of the sea. The team-work of the men exceeded the trained tactics of any football squad or shell crew that ever was seen.

The yellowfin taken that day ranged from forty to 300 pounds, the average being about seventy pounds. The bait was drying out rapidly because of the temperature of the sea. Sometimes the heat of the ocean water reached eighty-nine degrees. On Monday, April 14, the bait tanks were depleted and the *Navigator* headed southward for James Bay on San Salvador Island. From there they went on to Santa Cruz Island. Crane and Upjohn were impressed by the utter lack of fear of human beings evidenced by all of the creatures which they found on the islands. The animals, birds and reptiles had seldom been molested, except for occasional visits by the whalers.

Bait tanks filled once more, the *Navigator* headed back toward Redondo Rock and found that the schools of yellowfin had vanished. Reports of tuna at Cocos Island drew them 420 miles northward. Crane wrote:

Easter morning, April 20, we awoke early ... That afternoon we reached Cocos, which belongs to Costa Rica. It is a beautiful tropical island thirteen miles in circumference, covered with dense foliage, cocoanut palms and many other kinds of trees and plants. The sweet, scented odors of the tropics drifted out to our vessel. Waterfalls cascaded from the tops of cliffs.

This is Charles Island, one of the most southern of the Galapagos group. It also is known as Floreana, where many refugees from civilization staked out tiny settlements and enacted strange dramas of life and death.
This island became familiar to the tuna fishermen. A description of one of the early voyages recorded how fourteen tons of tuna were taken by poles in a few hours.
Sometimes the ocean temperature reached to almost ninety degrees.

Cocos Island is fabled as a hiding place of pirate and Inca treasure, none of which ever has been found.
The island became well known to crews of the tuna clippers from San Diego and San Pedro on their long cruises to southern fishing waters.
Here two tuna clippers lie in the lee of the island, between sessions of fishing.
Approaching the island the fishermen were met by the sweet, scented odors of the tropics.

Crane and Upjohn hurried ashore to make their own hasty search for treasure supposedly buried by pirates or concealed by Incas driven from Peru by the Spanish conquerors. They were frustrated, as many were to be after them. Crane continued his story, however:

That evening we exchanged greetings with the crews of the *Atlantic* and the *Stella di Genova*, both of which had arrived that day after a week's separation. The *Atlantic* transmitted wireless messages to home and received others in return, for which we were very grateful, then being four weeks that we had been out of touch with civilization.

After about a week of fishing, the *Navigator* turned homeward, and for seven days the weather was delightful. Then they ran into the storm belt and encountered severe conditions. The first land they saw in days was near Manzanillo, Mexico, above Acapulco, and they finally docked at San Diego on May 7, after an absence of two months.

The yellowfin had been plentiful; the tropics had warmed their bodies; but the storms had given warning that the Pacific expected to exact a toll for everything that it gave up.

In a few years the fishing fleet had established a pattern of operation based on the little-understood movements of tuna. A study by the California Bureau of Marine Fisheries reported that in the winter months from November to the end of February, the fleet exploited the Galapagos Islands. Through March, April and May the boats fished off the Central American mainland. In June and July they often fished in the Gulf of California and around Cape San Lucas. In August and September the fleet scattered along the Lower California coast and the neighboring banks and islands as far as Clipperton Island. Through the Fall they mostly reverted to the Central American mainland. And then they began the cycle again with the coming of winter.

The method always was the same. Upon sighting a school the course of the ship was changed to intercept the fish and bait from tanks was thrown into the sea by the "chummer." In a fast-biting school there was a steady rain of fish upon the decks, and it became not uncommon to take thirty to forty tons of tuna in a single day. On an average, however, a crew could count only upon two or three good days of fishing with a daily catch of twenty to fifty tons. The balance of the catch often came agonizingly slow. As H. C. Godsil in the state report on tuna fishing related:

> Tuna fishing is never a continuous process. The school will stay with a boat for an interval varying from a few minutes to half an hour, and then suddenly move on or down. The tuna boat then pursues the school if it remains on the surface, chums it up again and starts to fish. If the fish will not bite, the vessel after two or three such tries will abandon it and seek another ... In the log book of a tuna boat will be seen repeatedly the statement: "Lots of fish—won't bite," and to one who knows, this terse excerpt tells a tale of an irritated crew in enforced, exasperated idleness with days and profits slipping by.

In the tales of the sea the cruises of the tuna clippers did not receive as much attention as the cruises of the historic whalers or the New Bedford cod fleet which penetrated the Atlantic fogs of the Grand Banks. But danger was never very far away. It was the "chubascos" which held the most dread for the fishermen. Similar to the hurricanes of the Caribbean, they are born in the area of the Mexico-Guatemala border and generally move in a northwest direction, with an intensity ranging from seventy-five to 125 miles an hour. When they reach the latitude of the tip of Baja California, they can change directions, sometimes blowing out to sea and other times turning inland to lash the mainland with the fury of a thousand demons.

By experience the fishermen learned that the chubasco season was fairly long, from late June until mid-October, and the storms averaged seven or eight a year.

In the same area of the Pacific which produced the chubascos were the Tehuantepec winds. These winds are not hurricanes but they come up with little warning and rarely are accompanied by rain. From October 1 to May 1 these draughts of wind funnel down the Isthmus of Tehuantepec, in southern Mexico and upper Central America, from the Gulf of Mexico and the Caribbean and may blow from three to twelve days at seventy miles an hour.

The wind hits the coast with such force that it can blow the water out of the gulf over a vast stretch of ocean front. At the beginning of the blow the water temperature may be as high as eighty degrees. In a short time it can drop to as low as fifty degrees. Before a skipper realized what was happening the entire afterdeck of his boat would be under water.

But the sea was in the blood of the Portuguese and they knew little of fear. It was said that Captain Guy Silva, sailing out of San Diego, was fishing off Cape San Lucas when a huge leopard shark rose to the surface and drew alongside. Acting upon impulse, Silva jumped overboard and landed on the shark's back. Shouting to his men to clear the deck, he ran the length of the shark's back and then clambered back on board.

The loss of time searching for bait led in 1931 to experimental use

Yellowfin tuna are not to be taken lightly. Here, four poles are required to flip a large tuna to the deck into the hold of a tuna clipper, where it can be frozen for the long journey back to the canneries.
Four lines converge on a single barbless hook baited with a sardine.
On one voyage down the coast of Baja California, fishermen reported the tuna to be so thick that it "looked as if one could have walked across the ocean on their backs."

Guy Silva

Machado Medina

of an airplane as a spotter. Guy Silva and his son, Grey, fitted a small plane with pontoons and carried it into Central and South American waters atop the deck's bait box of the ninety-five-foot *Emma R.S.* The practice of airplane spotting was rather widely adopted, though later it was carried out by planes based on the mainland. As the range of the fleet increased far out to sea, the small planes lost their usefulness.

The first of the tuna clippers to be lost was the *Greyhound*, owned by Machado Medina. In August of 1929 it went ashore and was abandoned at San Hipolito Point, 300 miles from San Diego on the Lower California peninsula below Turtle Bay.

It was in 1931, two years after the southern waters had been reached, when disasters began to mount. A double wreck involved two of the five Medina brothers. Captain Joe Medina was skipper of the *Patria* and Machado Medina, who now had the *San Salvador*, were in the vicinity of San Benito Island, just west of the Cedros Island, 300 miles south of San Diego in Mexican waters. Joe Medina told the story:

The *San Salvador* was in the lead; I followed somewhat astern and to one side. The weather was calm, the sea smooth and the night a good one until about 2:30 a.m. when we ran into heavy fog. Visibility got worse and worse; we had to run by dead reckoning entirely. Well, at 4:45 a.m., we struck—hit the rocks of San Benito Island.

The *San Salvador* actually had struck the rocks first, but the prow of the *Patria* hit the rocks a glancing blow, veering outward enough so that it lay parallel to shore in a cradle of jagged stone. In the morning, when the fog had cleared, the two boats discovered they were on the rocks within a few hundred yards of each other. Both boats were worked free, but being severely damaged, had to wait for towing craft to return them to San Diego.

On another occasion in October 1931 the *San Salvador* encountered serious trouble. She battled a four-day chubasco about 1350 miles down the coast, off Clarion Island, one of the worst storms in the memory of Machado Medina. He related:

We lost our anchor and deck gear and had to run before the gale for four days and nights. Several times we almost capsized, but did not use our wireless. There was no use sending for another craft until we really needed aid.

Many of the tragedies occured in Mexican waters, or in the protected bays of Lower California, when bait or supplies were

110

being taken aboard. Newspaper reports told how six vessels were lost in 1931.

In February the *F.F.F.* sank off Cape San Lucas and a month later the *Morgan* overturned and sank when the cargo shifted while fishing at the Uncle Sam Bank in Lower California waters, 425 miles from home. Mike Ballestieri's *Lisboa* was destroyed by fire in Magdalena Bay on April 14 and on May 16, the *San Gabriel* caught fire in local waters and was abandoned. On September 23, M. Crevillo's *G. Marconi* was destroyed by fire off Santa Barbara. The last ship to meet grief that year was the *Abraham Lincoln*, which went down at a loss of $30,000.

The next year was a bad one for the clipper fleet. On July 2, 1932, the *Point Loma* crashed on the fog-shrouded reefs of tiny Asuncion Island, located near San Roque Island. On the same day the *Yolando* was destroyed by fire in Turtle Bay. Fire destroyed the 115-

One of the early tuna clippers to be lost in the southern seas was the St. Veronica. *She is shown here grounded on the rocks of Isabela Island, also known as Albemarle, the largest of the Galapagos group.*
This occured in 1932, one of the most disastrous years for the tuna fleet.
In a decade half of the clippers which had made up the original long-range fleet, had been lost.

foot *Adventurer* on November 14, in Magdalena Bay at a loss of $85,000. The crew was saved by Captain John Gabelich who two years later was to disappear without trace. The following day the *Continental* burned off Cocos Island. On the 30th the *St. Veronica* struck a reef on Isabela Island in the Galapagos.

In 1933 the clipper *Huntress*, a converted submarine chaser, was destroyed by fire near Ensenada on February 20. In June, Denny Moore's *Del Mar* went down off Cape San Lucas, gutted by fire. Fire also claimed the *Trojan* on July 29 in the Gulf of California. On November 22 the *Neskleetia*, with a reputation of being the jinx ship of the fleet, was lost when a seacock gave way while the crew was fishing at Alijos Rocks 150 miles from shore and 520 miles south of San Diego.

The story was the same the following year. The *Uncle Sam* caught fire in Turtle Bay and sank. The *Vasco da Gama* exploded and sank off Cape San Lucas. The *Lois S.* hit rocks in Magdalena Bay and three persons, including Captain E. Edwards, were drowned.

An enduring mystery of the sea involved the *Belle Isle*, skippered by John Gabelich and valued at $75,000. On June 25, 1934, she was off Costa Rica, where she was in radio contact with the San Diego clipper *Alert*. That was the last ever heard of her. Whether she foundered in a hurricane or was destroyed by an engine room explosion was never learned. Local fishermen believe it was caught in one of the equatorial hurricanes along the west coast of South America and went down with all hands.

In the decade since offshore tuna fishing began in 1925, nearly half of the first fifty clippers to be built had been lost. The lost ones were replaced, and often bore the same names, time and again.

The loss of life was not as great as might have been expected, as the vessels so often fished close together or within a short radio range of each other. To the fishermen, the greater hazard was in the actual fishing. Flying barbs could strike the men in the face or jerk them into a sea literally boiling with frenzied tuna and sharks, where the chance of getting back on board without the loss of an arm or leg was remote.

By this time the clippers had been converted into small liners and their range expanded to more than 7000 miles. The *Cabrillo*, launched on May 6, 1935, and owned by Joe and M. O. Medina, and David and George Campbell, cost $135,000. Quarters for a crew of twenty-one were clean and comfortable, and the captain's cabin was furnished with a desk, radio, easy chairs and a bed. A licensed radio operator and cook were on salaries but the rest of

George Campbell

the crew shared equally from the profits of a trip. She carried 600 huge blocks of ice for refrigeration.

Just aft of the wheel room on the port side was the chapel, a common feature of most of the larger clippers. It had a small altar with images of the Sacred Heart, St. Joseph and St. Anthony. On the walls were miniature reproductions of the Stations of the Cross. There always was time for prayer, and too often a moment when help was needed.

Regardless of the losses of clippers and the threat of imported Japanese tuna, and the troubles of the early years of the depression, the use of tuna gradually increased across the country. The five canneries at San Diego had their busiest year in 1935. And for reasons unknown, albacore suddenly began to reappear in their coastal haunts after a mysterious absence of almost a decade.

Chapel of later tuna boat

Though the white meat of the albacore was still prized, an expanding market had been built on other varieties and the fickle and elusive albacore no longer could dominate an industry.

CHAPTER SIX

MARY PICKFORD

SAYS:

"We take a personal pride in the present beauty and future development of

San Diego

In fact, if one were dreaming of a city it would be difficult to make the dream more alluring than the real.

Happily for us our ranch is near enough to make San Diego our very own"

Mary Pickford and Douglas Fairbanks have bought a large tract of land in Rancho Santa Fe near San Diego, and are planning to build an early California hacienda there. They have also purchased splendid ocean frontage at Solana Beach nearby.

You will like San Diego too.

You will like the trip down.

You will like the enchanting panorama from Point Loma.

You will like the way San Diego spreads out from the bay.

You will like Balboa Park around which the city is built.

You will like the clean, wide streets.

You will like the historic points to be visited.

You will want to stay in San Diego . . . and why not? You are invited.

for information-address

San Diego
California Club
Chamber of Commerce Bldg.

Above. Lily Pond and Museum
Balboa Park, San Diego.

The boom was at its height.
The San Diego-California Club was placing a large part of its advertising
in Los Angeles, to lure tourists and prospective settlers who already had been
drawn to the coast by other means.
The glamour of Hollywood was combined with the extravagance of the booster
to assure one and all that San Diego was truly the dream city of every person.
The film stars Mary Pickford and Douglas Fairbanks had acquired acreage
in Rancho Santa Fe, to build their own romantic hacienda.

THE BOOM FADES

The fight for Boulder Dam and the All-American Canal was coming to an end. After eight long years of frustration and defeat, Representative Phil Swing finally maneuvered the Swing-Johnson Bill to the floor of the House of Representatives.

A last-minute effort to send it back to committee, and thus doom it for at least another year, was defeated 219 to 137. Within a few hours the bill was overwhelmingly approved by a roll call vote on May 25, 1928. The next day Swing took the floor to thank his colleagues:

The future will justify every assertion that has been made in behalf of the Boulder Dam project, and on a roll of honor will be spread the names of those men who had the vision and the courage to make its construction possible. Time will dispel all doubts and fears which the opposition has sought to throw around it, and leave it standing in magnificent grandeur clear cut against the sky, the greatest accomplishment of our generation in this or any other country in the world.

The news was received with great excitement in San Diego and Imperial Valley. But the battle was not over. Now it was up to Senator Hiram Johnson. He forced the Senate into continuous session, in an effort to force the bill to vote before adjournment, despite a fillibuster conducted by senators from Arizona and Utah.

Debate was prolonged and acrimonious. At one point Senator Henry Ashurst cried out that Arizona was being strangled and

Johnson was a "bifurcated, peripatetic volcano, in perpetual eruption, belching fire and smoke ..." Despite Herculean efforts Johnson was unable to break the fillibuster, and an impatient Senate adjourned. Johnson warned his fellow senators: "Yes, I am whipped, but, by heaven, another day is coming and then someone else will be whipped."

In December the bill came up again, and by this time it had captured and fired the imagination of the entire country. It had a clear majority of support in the Senate. Upon Johnson's acceptance of an amendment limiting California's share of water from the Colorado, a clause that would lead to decades more of misunderstanding and dispute, the battle came to a quiet end by a vote of sixty-three to eleven, on December 14. A week later while Swing and Johnson watched, the Boulder Dam Project Act was signed into law by President Coolidge. The California Legislature accepted the limitation and ratified a six-state compact. Arizona, however, was to hold out for fifteen years.

To San Diego the signing of the bill meant it had a future source of water on which to rely when its own resources were exhausted. To the farmers of Imperial Valley it meant that at last they would have their own canal and that it would run entirely within the United States, and their supply would no longer be subject, or so they thought, to the demands of Mexican lands.

The size of the threat posed to their available supply of Colorado water was evident in an article written in 1929 by the manager of the 800,000 acres of the delta owned by the Chandler syndicate in Lower California. Though only a portion of the land was being irrigated, H. H. Clark wrote:

During the past year we have employed from 4000 to 8000 laborers constantly. In addition to man power, we use 8000 head of mules, 20 big tractors and 11 dredges for cleaning of irrigation canals. There are 3000 miles of ditches on the ranch.

Mexican ranchers had their own irrigation systems. Chandler paid the Imperial Irrigation District from $550,000 to $650,000 a year for the delivery of water under Mexico's share written into the agreement by which water was delivered to the valley through Mexican territory. This one ranch was larger by 200,000 acres than the Imperial Irrigation District. Of the nearly one million acres of potential farm land in the area, only 156,000 acres were under irrigation in 1927. The figure in 1928 was 191,000. The next year, the acreage declined to 165,000.

The election of Herbert Hoover as President only seemed to

assure the progress so happily envisioned with the prospect of Boulder Dam. A title company advertisement, signed by John F. Forward Jr., caught the spirit of San Diego:

Life's need of drama created the pyramids; it will build Boulder Dam. The mighty army of visitors and landseekers attracted by Boulder Dam should naturally come over the Broadway of America, the new national all-year highway, from Broadway, New York, to Broadway, San Diego. With Mr. Hoover in office, with farm relief assured, with Boulder Dam to be built, attracting national attention and travel to the Great Southwest—San Diego, during the decade of 1930 to 1940, will undoubtedly enjoy the greatest prosperity in history.

While the Swing-Johnson bill was riding to its final triumph, 1927 was a year of substantial building and development in San Diego. A large new hotel, El Cortez, was being erected high on Seventh Street by a company headed by Richard T. Robinson, and its tower would be a welcoming beacon for ships at sea. A second hotel, the Pickwick, was opened on Broadway. Under construction on Broadway was another bank building, for the San Diego Trust & Savings Bank. In September the Spreckels companies announced the sale of the John D. Spreckels Building and all stock in the First National Bank to a local syndicate headed by the bank's president, F. J. Belcher Jr.

Within six months the J.D. & A.B. Spreckels Companies had disposed of their most influential properties, *The San Diego Union* and *Evening Tribune*. They were purchased early in 1928 by

By the late Twenties the skyline of San Diego took on an appearance that would change but little in two decades.
This is an air view which shows the major business buildings. The largest along the south side of Broadway had been built, or started, by John D. Spreckels. The Navy ships moored in the bay indicated the growing importance of the military to the economy of San Diego.

Colonel Ira C. Copley, of Aurora, Illinois, who had become well acquainted with San Diego as a frequent visitor. He was a former owner of Midwest utility companies and a congressman from Illinois, who had entered the newspaper publishing business in both California and Illinois. At a dinner in his honor at Hotel del Coronado, Copley outlined the policies for the two newspapers:

> These papers are not to be personal organs of myself or anyone else. I have no political ambitions. I have no connection with any public utility anywhere and no connection with any other business than the newspaper business anywhere ... it shall be the purpose of these papers to present the news on the basis of its honest news value. They will have neither enemies nor friends in that respect. No newspaper has ever been really successful that has not delivered the goods in an honest and constructive way.

Ira C. Copley

Soon afterward Copley purchased and eliminated the *Independent*, the newspaper that had been started by George Marston, Ed Fletcher and others, as a locally owned voice of civic opposition to the plans and domination of Spreckels. It had lost money heavily and its owners were glad to be rid of it. He also purchased the twenty-room Spreckels home in Coronado. While the Spreckels interests would continue to exert an influence on the affairs of San Diego, it would not be as personal nor as persuasive. As in so many other cities, an era of personal journalism also was disappearing and newspapers were becoming more institutional and more representative of the interests of their communities and regions.

The trans-Atlantic flight of Charles Lindbergh had greatly stimulated interest in commercial aviation. In July of 1927 W. B. Mayo, chief engineer for the Ford Motor Company, flew into San Diego with Jack Maddux aboard Ford's new trimotor, all-metal transport, a "Leviathan of the Air." Maddux announced his plans to establish a passenger, freight and airmail line from San Francisco to Texas, by way of Los Angeles, San Diego, El Centro, Phoenix and El Paso. He said:

> Of course, the service will depend upon the cooperation we receive in locating suitable landing fields, and the patronage of the traveling public.

Lindbergh himself returned to San Diego for a visit on September 21, to receive the tribute of a record crowd of 60,000 packed in the stands and on the floor of the City Stadium. He also visited with the men who had worked on his plane at the Mahoney plant and told them:

> At this time I want to thank all, especially the older employes, for the work you did in constructing the plane. It is this organization which can do so much to keep San Diego and California in the forefront of aviation.

*When Charles Lindbergh finally returned to the scene where his triumph
had its beginning, nearly all of San Diego turned out to see him.*
*He rode a flower-decked auto through the city streets and then was driven
around the floor of the city stadium before a crowd that jammed almost every
foot of standing space.*
*He did not, however, forget the men who had built the plane which had
carried him safely across the ocean. He visited the Mahoney plant where it
was built and said he wanted particularly to thank its older employes.*

On the strength of the performance of the Ryan airplane, and
the added publicity arising from the flight of Lindbergh, the Mahoney plant was turning out airplanes that were being sold even in
foreign countries. In another section of the same plant, a converted
fish cannery, another company was beginning the manufacture of
still another, and much larger, airplane.

George H. Prudden, who had assisted in the design and manufacture of the prototype of the Ford all-metal airplane, had moved
to San Diego, because of its exceptional flying weather and the
promise of a major airport, and designed a new six-passenger trimotor, all-metal monoplane.

A San Diego syndicate was formed to finance the Prudden-San
Diego Airplane Company, with a capitalization of $60,000. Its
engines were to be supplied by Claude Ryan, who had organized

the Ryan Aeronautical Corporation after obtaining the rights to a German-designed engine and again was in business on Dutch Flats. He told San Diego:

There are thirty aircraft manufacturing plants in the United States today, virtually all of them operating at capacity . . . the all-metal plane being built at the Prudden factory here will be equipped with three of our motors.

Prudden's first airplane, with Ryan-furnished engines, made its maiden flight, a successful one, in October of 1927, attaining a speed of 135 miles an hour. The airport that Prudden desired, and which Maddux had said would be necessary for improved commercial air service, was approved by the voters in November of 1927. A bond issue of $650,000 was passed to deepen submerged areas of the bay and to use the fill to reclaim land lying between high and low tides at the waterfront site for an airport suggested in the Nolen Plan. At the same time the Navy requested that areas to be dredged be made sufficiently deep to provide a future turning basin for the new giant aircraft carriers, the U.S.S. *Lexington* and the U.S.S. *Saratoga*. The Navy's first experimental aircraft carrier, the U.S.S. *Langley*, had been a familiar sight in the harbor. It was a

While public attention was being focused on Lindbergh and his flight, military aviation continued to break through new barriers.
The Navy's first experimental aircraft carrier, the U.S.S. Langley, *became a familiar sight in San Diego harbor and was affectionately known as the "covered wagon."*
Here, a Navy plane lifts off the flight deck while the Langley *was moored to a North Island dock. Soon afterward the* Langley *was replaced by new giant carriers, the* Saratoga *and the* Lexington.

converted collier and because of her silhouette she was affectionately known as the "covered wagon." San Diegans began referring to their city as the "Air Capital of the West."

Over a period of half a century San Diego had lost the railroad connections by which it had hoped to match the growth and influence of Los Angeles and San Francisco. Its commercial shipping had lagged behind that of an ambitious Los Angeles. The competition for transcontinental auto traffic had found San Diego at a disadvantage compared to the more politically astute northern cities.

Aviation in 1928 represented a new chance and a new way to metropolitan importance. But the inauguration of promised commercial air service, which could make San Diego an important transportation center, agonizingly was delayed time and again. The Chamber of Commerce acknowledged that in some respects San Diego seemed to be losing ground, but expressed confidence that the bay would be made the home port for the Navy's aircraft carriers.

In spite of the concern over the lack of air transportation service, the aircraft manufacturing industry in San Diego seemed to be struggling toward permanence. An average of twenty-seven airplanes were being manufactured daily in the United States. The Mahoney company alone in March produced fourteen airplanes and expected to produce seventeen in April. The Prudden company set a goal of thirty-two for the year. Ryan was supplying engines to twenty American aircraft companies.

Meanwhile, interest in aviation continued to develop. The Army refueled the *Question Mark* at night over San Diego in a record endurance flight over Southern California. Amelia Earhart, with two co-pilots, became the first woman to fly the Atlantic. At Rockwell Field on North Island, the Army Air Service established permanent pursuit units which brought the operations there up to the level of World War I. In June the Navy began assembling more than 200 airplanes of various types, with supporting units of the Battle Fleet, at San Diego for joint air maneuvers with the Army.

The airport for which San Diegans had voted and which, it was hoped, would launch San Diego as an important transportation center, was dedicated on August 16, 1928, and officially named Lindbergh Field. The 142 acres comprised only one unit of a projected development that would embrace land held by the Marine Corps. In the dedicatory address, Lieutenant Governor Buron Fitts stated:

Amelia Earhart

An air force cannot be created overnight . . . San Diego leads California in aviation—it is the home of the industry—and California leads the world. I do not believe, nor does any other thinking man, that government subsidies should be provided for aircraft building, but I do believe that it is the duty of governments, national, state and municipal, to provide air routes. We do not give money for building automobiles—but we do for roads. And I believe that it is the obligation of the government to provide airways, fields, aerial beacons and the rest, just as it builds roads.

A mass flight of 400 airplanes had been planned to bring together in one formation the Navy air units which had been assembled at San Diego, and all Army Air Service units on the Pacific Coast. All hotels were filled with visitors, and the coastal steamer *Harvard* had arrived from San Francisco with every stateroom reserved. Because of low clouds all along the coast, however, the mass flight was reduced to 222 planes, 140 from the Navy and eighty-two from the Army.

The flight was described in detail over a public address system by Rear Admiral Joseph M. Reeves, commander of aircraft squadrons

The stimulus of Lindbergh's historic flight resulted in final voter approval of a first class airport for San Diego.
The left picture shows how the airport, named in honor of Lindbergh, was to have appeared. At the right is the dedication celebration of the first section which took place in 1928.
The airport was located on filled tidelands as suggested by the planner John Nolen. The fill was obtained from harbor dredging operations which at the same time provided a turning basin for new and larger aircraft carriers.

LINDBERGH FIELD
SAN DIEGO

of the Battle Fleet, who, in a previous talk to San Diego businessmen had pointed out that naval aviation maneuvers being conducted at San Diego were creative in the sense that there were no traditions to guide them in pioneering for air war at sea. Anchored off the Coronado Roads were the Navy's two carriers, the *Lexington* and the *Saratoga*. The first landing on the soft ground of the new field, as yet unoperational, was made the day before by Frank Seifert, a city councilman and pioneer Army reserve flier.

With all of the interest concentrated on aviation and its promise for the future of transportation, there was little concern over the efforts of Los Angeles and San Francisco to bring about improvement of highways benefiting their respective communities. The San Diego Chamber of Commerce, according to Ed Fletcher's memoirs, refused to finance a caravan, but did send a representative to a highway convention in Memphis, Tennessee, to publicize the new route called the "Broadway of America."

The "Broadway of America" ran from New York and proceeded to Memphis, and in Texas joined Highway 80 to San Diego. Fletcher invited Mayor Clark and Rear Admiral J. S. McKean, commandant of the 11th Naval District, to go as his guests, and 108 San Diegans in twenty-eight autos left San Diego in April of 1928. By the time the caravan reached El Paso, it had grown to 150 autos and 654 delegates. All along the route the caravan was welcomed and feted, and at each stop Mayor Clark and Admiral McKean explained the economic virtues and military necessity of

national highways, and the beauties and advantages of San Diego. It arrived at Memphis with 1564 delegates. Upon returning to San Diego, Fletcher wrote:

Substantial gains in tourist travel to San Diego have been made during the last two years by reason of the replacement of the old plank road over the sand dunes (in Imperial County) by a hard surface pavement, and still more recently by completion of the Mountain Springs paving, formerly a terror for timid motorists.

However, he was not satisfied all was being done that should be done to attract highway traffic to San Diego. Instead of using most of its funds to advertise San Diego in eastern newspapers for new settlers, and in Los Angeles newspapers for tourist business, the San Diego-California Club, he thought, should cooperate with all cities along the Broadway of America, Highway 80, the Old Spanish Trail and the Dixie Overland Highway, in distributing literature and placing billboards.

Autos were bringing more people into Southern California through Yuma than Southern Pacific trains. But seventy percent of the autos were being diverted at Yuma to Los Angeles, by way of

While attention was directed toward the development of aviation passenger and mail service, national highways also were being put together to meet the demands of the auto age.
The Broadway of America ran from New York through Memphis, Tennessee, to Texas, where it joined Highway 80 to San Diego.
A caravan that began at San Diego reached Memphis with 1564 delegates who pledged themselves to promote travel on the "Broadway of America."

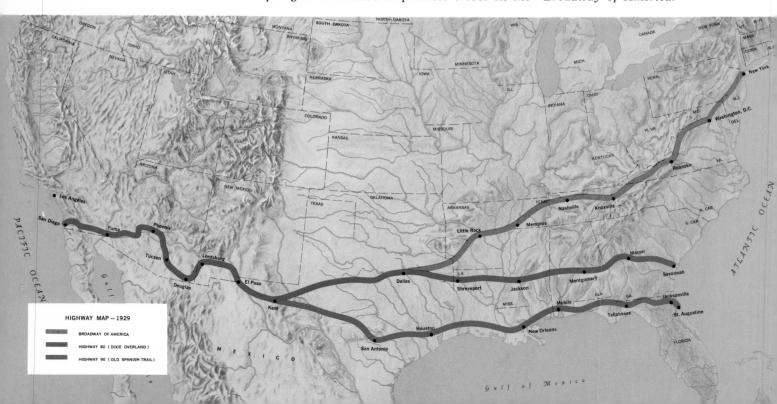

HIGHWAY MAP – 1929

BROADWAY OF AMERICA

HIGHWAY 80 (DIXIE OVERLAND)

HIGHWAY 90 (OLD SPANISH TRAIL)

the Salton Sea and the San Gorgonio Pass. In one year, 1927, a total of 61,699 cars entered California at Yuma; in 1928 travel traffic was reflecting an increase of thirty to forty percent, averaging 135 to 140 cars a day.

Even at that, the tourist business was San Diego's second largest industry, behind that of the military and ahead of agriculture. Much had been expected of the aviation industry. However, late in 1928, after the dedication of Lindbergh Field, which was expected to provide sites for additional aircraft production, the Mahoney plant was purchased by a group of St. Louis investors and relocated in Missouri. Perhaps fifty of the M-1 and M-2 Ryan planes had been produced in San Diego. The Prudden company produced two airplanes, the second being converted from a trimotor to a single motor ship, though sixteen were on order, and then encountered financial and technical difficulties. T. Claude Ryan now was principally concerned with a flying school, one of three in the area.

Arriving in San Diego at about this time was Edmund T. Price, age thirty-three, who had been in the investment business in the East and Michigan. In 1915 he had visited the Panama-California Exposition with his family and promised himself that someday he would return to San Diego and make it his home. He stepped into the Prudden organization, at first without pay, and by October had been placed in charge of a reorganized company, the Prudden Aircraft Corporation. In April 1929, it became the Solar Aircraft Company.

Edmund T. Price

With the development of larger airplanes and the lighting of airways, new companies rushed into competition for routes and government airmail contracts. In 1929 San Diego was being served by four airlines: Maddux Air Lines, Western Air Express, Pickwick Airways and Continental Air Express. While the air lane between San Diego and Los Angeles became the busiest in the nation, according to a Bureau of Aeronautics Report, with eight scheduled round trip flights a day, San Diego was not a major terminal but a "feeder" point.

The airlines were still using Ryan Field on Dutch Flats. Lindbergh Field did not go into full operation until 1930, though it was used by private fliers and for unscheduled flights. The Ryan Field recorded 390 trimotor landings and takeoffs a month.

The hope that the Maddux line would make San Diego the main terminal for service north to San Francisco and east to El Paso for direct connections with New York had not materalized. Its planes were shuttling eastward only as far as Phoenix, Arizona. On the plea of San Diego businessmen, Maddux began operation on a loop

Land was being sold and the people were still coming and the countryside was being blessed with rain, so why worry about tomorrow.
The building of Sutherland Dam on a tributary of the San Dieguito River had been started and then halted because of poor foundation conditions.
It was moved up stream, and then when the city ran out of bond money the work was halted. The dam remained unfinished for twenty-five years.

that included Agua Caliente in Lower California and the Imperial Valley. One of these flights ended in San Diego's first major commercial air crash. A stunting Army plane collided with a Maddux air liner and the trimotor plane crashed near Thirty-ninth and Spruce streets, with a loss of six lives. San Diego's claim to be the "Air Capital of the West" rested with military flying. When Army and Navy flights were included, the weekly average of flights over the city was 540.

With east-bound air service stopping far short of the transportation center of El Paso, San Diego feared that the gate to the East had been almost shut once again. Even the San Diego & Arizona Railway, which Spreckels had forced over the mountains at such great cost, had never fully opened the gate to rail traffic. And west-bound national highway traffic gradually was being diverted into arteries leading into Los Angeles.

Disappointments were nothing new to San Diego, but the boom now made them seem less crucial than in the past. There was too much money to be made in real estate to worry about what might have happened, or over what was happening within their own community. The city ran out of bond money in 1928 and was forced to halt construction work on Sutherland Dam on the San Dieguito River system. Hiram Savage had been rehired as the city hydraulic engineer, and with his dislike of the multiple-arch type dams, the unfinished structure was neglected and passed from public attention. It was to stand uncompleted for twenty-five years.

The loss of 385 lives in the collapse of the St. Francis Dam in Los Angeles County in 1928 aroused the fears of residents of San Dieguito Valley below the high Hodges Dam with its twenty-three graceful arches, so disliked by Savage. Cracks had been reported in the structure.

An examination by a board of consulting engineers appointed by the State at the request of the Board of Supervisors, disclosed a number of cracks due to shrinkage and temperature stresses which were slowly but steadily widening. The board held there was no immediate danger except in event of a major earthquake or a very heavy overflow going over the top of the dam. Strengthening was recommended. But it was 1936 before anything was done about it.

While federal statistics could be summoned to prove that industry was expanding faster in San Diego than in the other large cities of the Pacific Coast, the percentage figures were misleading, in that the town had little industry to start with and no new large industrial capacity was represented. The industrial payroll was only about $7,000,000 in 1928 compared with the $18,000,000 annual payroll of local military establishments.

The more realistic members of the business community began to realize that at least in their lifetime they might not see a significant expansion of industry. The 650 acres of waterfront property in the National City and Chula Vista areas, which had been purchased through the Chamber of Commerce, as sites for new plants, were sold to the Santa Fe Railroad Company to pay taxes that were due and to finance a new Chamber building.

Selling land still was the major concern of the moment. With no real expansion of industry, and thus with few jobs to offer, a change was necessary in the type of advertising being placed by the San Diego-California Club. Jobless as well as people with incomes barely adequate to sustain them had been drawn to the city by the lure of the ease of life in Southern California. The City Council appropriated $10,000 to try and build more commercial interest in its port and Lindbergh Field, while the San Diego-California Club concentrated its appeals for new residents in class magazines with the highest income readership. Civic "gold" was to be found in the sun but those who wanted to enjoy it were expected to pay their way.

Abelardo Rodríguez

Even across the international border the speculative fever had taken hold, and American money was greatly influencing economic and social conditions. In Tijuana the number of American visitors exceeded 1,000,000 annually. Under the leadership of Governor Abelardo Rodríguez, the northern district of Baja California was

Wirt G. Bowman

James N. Crofton

put on a self-sustaining basis. At the hot springs on land once the Spanish rancho of the famed Arguello family of Upper and Lower California, a new resort was being built that would become known as the playground of Hollywood.

The Agua Caliente resort, race track and golf course were built by a syndicate whose principals were Wirt G. Bowman who had owned the Foreign Club, a gambling establishment in Tijuana; Baron Long, a California night club and hotel operator; and James N. Crofton, who once rode a horse through the streets of San Diego advertising horse racing at the old Tijuana track of James W. Coffroth.

The first unit, the hotel and casino, built at a cost of $1,500,000, was opened formally the night of June 23, 1928. Crowded around its gambling tables were the current elite of the movie colony, with the ready money of the days before heavy income taxes, among them Al Jolson, Charles Chaplin, Dolores del Rio, Sid Grauman, Joe Schenck, Mabel Normand, Lupe Velez, Jackie Coogan, and the boxing champion Jack Dempsey.

In the language of the day, it was "America's Deauville," and its advertisements read:

In a quaint setting under the great oaks in the valley of the Tia Juana River, flanked by the purple hills of two nations, has risen this new play spot of the Southland ... Nothing has been left undone which will add to the comfort and pleasure of the guest at Agua Caliente. Although the achievements of the past year in transforming the brush-covered hills into a place of infinite charm and beauty seem nearly a miracle, they are matched by even a more ambitious program for 1929—greatly futhering the work of creating, in Agua Caliente, a place which will attract travelers from all the world to the Southland.

The boom was beginning to run down, but nobody had noticed it as yet, when one of the most famous tourist attractions of the Southland was opened.
This was the Agua Caliente resort just below Tijuana in Baja California, at a site of a hot springs on what was once a historic rancho.
This photograph was taken at the time of the resort's opening in 1928.
Building of the hotel was followed by the addition of a spa, race track and dog track.

This shows the famed Gold Room of the Agua Caliente resort.
In the resort's relatively short life, movie stars from Hollywood and the
"international set" gambled away the easy money of the boom.
Advertisements hailed it as the "Deauville of America." Profits from gambling
tables repaid the original investment within a short time.

While in the United States as a whole speculative gains had increased 312 percent in five years, wages had risen only twelve percent, and there were signs that the tides of migration were beginning to ebb. In Florida the total value of building permits for all its cities dropped from $171,000,000 in 1926 to less than $30,000,000 in 1928. That the westward tide also was slowing was becoming evident in San Diego, even if there was no one to believe it. The value of building permits dropped $2,000,000 in 1928, from $14,000,000 the year before. At that the value of permits issued in San Diego in January were equal to that of Miami's for all of 1928.

A year-end review disclosed that twenty-four office buildings had been erected, and fifteen schools, nine churches, forty apartments and 107 stores. The valuation in building permits reflected continuing business and commercial expansion. The number of homes being built told a different story.

Though more than 20,000 lots had been sold in less than a decade, the demand for houses was lessening dramatically. In 1924, 3500 homes had been built and it was estimated that there was a need for 4000. In 1925, more than 4000 had been built but the need was estimated at only 3500. The situation was about the same in 1926. In 1927, however, only 2500 homes were built and there was an apparent need for just 500.

The high tide of the population growth of the 1920's was reached in 1928 when San Diego added more than 10,000 new residents. In 1929 the population increase was only a little more than 2000 persons. In two years the number of lots sold and the filing of new subdivision maps dropped fifty percent. The ups and downs of the real estate market, and the ebb and flow of population migrations, however, were considered merely temporary phenomena in an ever-unfolding pageant of Western expansion. Tomorrow was another day.

In a full-page advertisement at the beginning of the New Year of 1929, the Board of Supervisors proclaimed San Diego County "an empire complete." In an article for the Chamber of Commerce magazine, the editor of the *San Diego Sun*, Paul C. Edwards, reassured San Diegans that commerce, industry, transportation, new buildings, bank deposits and post office receipts were not all the elements that make a great city:

No city in America of similar size has as much in culture as San Diego. Perhaps no city has so much to build its culture on . . . First attracted by her natural beauties, many new residents come to San Diego. Obviously those who choose a new home because of its beauty are persons who value all the higher qualities of life. So the development of these qualities has had unusual encouragement. And as the old develop, new are added, bred by a genuine civic ambition to make San Diego in fact a modern Athens in a new Western World.

"Athens" had its price. As new residents were still arriving, though perhaps not in the numbers of prior months, San Diegans were placed on the alert that "there should be a barrel of money for you in Point Loma investments."

Prospective land buyers were brought to San Diego by the trainload and then driven to Point Loma.
There, the John P. Mills organization fed them in a large tent and described the wonders of Azure Vista and Sunset Cliffs.
John P. Mills and his fellow investors spent a fortune putting in streets and sewers and insisted on high building restrictions. Everybody rushed to buy land but not very many people rushed into building.

The John P. Mills Organization, sales agent for Pantages, Mills and Shreve Company, described Point Loma as taking on a "setting such as only to be found, perhaps, on the Riviera coast of the Mediterranean Sea." It was decreed that all houses on Sunset Cliffs had to be of light color and with red tile roofs, and cost from $5000 to $25,000, depending on relationship to the ocean front. In his unpublished memoirs, John P. Mills recalled:

We put in all the improvements, paved the streets, paved the curbs ... underground utilities, everything you could think of. We gave all the waterfront to the city of San Diego for a park. When I opened it for sale the first day we did over one million dollars. I sold between three and four million dollars worth of land. I chartered trains four days a week and brought hundreds of people into San Diego, where buses met them and they were escorted out to the property by the police. They were given luncheon and a lecture afterward.

Developers of La Jolla Hermosa hurried to advise investors that "more cash profits have been collected on this tract than from any similar property."

An original Spanish land grant twenty-five miles north of San Diego that had been planted to eucalyptus trees by the Santa Fe Railroad, in a disappointing experiment for producing railroad ties, was converted into productive citrus groves and homesites and became known as Rancho Santa Fe. An advertisement of 1927 claimed that almost eighty percent of the land had been sold in estates ranging from five to fifty acres, and that residents included motion picture stars, the owner of the Algonquin Hotel in New York, a member of the New York Stock Exchange, the scion of one of Boston's oldest families, a former South American representative for the Dupont interests, and many other wealthy and important executives from around the country.

Farther up the coast a former mayor of Seattle named Ole Hanson formed a syndicate and laid out an entirely new town on the ocean, halfway between San Diego and Los Angeles. It was named San Clemente and it was decreed that every building had to be in the style of "Old Spain."

When the voters rejected a site in Balboa Park for the new State College, another area overlooking Mission Valley and the crumbling ruins of the San Diego Mission was chosen. Dr. Edward L. Hardy, its president, said the college would arise as a new expression of the architecture of Spain with its Moorish and Arabian influences. The selected site also caused a new round of speculation in nearby land. The promoters of Talmadge Park Estates pointed out that when it was announced that a branch of the University of California would be located at Westwood, Los Angeles, lots which had been purchased for nearly $4,000,000 were quickly sold for $6,000,000.

Communities in the county vied with each other in describing their advantages and the possibilities for gain. In the north county Carlsbad, with a population of 2500, was the "Avocado Capital of the World." It had 40,000 bearing avocado trees and 15,000 more

Dr. Edward L. Hardy

were planted in 1928. Encinitas was the "Home of the Mid-Winter Flower Show."

Inland, La Mesa was the "City of Beautiful Homes," and its 3000 population "invites the world to share in her manifold blessings." Escondido was the "Sunkist Vale" and Ramona the "Turkey Capital."

To the south of San Diego, National City was "Where Rail and Water Meet," with industrial sites waiting the certain coming of industry. "Truly California at its Best" was the boast of Chula Vista, the most southerly community, with a population of 5543, and for investors it was the "Harbor of Opportunity." With the formation of the Chula Vista Mutual Lemon Association, Chula Vista advertised itself as the "Lemon Capital of the World."

The population of Imperial Valley in 1928 reached 65,000 and its farms shipped 65,000 carloads of produce, a carload for each man, woman and child.

New tracts of land and new subdivisions were being opened, with paved streets and lighting, under special assessment districts, one of which was known as the Mattoon Act, which permitted pyramiding of assessments, taxes and interest. This act originated in Los Angeles and was widely applied over Southern California. Its original intent was to provide the means by which necessary roads could be constructed across various and often jealous taxing jurisdictions by employing the county tax structure. It was never intended to apply to the opening and selling of vacant land. As with the general county taxes, those who paid had to carry the burden of those who did not.

The inherent possibilities of abuse were not realized while land was being sold and resold at speculative prices. Among the roads built and improved under these acts, and which reached from the central area to surrounding developments, were the Causeway to Crown Point; the Market, Broadway, Fairmount and Euclid street extensions; and National and El Cajon avenues. A tenth of all taxable property in the county fell under these acts. Each piece of property benefited was made liable for all assessments of all property in the district. This was satisfactory as long as all owners were paying their levies. No thought was given to what would happen when they didn't.

Though building of homes was slowing down, business expansion continued. Among the new business buildings completed or being planned in 1929 were one for a nation-wide department store at Twelfth and Broadway, the Samuel I. Fox Building at Sixth Street and Broadway, and the Guilford H. Whitney building which replaced the old Isis Theater on Fifth Street between B and C streets. The Isis Theater had been a landmark for thirty-five years. The Bank of Italy, which was to become the Bank of America, purchased the former John D. Spreckels Building from the local syndicate which had acquired it from the Spreckels estate. The price was $3,000,000.

There was no lack of confidence in business, and San Diego was a long way from the financial centers of the East. In June of 1929 national industrial and factory production indexes turned downward, and freight car loadings declined. This was not particularly worrisome news to the average person though the stock market reacted nervously.

At about the turn of the tide, from boom to depression, this is how San Diego appeared to the artist from a high vantage point.
The areas bounding Balboa Park were relatively thickly settled. Point Loma was just beginning to be built up. Mission Beach was sprouting houses and Tent City on the Coronado Strand was still a popular summer resort, particularly for residents of Imperial Valley.
Sparsely developed North Island was connected to Coronado by a bridge.

The growth of the city for the next decade or so seemed assured when the long fight over rights to the water of the San Diego River came to a sudden end. On June 20, 1929, the State Supreme Court handed down a decision after nineteen years of controversy and ruled that San Diego City was entitled to all of the water that coursed through the boundaries of the original Spanish pueblo. The decision stated, in part:

... San Diego ... is the owner in fee simple of the prior and paramount right to the use of all the water (surface and underground), of the San Diego River, including its tributaries, from its source to its mouth, for use of the said City of San Diego and of its inhabitants, for all purposes.

In the next year the Supreme Court reaffirmed its decision and granted the city the right to proceed with the construction of El Capitan Dam. The decision was a difficult one for Fletcher to accept. He always believed that the rights he acquired on the upper river, and which had passed to the La Mesa, Lemon Grove and Spring Valley Irrigation District, and the riparian rights he had claimed on the lower river, were valid and that the protracted legal action had been unnecessary.

William Templeton Johnson

The decision reversed the finding of the Superior Court in San Diego that while the city did own the paramount rights it had allowed the Cuyamaca Water Company to use water which now could not be taken away. However, it was agreed that the irrigation district could continue to take water from the river as long as it was not needed by San Diego. In the end, in the best interests of the city and the county, an agreement was reached granting the district the right to appropriate 2,000,000 gallons daily.

The 160th anniversary of the founding of the first Franciscan mission in California, on Presidio Hill in 1769, was celebrated in 1929 with the dedication of Presidio Park and Museum on July 16. The park and museum, created by George W. Marston, were transferred to the city. The museum building was designed by William Templeton Johnson, the architect who had conceived the Fine Arts Gallery in Balboa Park.

The same month recorded the death in Europe of Katherine Tingley, the "Purple Mother" who had established the Theosophical Society headquarters on Point Loma. Even before her death the society had been falling into hard times and blocks of land were sold to meet debts and operating expenses.

Until September, declines in the New York stock market had been relatively modest. On Saturday, October 12, stock market trading was the heaviest of any Saturday in the exchange's history. On Monday, heavy selling continued, until on Thursday, the worry turned into panic and nearly 13,000,000 shares changed hands. Marginal investors were shaken out and many ruined. The heavy slide continued into the following week and Tuesday, October 29, probably was the most devastating day in the history of markets. Secondary headlines in the newspapers in San Diego announced the loss of billions of dollars in listed values, but there were editorial inclinations to dismiss them merely as "paper values." But in the East and in other financial centers, it was now the turn of the well-to-do to be shaken out, and many of them were seeing fortunes vanish.

It was in that same month that the Chamber of Commerce magazine stated that probably there was no better evidence of the business opportunities in San Diego than the quick success recorded by the Gildred brothers in a large building and leasing project undertaken virtually at their first sight of the city. The Gildred Building covered a full block bounded by A, B, Seventh and Eighth streets. One portion housed a ten-floor garage, another a four-story department store, and another portion, the third largest theater on the Pacific Coast. With this structure, the skyline of San Diego assumed an appearance it would hold almost unchanged for the next three decades.

The Gildred brothers, Philip L. and Theodore Gildred, had recently come up from Ecuador in South America. Philip Gildred was quoted as saying:

Although I had traveled for many years, I made my first trip to the West Coast of the United States in 1927—and stayed. I was amazed at the beauty, and visualized the enormous possibilities of the city of San Diego, situated in a temperate zone which makes its climate ideal. The greatest possibilities yet to come to San Diego will be from its port—one of the finest in the world ... This city, whilst a metropolis, had not yet the hustle and bustle of other cities, and I know that in that respect, in our lifetime, this feature will attract many people to come and live and enjoy the beauty of our city and surroundings.

Philip L. Gildred

Though an expected stock market recovery in November failed to materialize, thousands of San Diegans turned out to see a parade for the formal opening on November 8 of the new theater in the Gildred brothers' building, which became part of the Fox Theater circuit. A special train brought Hollywood film stars to San Diego, now suddenly being described in advertising literature as "the playground of America" and "the capital of the Southland's empire of amusement." The inaugural presentation was a specially created stage performance of the Fanchon and Marco company and Will Rogers' first talking picture.

The population of San Diego was being estimated at 170,000 and there was a significant effort to modernize the city administration and to institute civic reforms that had had their beginning across the country with Theodore Roosevelt and in California with Hiram Johnson.

Over the years there had been repeated revelations of laxity in the enforcement of laws against gambling and vice, and of cases of actual corruption in city and county governments. A board of freeholders was elected and presented a proposed charter for an election on December 19, 1929. It would have placed all city authority and departments with a city manager, including the harbor department which had been governed by a commission, and would even have made the city attorney an appointive instead of an elective official. The grant of such powers met strong opposition and the proposed charter was rejected by the voters.

Opposition to any civic changes was easily aroused. Two years before the proposal to locate the Civic Center on the tidelands, on land already held by the city, had barely won approval. The "little people" who had come for the climate were not particularly concerned about what was happening beyond their immediate neighborhood. But the city manager form of government was taking root everywhere and a new board of freeholders would submit another and less sweeping charter.

The year ended with public optimism, though building permits had dropped another million dollars. The Agua Caliente Jockey Club inaugurated the new race track on December 28 and announced a $100,000 added handicap to be run in March. A $25,000 golf tournament, the richest on record, was scheduled for the opening of the new Agua Caliente golf course.

Meanwhile, the State of California was releasing funds for road construction to relieve growing unemployment. Bank clearings, the indicators of the flow of business, were dropping sharply. The number of homes for rent and sale lengthened in the columns of San Diego newspapers. There were long comforting lists of building projects still planned by local companies and out-of-town investors for 1930. *The San Diego Union* assured its readers that they could cheerfully undertake the responsibilities of the new year.

CHAPTER SEVEN

The Great Depression was not all sadness.
While Southern Californians escaped some of the hardships of people in colder
and more industrial areas, there were "breadlines" and severe personal and
business losses.
But at the same time, it was a period of the quiet of earlier years, and, too,
of rebirth.
San Diego, for example, acquired some of its enduring civic attributes as a
result of emergency projects, the harbor was deepened and prepared for a
future nobody at that time foresaw, and parks were acquired or improved.
It was during the depression that the Anza-Borrego Desert Park was created
and became a playground.

THE QUIET YEARS

The Great Depression settled swiftly and sadly over Southern
California. With it came the end of the first great internal migration of the auto age. In ten years 2,000,000 new settlers had moved
into the state, nearly three-fourths of them into Southern California.

The rate of bankruptcies was the highest in the nation and
reflected the collapse of many speculative land promotions and oil
and other wildcat stock schemes. In San Diego in one year the
value of building permits abruptly dropped by half and bank debits
sank a hundred million dollars.

It was difficult for the people of Southern California, who had
prospered for a decade from the tide of new settlers and investors,
to accept the prospect of a long period of economic and population
stagnation. They were convinced that it all must start up again,
and soon. San Diegans drew comfort from the newspaper oracle of
the day, Arthur Brisbane, an editor and columnist for the Hearst
newspapers whose writings also appeared in scores of other publications, generally on the front page. He visited San Diego on March
19, 1930, and then wrote:

Everything you have ever thought about or wanted is here, and many
things that you never imagined . . . every man, woman and child says: "Why
anybody able to come here should live anywhere else, is a mystery." They are
right, it is a mystery.

By way of prediction, which please write down on your cuff, this writer wishes to say that fully developed air travel, with 24-hour round trip, from ocean to ocean, will build up a permanent and transient population in this city and territory surrounding it as no place on earth has ever been built before.

As far as San Diegans were concerned, it was still a mystery why more settlers preferred Los Angeles to San Diego. The census of 1930 showed that over a million more persons resided in Los Angeles. The population of Los Angeles was 1,238,048 and that of San Diego 147,897. During the past decade San Francisco's had risen only 128,000, to 634,394. Though San Diego's population had doubled in ten years, the county as a whole had grown less rapidly, from 112,248, to 209,659. More than half of the state's population now lived in the eleven counties generally assigned to Southern California.

The depression had not touched bottom and George W. Marston was able to write that San Diego was not as yet in a precarious situation, though he informed the city planner, John Nolen:

San Diego is not only suffering from the general depression in business, but it is in the end of the first year of a reaction from the boom of the preceding five years. More than this we have had through the operation of the Mattoon Act an iniquitous tax bill levied upon many of our undeveloped properties. This has resulted in many people losing their holdings. This and the general high rate of taxation has produced a very irritable feeling among the people and I have never known such a difficult period for voting upon improvement bonds.

Large areas of land within the city were unsalable even if the realty market did improve, because of the pyramiding of special assessments. A dead hand had been laid upon growth, and it would take years to lift it. The list of tax delinquencies published in *The San Diego Union* grew to sixty-four pages.

A way to cut the tax burden was suggested to the City Council in 1930 by the treasurer, Jack Millan. He proposed a revision of the new City Charter to permit the sale of remaining pueblo lands. The 7000 acres north of the San Diego River represented all that was left of the 48,000 acres that had been conveyed to the city with United States recognition of the Spanish boundaries of the original pueblo. In 1889 the voters had prohibited further sale of these lands until 1930, and in 1929 this had been extended until 1940.

Millan argued that San Diego taxpayers were carrying a burden of $23,000,000 worth of vacant and dead lands, for parks, playgrounds, churches and schools, and that the sale of only half of the pueblo lands would relieve taxes by about $2,000,000. However, it was feared that the dumping of such a large amount of land on the market, at sacrifice prices, would further depress real estate values on which the community rested so much of its hopes for recovery.

Federal and state public works projects were instituted or undertaken before scheduled to provide jobs and bolster the economy. President Hoover signed a deficiency bill appropriating $10,000,000 for the preliminary construction work on Boulder Dam.

Improvements in the city's water distribution and storage system were being carried out with funds from a successful bond issue in 1929. A new gateway into San Diego from the north was provided through city-state cooperation. A new highway was constructed through Rose Canyon, removing La Jolla from the main route into the city, and work was in progress on a substitute Torrey Pines grade to eliminate the narrow curving road that led from Sorrento Valley up to the mesa. The Broadway pier was length-

Construction of Boulder Dam was begun during the depression.
President Hoover signed a deficiency bill providing emergency money to begin the project that had taken a decade to get written into legislative law.
Here, in a photograph taken in 1932, is shown the upper cofferdam which diverted the Colorado River through canyon wall tunnels and around the actual site of the dam.
Men and machines are placing and compacting earth material to form the temporary diversion dam.

ened 200 feet and a two-story transit shed erected. However, a proposal that both the city and county approve bonds to construct a combined Civic Center building on the waterfront was defeated.

The federal government authorized additional funds for dredging the harbor and the material would add 122 acres to Lindbergh Field. By the summer of 1930 airlines began operating from Lindbergh Field, though companies were constantly entering or going out of business or merging with other lines. The Maddux line became Transcontinental Air Transportation-Maddux and was

Airlines struggled to survive during the depression and companies disappeared or merged with others in a picture of change and confusion.
San Diego's fear that it might be cut off from regular service was alleviated when the Pacific Air Transport inaugurated the first airmail and passenger express service along the entire Pacific Coast.
Here the first plane from San Diego prepared to take off from Lindbergh Field. The runway was crowded with cheering spectators and the flight was considerably delayed.

offering connections at Phoenix to El Paso and eastward all the way to New York. Western Air Express and Pickwick Airways were still in business.

Pacific Air Transport received permission to extend its original Seattle-Los Angeles service to San Diego as the southern terminus. The first flight was scheduled from Lindbergh Field on July 1. A celebrating crowd of several thousand blocked the runway and the takeoff had to be delayed. Pilot R. L. Remlin finally lifted off a single-engine Boeing 40-B, with space for four passengers and a quantity of airmail, at 10 o'clock at night. Searchlights from Navy ships in the harbor outlined the plane in the sky and an escort of nine Navy planes, authorized by Admiral Reeves, accompanied the plane northward.

Pacific Air Transport soon became a part of United Air Lines and the others serving San Diego disappeared or were replaced by new companies, and the shuffling went on. For one brief year San Diego had a direct flight eastward as far as Phoenix. In response to pleas from San Diego, American Airways, predecessor of American Air Lines, added a conditional San Diego-Phoenix shuttle connecting with its Atlanta-Los Angeles airmail route. Fifty pounds of airmail a day were required to maintain the service. Even though Thomas Bomar, manager of the aviation department of the Chamber of Commerce, airmailed packaged bricks, the weight requirement could not be maintained and the service was discontinued.

Flying was still a challenge to the brave. A local girl named Ruth Alexander, who had been flying for only a year and held a woman's altitude record, was to attempt a one-stop flight across country, from San Diego to Newark, New Jersey. She lifted her heavily-loaded monoplane from Lindbergh Field. It staggered toward Point Loma in the fog and failed to clear the summit. She died in the wreckage.

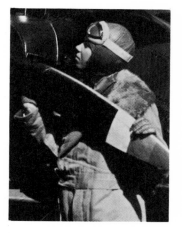

Ruth Alexander

In San Diego the aviation industry which had been started so audaciously virtually vanished. Edmund T. Price had assumed the presidency of the Solar Aircraft Company but the third all-metal plane which the company produced, and on which so much had been depended, found no immediate buyers. Aviation companies elsewhere also were disappearing. The depression began with 300 and when it ended, there were only about fifty. But interest in flying did not abate.

In the summer of 1931 Price took his wife, three children, a pilot and a mechanic and with the Solar plane flew 7000 miles across country, from San Diego to New Bedford, Massachusetts, touching down on fifty airports in twenty-five states. Newspapers dubbed the plane the "Flying Nursery." It was great publicity but sold no airplanes. The third and last plane produced by Solar Aircraft eventually was sold to a Mexican firm for use in the coffee trade.

Solar turned to producing pots and pans for the Navy. Claude Ryan moved onto Lindbergh Field and was conducting a flying school.

The distress in the United States, limited perhaps to certain classes as it might have been, had no effect on the Mediterranean-style playground below the border. On July 27, 1930, the latest addition to the Agua Caliente resort, a spa with its pools and mineralized waters, was opened with dedication ceremonies and a water festival. Sixty miles farther south a hotel and gambling casino were opened at Ensenada, with the former heavyweight boxing champion, Jack Dempsey, as a heavy investor.

The little aircraft companies in San Diego had their troubles during the depression. The market for airplanes was dwindling. The third plane produced by Solar Aircraft found no buyers.
The company president, Edmund T. Price, picked up his family and flew from city to city across the country, for a total of 7000 miles.
Newspapers dubbed the plane the "flying nursery." However, the flight produced no buyers and the airplane later wound up in the coffee trade in Mexico.

148

The Agua Caliente complex then consisted of a hotel, casino, a bungalow court, so popular in those days, a bathhouse, golf course and cafe, and the spa, representing a total investment of $6,000,000. A greyhound racing track was added later. Money flung across the gambling tables repaid the investment almost as fast as it was spent. As a writer familiar with the scene wrote:

Diplomats from the East and West, potentates from the Orient, American business tycoons and political leaders, famous names in sports and show business, even gangsters spawned by the prohibition era, all felt the spell of Agua Caliente.

That San Diego seemed to have escaped the worst of the consequences of the depression was expressed editorially by *The San Diego Union* on January 1, 1931:

The contrast between our sun-warmed spot of earth and the snow-bound streets of the average eastern city, is no greater than the contrast between the tone of business here and that reported from the East. It would be silly to pretend that San Diego, alone in all the United States, was free from any effects of the general business depression. But it is perfectly accurate to say that the effects here are nothing like as severe as those reported from industrial and agricultural centers in other parts of the country.

For the first time, perhaps, there was a general relief that San Diego had not become, as so many had hoped, an industrial city. The thought was stated openly in the editorial that the city's chief asset was a way of life which no shift or change in economic conditions could impair.

By Spring conditions had worsened and there were 4835 persons actively looking for work in San Diego and nearly 900 others had been laid off but were hopefully waiting to be recalled to their old jobs.

The mild climate alleviated the suffering experienced in the East, though contrary to post-depression reports, there were "breadlines." Food was dispensed to the hungry from four depots. A city bond issue provided $300,000 for numerous recreational projects, including a golf course and tennis courts in Balboa Park, which helped to provide jobs for the most needy of the unemployed.

The flush of the boom years had all gone by now, and there was a turning inward. San Diego in a way settled into the routine of a town in the shadow of the new giant of the Pacific Coast, Los Angeles. Times were hard and they were to get worse.

The necessity of reform in city government, so obvious for years in the politics surrounding water development and in the administration of the police department, produced a new City Charter submitted by a board of freeholders. It was a compromise of the 1929 plan which had proposed unacceptable powers for the city manager.

The compromise, however, did initiate a clear-cut city manager system. The city manager was to be appointed by the Council and vested with broad administrative authority over the fire, police, health and other city departments, but not over the harbor, city attorney, city clerk, auditor and controller, and civil service. City commissions were continued for supervision of the harbor, parks and planning, and for civil service.

Walter W. Austin

It provided for a Council of six members to be nominated by districts and elected at large. The mayor was to be nominated and elected at large and become the seventh member of the Council, as presiding officer and ceremonial chief of the city. It also provided for a hydraulic engineer, a water department, and an accounting system to determine how much water cost and who paid for it.

A new method of financing development of the harbor also was provided. Since 1912 San Diegans had never refused money for a port which carried so many of their hopes for the future. There had been seven bond issues between 1912 and 1928. In 1929, however, the citizens had decided that ten cents of each tax dollar collected was to be allocated for harbor work. The new Charter provided a fixed sum of $150,000 a year. Under a commission with a large measure of independence, development of the harbor on a long-range program proceeded free of most of the troubles which continually beset the development of water resources.

The Charter was approved at a city election on April 7, 1931. The same election saw the defeat of Mayor Clark and the election of a businessman, Walter W. Austin, as his successor. In the campaign it was charged that since 1924 the people had voted $8,650,000 for water with little results to show for it. Two new city councilmen also were elected and they pledged to support the program of the city's hydraulic engineer, Hiram Savage.

Once again Savage was recommending that the next dam should be built in Mission Gorge on the lower San Diego River, in preference to one at the El Capitan site which figured so prominently in the years of legal struggle with the Fletcher interests.

The site recommended by Savage was about a half mile below the old Padre Dam. A second site in the gorge a mile below the one favored by Savage, and two miles above the San Diego Mission, was owned by Fletcher. Fletcher pressed the city to

150

*The fear of a shortage of water finally brought an end to a long dispute as to
where the first dam on the San Diego River should be placed.
A site in Mission Gorge lost out to a site farther upstream near El Cajon
Mountain.
The voters approved transfer of bond money in 1931 to begin the construction
of El Capitan Dam. This photograph, taken in 1934, shows construction work
on the spillway extension.*

acquire his site and contended that a dam farther upstream would
flood a large section of El Cajon Valley. The site urged by Savage
was rejected at the polls, and San Diego was warned that it
possibly was facing a water emergency, with its five reservoirs only
half full. All factions were brought together and it was agreed to
proceed with El Capitan Dam. It was estimated that in forty-eight
years 20,000,000 gallons daily had flowed past the site and been
lost to the people. The voters in December of 1931 approved the
transfer of $3,600,000 in bond money to construct a rock-fill dam.
The largest share of the bonds represented money which seven
years before had been voted for another type of dam at the same
site.

The question whether the city manager system instituted by the
voters was to survive, let alone govern, remained in doubt during

John F. Forward Jr.

George Burnham

much of the depression. Underlining the struggle, too, was whether San Diego would be an open or closed town. City councilmen, long accustomed to personal powers and the manipulation of the police department, were wary of the city manager system approved by the people.

Some time elapsed, and a new mayor, John F. Forward Jr., had been elected in April of 1932, before the first city manager was hired in May. He was a former public works commissioner from Detroit, Horace H. Esselstyn. Councilmen found themselves stripped of daily responsibilities. Esselstyn lasted three months. The city purchasing agent, A. V. Goedell, was named acting manager, but he was to remain in the office only about ten months. He was succeeded by Fred Lockwood, who had been a manager of city operations under the former system of government, and he held the office for about fifteen months. Police chiefs came and went, amid continuing and often conflicting charges of political interference with the police department and corruption within the department.

Another effort for a Civic Center came to nothing in 1933. When a bond issue was proposed once again to build a city-county administration building, opponents of the waterfront site forced two other possible sites onto the ballot. Voters were given a choice of the tidelands, the southwest corner of Balboa Park, or the Broadway site of the existing Courthouse in the heart of the city. The tidelands site won, but city voters at the same time failed to deliver the necessary two-thirds majority for a participating bond issue.

The general national discontent brought the end of the Progressive movement in California that had taken Hiram Johnson to political power. Governor C. C. Young was defeated for renomination in the Republican primary by the conservative and "wet" mayor of San Francisco, James "Sunny Jim" Rolph Jr. In San Diego, however, a Republican majority stayed with Young. Rolph took office in January of 1931 and talked of the "bright days which I see just ahead," and promised no new taxes and that the $30,000,000 surplus in the state treasury would be used to help alleviate depression suffering.

Franklin D. Roosevelt, Democrat governor of New York, was elected President in November of 1932 and assumed office on March 4, 1933. In San Diego County Roosevelt had led Herbert Hoover by 10,000 votes, but Norman Thomas, the Socialist candidate, received more than 3000 votes. At the local level the Republicanism that had so long dominated San Diego persisted and sent George Burnham to Congress to replace Phil Swing, a Democrat.

Swing, with ten years of his life spent on the fight for Boulder Dam, had decided to return to the practice of law. His work was not done, however. As representative of the Imperial Valley Irrigation District he went to Washington and with several other western delegates was able to obtain a fifteen-minute appointment with President Roosevelt, to plead the case for an immediate beginning on the All-American Canal. The President listened but was noncommital. In his memoirs Swing wrote:

> I did not know it then, but learned later that after I left, Mr. Roosevelt put in a long distance call to Senator Johnson, then in San Francisco. The President said to him, "Hiram, do you want me to grant an allocation to start the All-American Canal?" Senator Johnson had never asked any favor of anyone and I had not asked him to endorse my P.W.A. application, but when asked by the President for his opinion of the merits of the All-American Canal, for which we had both worked so hard, he did not hesitate to say that it was worthy of an allotment. That settled it.

The next day, October 24, 1933, Swing was notified by an official of the new Public Works Administration that the canal had been approved as an emergency project and $6,000,000 allocated to start the work.

While the nation was awaiting the change in the administration in Washington, the financial situation reached a crisis because of heavy withdrawals of funds from banks. Bank shareholders as well as depositors were nervous and distressed.

Governor Rolph declared legal holidays in California which forced the closing of San Diego banks for four days early in March of 1933. They re-opened March 7 under the authority of the Secretary of Treasury, for limited transactions, and remained in this condition, and during the national bank holiday declared by President Roosevelt, until March 14.

Since the beginning of the Twenties only two banks had failed in San Diego County. A third one, in Oceanside, failed just before the bank holiday. A fourth bank, in East San Diego, did not re-open after the emergency. No signs of panic were noticeable in San Diego, however, and $5,000,000 in script, which had been printed to be used if the bank closing were extended indefinitely, was never issued.

James Rolph Jr.

Upon the re-opening, the number of new deposits exceeded cash withdrawals. San Diego County emerged from the bank holiday with eleven institutions in operation. A merger reduced the total to ten by the end of 1933, of which four were national banks and six state banks.

C. Arnholt Smith

Two other financial institutions, savings and loan companies which had flourished almost unregulated with the boom, were affected. One liquidated voluntarily and the other was declared bankrupt. Others remained open under restrictions.

Control of one of San Diego's major banks, however, changed hands in the Spring preceding the bank holiday. A group led by C. Arnholt Smith, an officer of the Bank of America in Los Angeles, acquired control of the United States National Bank. Smith had begun his banking career in San Diego as a messenger.

The largest downtown business to close its doors was Holzwasser's department store at Fifth Street and Broadway. The San Diego Athletic Club, which had been enlarged even during construction to include residence quarters, was bankrupt, and continuing losses had to be absorbed by a few individuals who had personally guaranteed loans. The La Jolla Beach and Yacht Club was opened in the summer of 1927 in a La Jolla Shores area then known as Long Beach, but plans to dredge a slough and create a yacht harbor had to be abandoned. Eventually the property and beach rights were sold to a retired newspaper publisher and regular summer resident of La Jolla, Frederick William Kellogg.

The statistics of the times tell the story of San Diego's continuing economic decline. Hearings before the California Unemployment Commission in November of 1932 indicated that in the county there were 16,000 persons unemployed and 4000 families on direct relief, out of a population of a little more than 223,000. By 1933 the unemployed totaled 23,000.

The value of manufactured products decreased from almost $38,000,000 in 1929 to about $16,000,000 in 1933. Industry was represented by food processing, packing and canning of various kinds, all exported; boat building, some furniture manufacturing, metal working, lumber milling and wood products related to building; and scores of other pursuits normally associated with community existence.

Throughout the state the total of unemployed had risen to more than 700,000 persons, half of whom lived in Los Angeles County. The value of farm products had declined from $750,000,000 to $372,000,000.

A certain stability was effected in the economy of San Diego by military spending, which continued to rise during the depression. Military payrolls rose from $16,000,000 in 1929 to $20,000,000 in 1934. However, the regular comings and goings of Navy ships, and their occasional long absences on fleet exercises, caused sharp fluctuations in business. It always was a big event when the ships

154

returned from distant waters. Income from agriculture was the county's second greatest source of income, and it remained so during the depression. The low decrease in income from sales, from $10,695,300 in 1930 to $8,168,021 in 1933, indicated that farmers were kept busy. The annual value of crops in the Imperial Valley, however, dropped from $40,000,000 to $19,000,000.

The value of canned fish products dropped from $7,351,781 in 1930 to $3,188,661 in 1932, but the demand continued strong and the number of persons employed in fishing and canning increased slightly during the same period. Cannery workers rose from 1415 to 1555. Tuna fishermen, however, were hard hit, not only by the depression but by Japanese imports. The tuna catch of California fishing boats had exceeded 100 million pounds in 1930 for the first time. The next year it fell to sixty million pounds. Recovery was slow until 1934 when the import duty on tuna canned in oil was raised. In one year the catch jumped to more than 125 million pounds.

The value of yearly city building permits, once more than $20,000,000, had sunk to a little more than $2,000,000 by 1932. Most of this represented repairs or alterations. In another year they would dip to $1,800,000. A special federal census in 1934 reported that of more than 39,000 single family dwellings, 2842 were vacant.

The percent of tax delinquencies reflected the collapse of the real estate market and the effects of the Mattoon Act. Property tax delinquencies in 1928-1929 were only 2.76 percent. Four years later in 1933 they were 17.1 percent.

The highest rates of tax delinquencies were in the road improvement districts. The value of the land and improvements in the fifty-six districts was nearly fourteen million dollars, and the total bond and tax liabilities were more than sixteen million dollars. City and county taxes were not being paid on half the properties and in 1935 in eleven of the improvement districts no payments on bonds were made. Under the law property owners could not pay their city and county taxes without at the same time paying the district assessments. Most of the other 32,000 owners soon abandoned payment of taxes and improvement levies and some of the bonds dropped in value to as low as fifteen cents on the dollar. As a result more than $2,500,000 in tax revenue was being lost, or added to the general tax burden of other property owners in the county.

Most of the land had been improved for speculative purposes, and the prospective buyers had never come. The assessed values in land and improvements in the Rolando No. 1 development had dropped to $31,651, but the bond and tax liability was $330,794. The land and improvements in Fletcher Hills were assessed at only $58,760, but the total of bonds, coupons and taxes against the property was $978,562. The Paradise Hills development had assessed values of $13,013 and a bond liability of $592,442. One owner whose property was assessed at $100 received a 1935 tax assessment of $43,816.

The Causeway project, the most costly improvement which obligated property with an assessed valuation of more than seven million dollars, was in relatively good shape, with a total liability of only $1,710,615. However, the deliquency rate was fifty-eight percent in 1934. In Rancho Santa Fe, one of the more prosperous developments, the bond liabilities were about three-fourths the value of all land and improvements, and the delinquency rate was only thirty percent.

Oscar Cotton, the real estate broker and co-founder of the San Diego-California Club, in his memoirs wrote:

Those were the days when building managers asked prospective tenants how much rent they could afford to pay, and that was it ... Sale prices were so low it was actually sickening. Level, half-acre lots in Bostonia, with water pipes, sold for $99. Good, five-room houses right in town went for $3000 to $4500 with 10 percent down, and others not so good, for $2500. Occasionally a smaller house would bring as little as $1500. Business properties were just as low in proportion. It was all most depressing, but the town had been much overbuilt and overexpanded during the lush Twenties, and here we were again, absolutely stranded with thousands of properties for sale, and only an occasional buyer.

The most spectacular real estate collapse involved Sunset Cliffs where more than $3,000,000 worth of lots had been sold on contract. The high building restrictions written into the deeds made the land unsalable and unusable in a time of depression. Contracts to purchase were simply allowed to lapse. John P. Mills and his partners also suffered experiences with the law, growing out of wild boom-time parties. Mills lost many thousands of dollars across the gambling tables at Agua Caliente and his home and yacht were attached. The fortune of $6,000,000 with which he came to San Diego disappeared.

The Spreckels interests still represented a large area of San Diego's economy and the depression had made it more difficult to liquidate properties. In 1932 Frank J. Belcher Jr., who had headed a local syndicate which purchased control of the First National Bank from the estate, became president of the J.D. & A.B. Spreckels companies at San Francisco. A year later the Spreckels companies sold their remaining interest in the San Diego & Arizona Railway to the Southern Pacific. This railroad, of all his achievements, had been John D. Spreckels' greatest pride.

For a period the City Council and the Board of Supervisors had tried to stem the economic slide by providing relief at the rate of $40,000 a month. When they came to the end of their resources, the burden was shifted to the state, and there followed one relief or public works agency after another, and they in turn were followed or supplemented by federal agencies.

Though the San Diego-California Club had agreed to reduce its appeals to new settlers, so as not to attract persons looking for work or for easy relief, the inflow of tourists and visitors continued fairly strong during the depression. The climate also proved to be a lure to the unemployed in other sections of California, particularly in the Central Valleys, and anyone who could provide some scrap of medical advice fled the interior for the cooler coast. They represented a goodly proportion of those on relief in San Diego County.

This experience was quite different from the sudden and devastating collapse of the Boom of the Eighties. In six months, in late 1888 and early 1889, San Diego's population dropped from 35,000 to 16,000.

The California Department of Agriculture checked 281,120 autos into Southern California in 1930, and they brought 759,923 visitors. Eighty percent of the cars were late models. Two years later, 80,000 out-of-state cars entered through Yuma on the Broadway of America. Many tourists always had been persons of moderate or high incomes who could afford to vacation or winter in Southern California. The tourist income in 1929 was calculated at about $15,000,000. No figures are available for the following three years, but in 1933 the income from tourists was estimated at about $13,000,000.

In a study of why tourists who visited San Diego decided to remain, the San Diego-California Club found that the beaches attracted twenty-six percent; gardening, seventeen percent; schools and other facilities for the proper training of children, seventeen percent; outdoor sports such as golf, yachting, tennis, roque and swimming, seven percent; and business opportunities due to the city's prospects for growth, sixteen percent. By questionnaires the comprehensive campaign concluded that approximately two-thirds of San Diego tourists and visitors chose to make the city their permanent home.

In the early reactions to the depression the voters had repeatedly rejected various civic projects but the city was being shaped advantageously nevertheless. In retrospect, it was a period of significant achievement as well as defeats.

On November 7, 1931, the aircraft carrier *Saratoga*, after waiting out a fog, steamed into San Diego Harbor with Captain Frank B. McCrary in command. The carrier had been built on the hull of a battle cruiser eliminated by a disarmament conference, and was 888 feet long and had a crew of 2000 men. She dropped anchor 1500 feet off the Broadway Pier in a turning basin that had been dredged while the city was obtaining material for the tidelands fill for Lindbergh Field.

A significant but little-recognized event for Southern California took place in 1931.
The Navy's new giant aircraft carrier, the U.S.S. Saratoga, *entered San Diego harbor.*
The historic port of California's Pacific Coast had been opened to the largest ships of the Navy and henceforth the Navy would concentrate air activities in the Southland.
Nine months later the Army joined with the Navy and Marines to put 420 planes in the air at one time over San Diego.

The *Saratoga* fired a thirteen-gun salute for Rear Admiral Thomas J. Senn, commandant of the 11th Naval District, and it was answered by the guns of the Naval Air Station. The historic bay of the Spanish explorers had been opened to the mightiest ships of the United States Navy and from then on it would be "home port" for the Navy's air force in the Pacific. Ten years and one month later Pearl Harbor would be attacked and the bay would be a principal port for the greatest war in history.

Nine months later Navy and Marine fliers joined with the Army in putting 420 airplanes in the air over San Diego. It was the greatest mass aerial flight in the world's history and was in honor of visiting members of the National Editorial Association and other news reporters on the West Coast to attend the opening of the 10th Olympic Games in Los Angeles. The date was July 28, 1932.

Captain John A. Towers, who led the first Navy flight across the Atlantic Ocean, was in command of 300 Navy planes in the mass flight, as chief of staff to Rear Admiral Harry E. Yarnell, commanding aircraft, Battle Force. There were twenty-eight "giant flying boats" capable of carrying a ton of bombs each and a dozen new torpedo-carrying bombers. Major Carl Spatz led the Army's 17th pursuit group of fifty-seven planes through intricate aerial "snake-dance" maneuvers.

*Rear Admiral
Harry E. Yarnell*

Following the air review, Amelia Earhart, the only woman to twice fly the Atlantic Ocean, participated in dedicating the new terminal and administration building at Lindbergh Field, which was being built privately by Claude Ryan, and in unveiling a plaque to Charles Lindbergh in whose honor the field had been named.

Several years before, the arrival of the *Saratoga* and the great air display would have brought an outpouring of predictions of San Diego's future. In the depth of a depression the mood of the public was more on the moment than on a visionary tomorrow.

The first buildings of the new San Diego State College were dedicated in a three-day ceremony, May 1, 2 and 3, 1931, and a visiting Spanish official pronounced them the finest and purest Spanish style of architecture he had found in any group of buildings outside of Spain. Classes already had begun and 2000 students enrolled. Though still technically a teachers' college, its curriculum had been expanded to 200 courses and the granting of bachelor degrees. Dr. Edward L. Hardy, college president, said that while teacher colleges should provide the same educational facilities available in other major population centers, there was no thought of attempting to have them become graduate or professional schools.

Three months later, through public subscription, a partial restoration of the San Diego Mission, the "mother mission" of the Spanish period, was completed under the direction of Albert S. Mayrhofer.

*Rear Admiral
Thomas J. Senn*

The San Diego Zoo grew from a meager exhibit of wild animals to an institution. Seamen from all parts of the world had brought contributions. Native animals, birds and reptiles were traded on all continents. Wealthy men from all over the Pacific Coast made long voyages in their yachts for specimens. San Diegans from all walks

The Spanish influence in architecture was still felt in the design of public buildings in the 1930's.
When San Diego State College outgrew its Normal Street site, attempts were made to place it within Balboa Park, but the voters refused to approve any further encroachments on park land.
The college then was relocated at the city's eastern edge and the first buildings dedicated in 1931. The sketch shows the college as it was originally conceived for some distant future.

of life contributed for the purchase of particular exhibits and facilities. The zoo also got its first full-time director. Mrs. Belle J. Benchley, who had been bookkeeper and then executive secretary, became the only woman zoo director in the country.

Until the Thirties the San Diego Zoological Society, under the leadership of Dr. Harry Wegeforth, had never quite achieved an independence that would remove an ever-present threat of being forced out of Balboa Park or subjected to the direction of other political or civic groups. The society had been defeated in its efforts to acquire permanent possession of park lands. It had won, however, a share of the tax revenues and then had lost them with the adoption of a new Charter.

In 1932 the county assessor, James Hervey Johnson, insisted that the San Diego Zoological Society was a private organization and thus owed the city $100,000 in back taxes on the animals and other collections in its possession. When the society refused to pay, Johnson set up a stand at the zoo and attempted to auction them off. No bids were received, so Johnson declared them all sold to the state.

It finally was ruled that the sale had been held on a holiday and therefore was not legal. To settle the doubts that had arisen, the zoo collections were deeded to the city and then in 1934 the people voted a permanent special tax of two cents on each $100 of assessed valuation for the zoo's support.

During the depression, in the later phases of the Works Progress Administration, new structures and cages were added and an amphitheater built.

The passage of the years had brought the exposition buildings, with the exception of the permanent California quadrangle, into decay. An architect, Richard S. Requa, later recorded their appearance in the Spring of 1933:

> Foundations of buildings and arcades were almost entirely decomposed; towers and facades were tilting forward drunkenly; and whole sections of cornices and parapets had broken away and dropped into the shrubbery at their base.
>
> Large areas of the stuccoed walls had fallen, exposing the skeletons of temporary construction behind. The danger to the public had become so apparent that spaces were roped off around the crumbling sections and the City Council ordered an investigation to be made by the Building Department.

The buildings were promptly condemned and their removal recommended. The proposed casting down of the buildings which had made Balboa Park the showplace of the West aroused a storm of indignation. A group of citizens led by Miss Gertrude Gilbert, who had been in charge of music at the exposition, suggested a campaign for funds to restore the buildings and was given one week to prove that they could be saved. A contractor, Walter P. Trepte, volunteered to determine the amount of money that would be needed, and it proved to be a third of that estimated by the city.

Newspapers, the Chamber of Commerce and hundreds of volunteers joined in a campaign. Within a month enough money had been raised to assure federal emergency financial contributions. Restoration was completed in about a year.

The San Diego Society of Natural History, oldest scientific organization in Southern California, had found a home in the exposition buildings, first in the Nevada Building and then in one of the large park structures, the Canadian Building at the east end of the Prado, on the south side. A desire for a permanent home led to a fund drive in 1931, just before the deepening of the depression. Ellen Browning Scripps assured its success with a donation of $125,000. The site selected was that of the original Southern California Counties Building, which had stood on the north side of the

Belle J. Benchley

Dr. Harry M. Wegeforth

Gertrude Gilbert

Prado at the east gateway to the exposition grounds and which had burned down in 1925. The stated purpose of the society was to explore and interpret the natural sciences in San Diego County and adjacent regions.

The new museum was dedicated on January 13, 1933. Miss Scripps, however, did not live to see it completed, though continuing support came from a foundation she had established. She died on August 3, 1932. An editorial of the time said:

> The daughter of a London bookbinder, who became a prairie farmer, gave a new glory to American womanhood by a life that added the best of the new to the best of the old.

The San Diego Museum, which began with the "Science of Man" and Mayan exhibits from the first exposition, for years was a depository for other random collections of no particular anthropological, archaeological or ethnological signifiance. In time, however, and quartered in the permanent buildings of the California quadrangle, the San Diego Museum Association changed the institution's name to the San Diego Museum of Man and later it was decided to specialize in the native cultures of the three Americas. Meanwhile, one of its staff, Malcolm J. Rogers, was roaming the deserts of the Southwest and slowly putting together a story of ancient hunters who had lived in the area 10,000 or more years ago.

When the Fine Arts Gallery was opened in the park in 1926, the only works of art it possessed were gifts of sculpture, tapestries and a few paintings contributed by Mr. and Mrs. Appleton Bridges, Mr. and Mrs. Archer M. Huntington, and Mrs. Alma de Bretteville Spreckels and her children. The collections increased rapidly, with gifts, and then through purchases made possible by the Helen M. Towle Fund created from a bequest by her in 1935.

A survey of the possibilities for more parks in California was made in 1928 by Frederick Law Olmstead, an internationally known landscape architect whose firm had been involved in some of the early planning for the 1915-1916 exposition. His report to the state described the fragile nature of deserts and how any man-made disturbances could affect changes that nature might require a hundred years to repair, if it ever could be done:

> As in the case of ancient redwood forests, only such public action by the present generation on an adequate scale can preserve this heritage for the people of the centuries to come.

The first plans for a park in the Anza-Borrego Desert, an arm of the vast Sonoran Desert extending deep into Mexico, and lying

Appleton S. Bridges

just east of the coastal mountain ranges, were submitted by Clinton G. Abbott, director of the Museum of Natural History in San Diego, and Guy L. Fleming of La Jolla, who had been instrumental in the effort to preserve the rare Torrey Pines on the coast between La Jolla and Del Mar.

Soon after the depression had begun, voters had rejected a bond issue to match state funds to acquire land for a park in Borrego Canyon; for a 1500-acre park on Palomar Mountain; a park on the Silver Strand which connected Coronado with the mainland; and for an estuary park between Del Mar and Oceanside.

George Marston, however, on his own initiative purchased 2320 acres in the desert, mostly in Borrego Palm Canyon, deeded them to the state, and induced other owners to sell 5500 more acres which were placed in trust for acquisition by the state. Then in cooperation with Marston and the State Park Commission, Representative Swing and Senator Johnson introduced a second Swing-Johnson bill in Congress that successfully transferred almost 200,000 acres of federal land to Borrego State Park in March 1933.

In 1929 the State Legislature also had designated Mission Bay as a state park and the city had prepared a suggested plan of development. This had been talked about for thirty years. The plan was modified from time to time but the project could not surmount the depression.

The years were quiet and life had a rhythm different from

The "floating palaces" were not yet on the way out on the Pacific Coast. One of the most famous of the coastal steamers, however, the U.S.S. Harvard, took herself out of the scene by running aground off Point Arguello in 1931. She carried 500 passengers, who were removed in lifeboats and taken to San Pedro by the cruiser Louisville. *The* Harvard *is shown settled deep in the water.*

*When time was not
so important*

that of the boom years. Even those who had come to speculate in land settled into a way of life that was to persist until World War II. The parks, beaches, bays and climate were free and there was room enough for everybody. For excitement there were always accidents of man and the occasional lash of nature.

Shortly after 3 o'clock on the morning of May 30, 1931, in heavy fog, the coastal steamer *Harvard*, with 500 passengers, ran on the rocks of Point Arguello, north of Santa Barbara, near where seven United States destroyers had gone aground in 1923. The passengers were removed in lifeboats and taken to San Pedro aboard the cruiser *Louisville*, where those originally bound for San Diego were put aboard buses. The *Harvard* and its sister ship, the *Yale*, had been familiar sights of the San Diego waterfront.

San Diego had the highest of hopes of becoming the West Coast base for the Navy's giant dirigibles. The U.S.S. *Akron* was brought to San Diego in May of 1932 on its trip from the Atlantic to the Pacific, and was to be moored at Camp Kearny on the Linda Vista mesa.

Thousands of persons were on hand to greet the silver ship of the air. Just when it seemed that the mooring was to be completed, the ship lunged upward in a wind and veered away. Three young sailors were carried aloft, still clinging to the mooring ropes. At 300 feet, two of them slipped and fell to their deaths. The third clung to the rope for an hour and a half before being pulled into the dirigible's cabin.

San Diego was never selected as a site for a dirigible base and the giant ships were to have but a short life with the Navy. Less than a year later the *Akron* dropped into the sea with a loss of seventy-three lives. In 1935 the *Macon* was lost off Point Sur in California.

A tremendous earthquake rocked Southern California the evening of March 10, 1933. Long Beach, less than a hundred miles north of San Diego, was the hardest hit, with fifty-six deaths and $25,000,000 in damage. In all, 121 persons died. While the shock was felt sharply in San Diego, there was no damage nor panic.

With the passions of war rising in Europe and Asia the Communists chose San Diego, as a military center, for a demonstration on Memorial Day, May 30, 1933. Representatives of the Young Communist League of Los Angeles had applied for a parade permit but it was denied when they refused to give assurances that the Red flag would not be shown.

Trucks carrying an estimated 300 Communists converged on San Diego on Memorial Day and unloaded them at New Town Park. Speakers described Franklin D. Roosevelt as a "Wall Street Presi-

This is one of the prize-winning photographs of 1932.
The Navy dirigible Akron was brought to San Diego, which had high hopes
of becoming the primary dirigible base of the Pacific Coast.
While being maneuvered toward its mast on Kearny mesa, with scores of
sailors pulling on mooring ropes, the Akron suddenly veered in the wind and
lifted upward.
Three sailors were carried aloft, as seen in this picture. Two fell to their deaths.
Soon afterward, the Akron and a sister dirigible, the Macon, also went to
their deaths. The dirigibles had but a short life.

Communism in the United States was reaching its peak of agitation during the 1930's.
San Diego was the scene of a riot on Memorial Day in 1933. Unable to legally march in Los Angeles, young Communists embarked in autos and trucks for San Diego, and with their supporters converged on New Town Park.
However, when they attempted to march, they were met by police and a struggle ensued. Here, a speaker urges on the crowd.

dent" and placards protested "imperialistic war," the "boss class" and the capitalistic system, and insisted that the military air maneuvers conducted over San Diego were helping to get the country involved in an international war.

When they attempted to form a parade line and march into the street, while singing the *Internationale*, they were met by a solid phalanx of police officers. A riot ensued in which two officers received broken bones, a number of others were injured, and an estimated thirty demonstrators hurt. It ended with the discharge of one tear gas shell.

Eight demonstrators were jailed and the rest climbed back into their trucks, taking their wounded with them, and were escorted to the city limits. It had been the first radical riot in San Diego since the I.W.W. troubles of 1912.

While the number of persons on relief in the state had jumped to more than 1,250,000, seventy percent of whom lived in Southern California, the depression seemed to touch bottom in San Diego County in 1934 and level out. The Navy was spending $1,400,000 on construction projects, the Army $1,800,000, most of it at Rockwell Field, and the Postoffice Department $755,000 for a new building. However, 13,671 men and 3132 women were still listed as unemployed. The Civil Works Administration found jobs for 6621 of them and was succeeded by the State Emergency Relief Administration. The SERA provided work for 5200 persons and at Christmas time in 1934 distributed food to 7600 families.

The depression had not defeated Edmund Price and his struggling little Solar Aircraft Company in the converted fish cannery. A tie vote on the board of directors, as to whether the company should die or live, had been broken by Price.

Price was aware of the danger to airplanes and pilots by the failure of engine exhaust manifolds, and began to experiment with new types. He was assisted by Fred Rohr, his plant manager who had helped to build Lindbergh's *Spirit of St. Louis* and had remained in San Diego when the Mahoney plant was removed to St. Louis. From the use of regular steel Price turned to heat resistant alloys and produced a series of stainless steel manifolds for the U.S. Navy. For one period employes went six weeks without pay. At the end of 1933 the company had orders which would take them a month to fill and had increased the payroll from a low of four to twenty-seven.

In his new location on Lindbergh Field, where he was operating a successful flying school and aircraft service, Claude Ryan returned to the production of airplanes. Though company after company had disappeared before the winds of adversity, Ryan knew that aviation was just emerging. He designed the Ryan S-T monoplane, America's first small airplane of all-metal construction.

Confidence was returning. There were indications that the worst was over in San Diego. There was talk of a county-wide movement for a bond issue to buy up Mattoon district improvement bonds and return $14,000,000 in property to the tax rolls and to the realty market. The value of building permits rose in 1934 by more than $700,000 above the depression's low point. Revenue from the tourist trade was up perhaps by $1,500,000. Vacant dwellings were being taken up. The city was continuing to grow in population. In four years it was estimated that the city had increased by 17,000 and the county as a whole by 32,000. Agricultural revenues rose $500,000 for the year, and the value of canned sea products went up $300,000.

In the Imperial Valley, after a struggle of a generation, 300 settlers assembled in the heat of midsummer of 1934 near Pilot Knob to watch a huge power shovel make the first excavation for the All-American Canal. At Pilot Knob the water of the Colorado would be turned away from its old route into Mexico and taken along the international border and then up into the Imperial and Coachella Valleys. At the levers of the power shovel was Mark

Frank Drugan

Baron Long

Rose, who twenty-two years before had begun the agitation to control the Colorado River.

The restoration of the temporary exposition buildings in Balboa Park was proceeding, when a suggestion was made that San Diego should hold another exposition. The idea came from Frank Drugan, a former salesman and promoter of newspaper features who had lost his home and office in the Long Beach earthquake and had moved to San Diego. Baron Long, operator of the U.S. Grant Hotel, and his partners in Agua Caliente, were ready to listen, as were representatives of the Spreckels interests and the San Diego Consolidated Gas & Electric Company.

Though San Diego already had an exposition plant that had been kept almost intact, his idea at first was received with little enthusiasm from the rest of the community. It was in the summer of 1933. San Diegans had heard it before, and a few persons once even had tried to arouse interest in it, without success. But Drugan was not easily turned aside. He decided to visit the Century of Progress exposition then being presented in Chicago and go on to New York and Washington to sound out the possibilities of industrial and government participation.

Across the continent in Buffalo, New York, a decision was being reached that would forever alter the course of the growth of San Diego. Consolidated Aircraft Corporation had begun producing flying boats for the Navy, but ice-choked water and freezing flying conditions had hampered testing and demonstration flights.

Nearly a hundred years before another resident of the cold lands of eastern New York state had turned his face westward in the search of a better climate. After a number of years in Wisconsin, he had gone to California. In 1867 he stepped ashore at San Diego and changed it forever. He was Alonzo E. Horton, founder of the modern city.

For more than five years Major Reuben H. Fleet, Consolidated's president, had carefully surveyed all cities in the United States having more than 100,000 population and finally decided on a location somewhere in Southern California. In his own summary Fleet later stated:

Twice each year I flew around the country examining localities and municipal airports. We wanted a site on a publicly owned and operated airport having a publicly owned waterfront on a good but not congested harbor, with a seaplane base and ramp on adjacent water, in a city large enough to furnish a reasonable supply of labor and materials, in a southern clime unhampered by snow and ice and yet not unbearably hot, with all-year-round flying weather for test flying and flight deliveries.

A strong effort to lure Consolidated to Long Beach was made by the Los Angeles Chamber of Commerce. But, San Diego, with its Lindbergh Field on the edge of the bay, met every physical requirement for seaplane as well as land plane operations, as the planner John Nolen had foreseen. And it was in this area where Fleet had learned to fly with the Army's Signal Corps at Rockwell Field. And here were friends of his former military flying days, Major T. C. Macaulay, who had been an instructor at Rockwell Field and now was manager of the San Diego Chamber of Commerce, and Thomas Bomar, who headed the Chamber's aviation department.

Consolidated signed a qualified agreement to come to San Diego, if a decision to move was made. The company had more than 800 employes and $9,000,000 in unfilled orders for airplanes. In one stroke San Diego could enter the realm of industry that had so tantalized its more energetic promoters for generations.

Just two years before, as the depression settled over the country, there had been expressions of thankfulness that San Diego had not become an industrial city. But now the Harbor Commission sent one of its members, Emil Klicka, to Buffalo to argue for a move to San Diego before the company's directors who were seriously questioning its advisability. San Diego won. Consolidated Aircraft would relocate on Lindbergh Field.

CHAPTER EIGHT

CREATING A FAIR

The years between the Great Wars were drawing to a close. In Asia, Japanese armies were driving into the mainland of China. In Europe, Adolph Hitler had taken control of Germany. In the United States, the recognition of Communist Russia gave impetus to a wave of radicalism.

Headlines in the newspapers imparted no sense of urgency. The world had not yet been drawn into the intimacy that was to come with the end of isolationism, the swiftness of transportation and the immediacy of communication.

The persistence of the depression was of more concern to the people of the United States. The number of unemployed had failed to diminish and the New Deal of President Roosevelt was running into trouble. The situation in San Diego may have seemed more fortunate. Roosevelt was expanding the Navy. A major aircraft company was moving to Lindbergh Field. Tijuana and Agua Caliente had survived the end of prohibition in the United States and were drawing more and more tourists through San Diego.

A merchant from Los Angeles, R. M. Walker, while flying over San Diego was impressed by the many lines of automobiles moving into the city:

Caravans they seemed, from all directions. Cars from the coast routes, cars from the mountain roads to the east of us, and more cars from our friendly neighboring republic to the south of us.

Soon afterward the Walker-Scott Corporation signed a twenty-year lease on the empty building which formerly had housed one of San Diego's two major department stores. It was reopened as Walker's department store with George A. Scott, a vice president of the Walker-Scott Corporation, as general manager.

The suggestion of another exposition began to be taken seriously. The first exposition had not only publicized the natural beauty and climate of the area but had brought the Navy and the Marines to San Diego to stay, and now in the White House was the man who largely was responsible for it, while he was Undersecretary of the Navy. What might a second exposition do for San Diego?

Frank Drugan returned from Chicago with colored slides and motion pictures of the Century of Progress and assurances that many of its exhibits could be made available for an exposition in San Diego. Tentative pledges of financial support had come from leaders of industry in New York and government officials in Washington.

The Chamber of Commerce directors in March of 1934 appointed a committee to study costs, financing and organization. Controversies over how the exposition was to be organized, and who were to be the officers and directors, consumed several weeks of time, even though there was an awareness that the exposition would have to be held in the near future, to take advantage of the availability both of federal emergency financing and the exhibits from the Century of Progress.

Frank F. Merriam

It did not seem to be a propitious time for such an ambitious undertaking. Governor Rolph had died and been succeeded in office by the lieutenant governor, Frank F. Merriam. Almost immediately Merriam was confronted with a spreading crisis of labor disturbances and radical agitation. While promising a broad program of social and economic relief for California, Merriam also pledged that the state government would resist the "subversive activities of avowed Communists." When fighting began in San Francisco, in connection with a coastwide longshoremen's strike, the National Guard was called out to protect state property.

In the Imperial Valley efforts to organize and bring about a strike of agricultural workers, mostly Mexicans, met with vigorous resistance. The American Civil Liberties Union intervened and obtained a court injunction in San Diego, but when the union's attorney, A. L. Wirin, went to the valley he was taken from his hotel room and deposited in the desert.

Wirin had been supported by a number of San Diegans who had organized a chapter of the American Civil Liberties Union. Among them was a daughter of George Marston, Helen, who had participated in various anti-war and social movements. Though Marston himself was not a pacifist, according to another daughter, Mary, who wrote the family history, he did defend the activities of his daughter and ignored a threatened boycott of his store by Imperial Valley customers.

Unrest and discontent was rising with the wind of economic despair. Howard Scott brought his Technocracy movement, which promised economic salvation through a dictatorship of science, from Columbia University to California. A rival known as the Utopian Society blamed the profit system for all the ills of society and contended that in a few hours of each day, people between twenty-five and forty-five years of age alone could produce all that was needed for everybody. An aged physician, Dr. Francis E. Townsend, began gathering adherents for an old age revolving pension plan that would give every person over sixty $200 to spend every month.

These movements were particularly attractive to older people dependent on small pensions or earnings on long-hoarded savings reduced by the depression. In San Diego, as in all Southern California, settlers had remained somewhat as aliens in a strange land, retaining their interest in their home states and cities and dividing into state societies or into other small, isolated social groups. Persons fifty years of age and over accounted for almost a quarter of the population. The average age of residents in San Diego in 1930 was 32.8 years as compared with a national average of 26.4 years. In another decade war and a new and younger migration would sharply reduce the age level.

There was a gulf between residents and the community's business interests that often was difficult to bridge. Through 1933 and 1934 the city government was embroiled in the continuing argument over the city manager system and who was to run the police department, though it was a series of unsolved murders that finally aroused public anger.

The city manager, Fred Lockwood, defended his choice of chief of police, Harry J. Raymond, who entered the office in January 1933. He was a private detective from Los Angeles who once had been in the office of its district attorney. He was the sixth chief of police in four years. Openly voiced suspicions that Raymond had kept questionable associations in Los Angeles were rejected by a Council majority. In an editorial, *The San Diego Union* stated:

People should assemble now to strike while the iron is hot ... first rate police protection is not a visionary hope. We believe a department headed by

Rutherford B. Irones

George M. Sears

Frank G. Belcher

an intelligent and experienced professional for the sole purpose of giving people protection under the law, would give San Diego better service than it is getting now, and better service than it has ever received before.

Before the year was out, Raymond was fired. Two citizens, Robert R. Hamilton and G. Edward Chase, were instrumental in obtaining 18,000 signatures for a special election in December of 1933 which successfully revised the City Charter to require five votes to hire or fire the manager and reduced the councilmanic salaries from $3000 annually to $10 a meeting, with a maximum of $600 a year.

This was designed to reduce the duties of councilmen to part-time policy-making as envisioned in the Charter. The mayor's salary, however, was left at $5000, as he was expected to devote a major portion of his time to ceremonial duties. Five months later Forward announced he was resigning as mayor to avoid further humiliation in his efforts to carry out Charter provisions in regard to the manager. Forward, a title company executive, was a second generation mayor. His father had held the office before him, in the early 1900's.

Again it was the issue of the police department that had split the mayor and the Council. The manager's selection of a chief was subject to Council confirmation and the Council majority was clinging to its control over the department.

A short time later Lockwood resigned as city manager. In August of 1934 the City Council appointed a medical doctor, Rutherford B. Irones, as mayor to fill out Forward's unexpired term.

With Irones came a new city manager, George L. Buck, a former city manager of Long Beach, and a new chief of police, George M. Sears, who had been with the police vice squad. Within four months, Irones was in jail. The mayor was driving the city's limousine when it struck a car driven by a sailor. The sailor's wife was seriously injured. Irones, who had been drinking, failed to stop. While rumors of his involvement spread throughout the city, the police did nothing. His arrest on a hit-and-run charge was forced by newspaper investigation and a civil suit for personal injury damages. Just before being convicted and sentenced to six months in jail Irones resigned as mayor, and the office was vacant again.

It perhaps was not surprising that efforts to raise money for an exposition were proving difficult. A name had been selected, the California Pacific International Exposition, and attorney Walter Ames was directed to organize a non-profit corporation. As no company had any profits against which donations could be written off for income tax purposes, it was decided that contributions would be in the nature of loans for which promissory notes would be issued.

G. Aubrey Davidson, president of the 1915-1916 exposition, was elected chairman of the board of directors, and Frank G. Belcher, son of the president of the Speckels companies, president. O. W. Cotton was chairman of the campaign to raise $500,000. He found that everybody wanted the exposition but few were eager to contribute.

At the first fund-raising dinner $300,000 was pledged by the City Council, Board of Supervisors and seven businessmen and institutions, but the pledges were contingent upon raising the entire amount. August came and went with no further subscriptions. Cotton and his committee placed a large advertisement in the newspapers which warned that the exposition "hangs by a thread":

The history of our city for the last sixty-seven years, since Father Horton bought San Diego's main business district for 26 cents an acre, shows five depressions with durations of from two to nineteen years. History also shows that we have never emerged from one of these depressions, except through some gigantic effort, such as the building of a railroad, large community advertising, or the staging of an exposition. Never have we drifted out.

The finest hour of inter-coastal steamer service came even as the multi-engine airplane was appearing on the horizon of transportation.
To San Diego, the inclusion of its port on the run of the Panama Pacific liners from New York to San Francisco, was a moment of triumph.
Here scores of San Diegans gather at the Broadway pier to watch the Virginia *tie up. They felt sure the port, too, had at last "arrived."*

One of the excuses for the San Diego 1935-1936 exposition was a celebration of the expansion of the West.
Despite the depression, the Bay Bridge and the Golden Gate Bridge at San Francisco Bay, the Grand Coulee Dam and power project in the Columbia River basin, and Boulder Dam and the Metropolitan Aqueduct were under construction.
This photograph shows the Bay Bridge while it was being built, looking back toward San Francisco from the Oakland side.

More than two decades before, when San Diego had a population of less than 40,000, its citizens had pledged $1,000,000 for an exposition and voted another $1,000,000 in bonds to improve Balboa Park.

The 1915-1916 exposition had been inspired by completion of the Panama Canal. As it was the first port of call in the United States northbound from the canal, San Diego had expected to become an important trading center for the entire Pacific. But the canal had merely shortened the route to California from Atlantic ports and the ships passed right on by for the busy terminals at Los Angeles and San Francisco.

In the years just before the depression civic hopes had been raised again when the Panama Pacific liners included San Diego as a stop every other Friday on their run from New York to Havana and through the canal to San Francisco. They were the *California*, *Virginia* and *Pennsylvania* and carried 700 passengers each. An arrival always was an event to be remembered.

But the waterfront strikes that were wracking California were to end the days of the Panama Pacific liners as well as the "floating hotels" which sailed between the coastal ports, with their oriental rugs, sumptuous buffet dinner meals and dance bands. The *Yale*, sister ship to the *Harvard*, which was wrecked on Point Arguello, was gone by 1936.

178

Though the railroads, too, had disappointed San Diego, the exposition might change the course of affairs. A survey showed that visitors to the Century of Progress had spent $750,000,000. Belcher predicted that an exposition in San Diego would attract an attendance of 5,000,000 with financial benefit to everyone in the area, and would "make a difference to all America, turning the minds of millions toward a bright future and away from a dull or even hopeless present."

By the end of September the fund drive had exceeded its $500,000 goal by $200,000 with 3300 subscribers. Telegrams were sent around the world with invitations to participate in the California Pacific International Exposition.

As San Diegans saw their exposition, it would celebrate development projects in the West that were costing a billion dollars. The Boulder Dam power and irrigation project promised cheap water and power for a vast area. The southland's Metropolitan Aqueduct was being constructed to augment the water supply for a future anticipated population of 20,000,000. At San Francisco the bridges across the Golden Gate and across the bay to Oakland were unparalleled in the world. The harbors serving Los Angeles, Long Beach and San Diego were being improved to handle a rising commerce anticipated for the Pacific Basin and through the Panama Canal. In the Northwest, the Grand Coulee power and reclamation project was under way on the Columbia River. Highways were being opened or improved up and down the Pacific Coast.

The scheduled opening was only eight months away, the last possible moment when exhibits from the Century of Progress could be obtained. Frank Drugan, who had suggested the fair, remained as executive secretary. Zack Farmer, who had been in charge of the Olympic Games in Los Angeles in 1932, was hired as managing director at the insistence of the Spreckels interests. J. David Larson was selected as executive manager and Richard S. Requa as director of architecture.

What kind of a state California would be, by the time the exposition opened, was thrown into doubt by the campaign for governor in the Fall of 1934.

Upton Sinclair, the novelist and Socialist, registered as a Democrat and announced his candidacy for governor on the strength of a booklet he had written, entitled, *I, Governor of California, and How I Ended Poverty: A true Story of the Future.*

His campaign to "End Poverty in California" became known as the EPIC plan. His candidacy split the Democrat Party. The conservatives deserted to the Republican Party. Socialists com-

Upton Sinclair

The politics of poverty

Symbol of scheme to "End Poverty In California"

179

plained that Sinclair had abandoned their cause. In a rally in San Diego, Sinclair stated:

> I know how to end poverty. For thirty years that has been my problem . . . I don't hanker for the job of being governor of California. In fact, I would rather be dog catcher right here in San Diego.

Nevertheless, he was waging a vigorous campaign and 1000 persons paid twenty-five cents each to hear him propose land colonies for the unemployed and the operation of idle factories under state supervision.

For the first time in twenty-five years the Democrat Party in California led Republicans in registration. Sinclair easily won the party's nomination for governor and his margin of victory in San Diego County was 3000 votes. The magazine writer, Walter Davenport, commented that five years previously these same people would no more have voted for Sinclair than they would have voted for Satan himself.

For the general election all conservative forces rallied behind the Republican nominee, Governor Merriam, while Democrat liberals threw their support to Raymond Haight, a Progressive Party candidate. Speaking before an overflow crowd in the Russ auditorium, Sinclair told San Diegans:

> All the massed privilege of the whole United States and Wall Street, and all that Wall Street means, is being concentrated here to decide this question: "Can you be lied to and will you believe lies?"

Merriam won, with 1,138,620 votes to 879,557 for Sinclair and 302,519 for Haight. In San Diego County, where *The San Diego Union* had described Sinclair as the Kerensky of the Progressive movement, Merriam led by 10,000 votes. In the local races it was a Republican sweep. George Burnham was re-elected to Congress and Ed Fletcher, with water problems laid aside, was elected to the State Senate. Anything to do with the city program, however, was rejected.

With the Metropolitan Water District already at work on its aqueduct to bring Colorado River water to Los Angeles and ten neighboring communities, San Diego in 1933 had executed a contract with the Secretary of the Interior for storage capacity in Boulder Reservoir for its allotment of water, and for its delivery near Imperial Dam which would also divert water for the All-American Canal. A second agreement in 1934 provided for sufficient capacity in the canal to carry water for San Diego as well as for Imperial Valley.

This agreement, however, was dependent on ratification by the people of San Diego. The issue put to the voters was whether or not they wanted Colorado River water. They were warned that all potential sources within the county would provide only for a maximum population of 500,000, and by ratifying the agreement the city would be assured of 100,000,000 gallons daily, whenever it was needed.

The proposal for participation in the construction of the All-American Canal, at a cost of $475,000 over thirty-five years, failed to receive the necessary two-thirds approval. Though El Capitan Dam was under construction, voters rejected a $350,000 bond issue for additional funds for a pipeline to connect it with the city's distribution system. Repair and strengthening of Hodges Dam, in which cracks had appeared, also was turned down.

Completion of El Capitan Dam resulted in the agreement with the La Mesa, Lemon Grove and Spring Valley Irrigation District, whereby storage facilities in the city's dam and the district's Murray reservoir were shared, in part, and the necessary pipelines jointly built with the aid of federal funds. The wooden flume which had brought water down from Cuyamaca Reservoir since 1889 was at last taken out of service.

The lack of confidence in the city administration drew a number of leading citizens into a Civic Affairs Conference to draft and support a slate of candidates for mayor and the City Council in the Spring election of 1935. Their candidate for mayor was Percy J. Benbough, an English-born mortician. He was not without experience in politics. He had once run unsuccessfully for mayor and served for a brief time as an interim chief of police.

The radical movement found itself aligned in the campaign with those favoring an open town, in opposition to the Civic Affairs Conference candidates. Radicals led by a San Diego State College teacher named Harry C. Steinmetz were trying to capture control of organized labor and he became a candidate for mayor on a fusion ticket, pledging public ownership of all utilities.

Steinmetz received the implied endorsement of the *San Diego Sun*, which favored public ownership of utilities. While Benbough was described as a good, honest businessman with a social outlook, the *Sun* commented that with other "thinkers who are not bolsheviks" it was intrigued by the ideas expressed by Steinmetz. However, Steinmetz was eliminated in the primary election. In the general election Benbough's opponent was A. Ray Sauer, son of the publisher of a weekly newspaper, the *Herald*.

All over the country other cities were in the midst of struggles to throw off antiquated systems of government built on patronage or on corruption. While in San Diego as elsewhere in Southern California everybody claimed to be for good government, thousands of persons had invested in real estate or were dependent on the tourist business and feared moves that might discourage any flow of visitors and settlers.

Examination of returns in the primary indicated that Sauer's strongest precincts were below Market Street in an area of Chinese lotteries and other forms of gambling. His candidacy was based on a plea for a "liberal" and "open" town, which he said would bring millions of dollars into the community from the entertainment of visitors expected for the exposition.

On the other hand, the Civic Affairs Conference said the election of its mayor and four councilmen would assure a majority pledged to good government under the City Charter. In the three years since the adoption of the new Charter, one mayor had resigned, another had been jailed, three councilmen had resigned, and there had been four city managers. *The San Diego Union* stated:

> It is our conviction that the people want a new deal at the city hall. They have every reason to want one . . . once we have charter government, a first-rate city manager, and a competent police department, it is going to be very difficult to coax, cajole or bulldoze us into accepting any other kind of outfit at the next election.

Percy J. Benbough

Though Benbough and the four council candidates supported by the Civic Affairs Conference were elected, the results were not overwhelming. Benbough led by 4000 votes out of 40,000 cast.

Anything having to do with increased taxes was rejected, except for the two-cent levy for support of the San Diego Zoo. As for the need to assure the city's future on water, voters for the second time failed to ratify the contract for participation in construction of the All-American Canal. For the fourth time city and county voters also failed to produce the necessary two-thirds majority for bond issues to begin building the Civic Center. All amendments to the Charter proposed by the city administration likewise were defeated.

Local political resentments, however, were surmounted by the enthusiasm for the exposition. The existing buildings were to be used for exhibit purposes and as far as practicable new structures were to be kept in harmony with the original Spanish-Colonial city that had been created in 1915 by Bertram Goodhue. The architect, Richard Requa, later wrote a book entitled *Inside Lights on the Building of San Diego's Exposition: 1935*. In discussing the original buildings and his plans for 1935, he wrote:

182

In the exposition group the endeavor had been to provide examples of all of the interesting styles used during the period of Spanish rule in America, from the plain, austere Mission style . . . through the more striking Churrigueresque . . . to the flamboyance of the Spanish Baroque.

In a search for a style that would combine novelty, beauty and authenticity and yet be in harmony with the old buildings, the exposition designers drew on the prehistoric and native architecture of the American Southwest, the Indian pueblos, and the impressive and massive structures left by the Aztecs in Mexico and the Mayans in Yucatan.

The area selected for the expansion of the original exposition plant extended southwest from the Spreckels Organ Pavilion and was known as the Palisades, and, as related by Requa:

The central postion of this mesa was laid out and graded for a spacious Plaza in the characteristic manner of the Latin American cities, around which were later located the new large exhibit palaces as plans for them were developed. These buildings were arranged in an order to exemplify the architectural progression from prehistoric to modern times.

On the west side of the Plaza were the buildings reminiscent of early Indian pueblo architecture of the United States. They were the Palace of Education, Hollywood Hall of Fame and Palisades Cafe. On the east side was the group designed in Mayan and Aztec styles. They were the Palace of Water and Transportation, the Standard Oil Building, and the Federal Building.

The next two large buildings facing directly on the south section of the Plaza were designed to establish a relationship between the ancient Mayan and a Twentieth Century treatment of masses and to demonstrate the progression from ancient to modern. The California State Building was on the west side and the Palace of Varied Industries on the east side.

This progression came to its point with the Ford Building at the extreme south end of the Plaza, as exemplifying the latest ideas in modern industrial architecture. The interest of the Ford company resulted from Edsel Ford's visit to the 1915-1916 exposition while on his honeymoon.

Edsel Ford

Confirmation of the participation of the Ford Motor Company came in February, with the opening of the fair only four months away. Its decision to participate brought many other industries, almost at the last minute. Plans for the Ford Building were completed and construction was about to start when the company requested changes that cost a month of time. As it was Ford's intention to import symphony orchestras for regular concerts, an adjoining ravine was converted into an open air bowl.

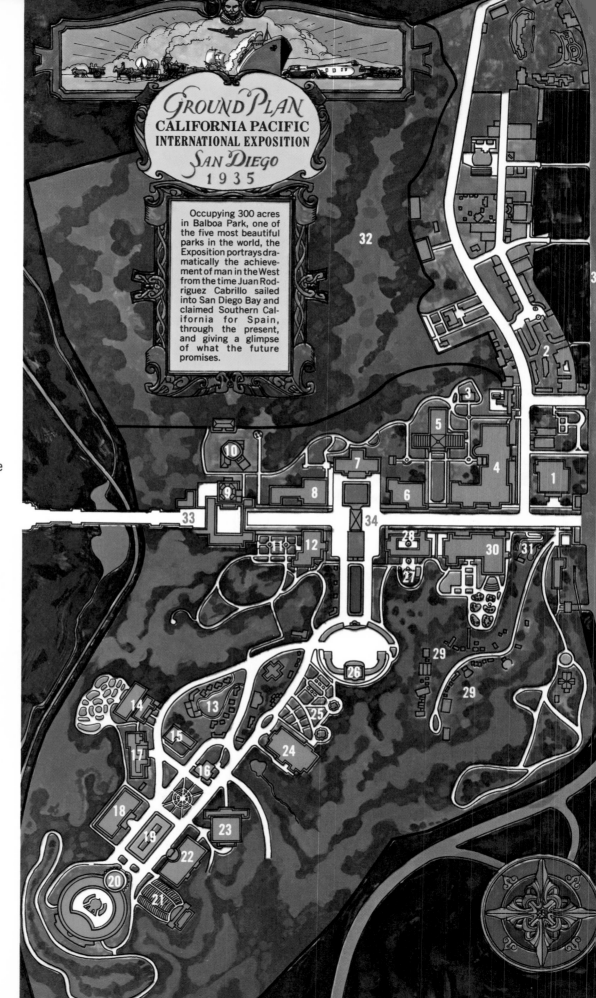

LEGEND:

1 Palace of Natural History
2 Spanish Village
3 Japanese Tea Garden
4 Palace of Foods and Beverages
5 Botanical Gardens
6 Cafe of the World
7 Palace of Fine Arts
8 Palace of Photography
9 Palace of Science —Museum of Man
10 Old Globe Theatre
11 Alcazar Garden
12 House of Charm
13 Foreign Nations Hacienda
14 Palace of Education
15 Palisades Cafe
16 Standard Oil Building —Tower to the Sun
17 Hollywood Hall of Fame
18 California State Building
19 Firestone Singing Fountain
20 Ford Building
21 Ford Music Bowl
22 Palace of Varied Industries
23 Federal Building
24 Palace of Water and Transportation
25 California Gardens
26 Spreckels Organ Pavillion
27 Casa del Rey Moro Gardens
28 House of Hospitality
29 Gold Gulch
30 Palace of Better Housing
31 Zoro Gardens
32 Zoological Gardens
33 Puente Cabrillo
34 Plaza del Pacifico
35 Park Boulevard

GROUND PLAN
CALIFORNIA PACIFIC
INTERNATIONAL EXPOSITION
SAN DIEGO
1935

Occupying 300 acres in Balboa Park, one of the five most beautiful parks in the world, the Exposition portrays dramatically the achievement of man in the West from the time Juan Rodriguez Cabrillo sailed into San Diego Bay and claimed Southern California for Spain, through the present, and giving a glimpse of what the future promises.

While the management was engaged in trying to meet Ford's requirements, Congress passed an appropriation bill for a federal building, but the government insisted that it had to be of permanent construction so that it could be converted into a theater after the fair had closed. It was built in two months and was the most outstanding of the prehistoric group. It was copied after the Palace of the Governors in Uxmal, Yucatan, one of the finest of the surviving Mayan structures.

It was through patios and gardens that the exposition was able to add to the Spanish-Moorish heritage left to San Diego by Goodhue. It was a more mature park than the one seen by visitors to the first exposition. The trees and shrubs planted twenty-five years before had filled the canyons, beautified the avenues and plazas and enriched the appearance of the ornate buildings and towers.

Three gardens known throughout the world for their beauty and interest were selected for duplication. The finest of these was in southern Spain, a few hours' journey from Gibralter in rolling country, in a small town called Ronda. In the old Moorish section, where ancient palaces and houses clung to the sides of hills, was a building known as Casa del Rey Moro, or the House of the Moorish kings, and below it the most exquisite garden Requa had ever seen. It was a comparatively recent addition by a French garden architect.

In renovating the park buildings, one section of the original Foreign Arts Building, which became known as the House of Hospitality, had been removed, and it was here, in a sloping area, that the garden at Ronda was recreated.

Another garden was inspired by a patio in Guadalajara, Mexico. The center of the same building had been cut out, in preparation for other uses, and now a patio was arranged in the usual Spanish manner, with a fountain in the center surrounded by wide paved areas. The corners were left open and filled with palms and shrubs. The patio itself was enclosed by arcaded galleries with iron railing across the arched openings.

The third garden of those found most interesting in the world

This map shows the ground plan of the 1935-1936 exposition at San Diego.
The original Spanish-Colonial buildings of the previous fair, in the center area,
were utilized for the second exposition and a new area was developed south
of the Spreckels Organ Pavilion.
Names of the buildings often were changed from year to year, depending
on their use, and the names on this map were those suggesting in most cases
their exhibition uses of 1935-1936.

was in Seville, Spain, adjoining the Alcazar. It was on level ground and was divided into many small plots by massive walls and hedges. The flower beds were outlined with box hedges and at each intersection of the paths there was a low fountain of unusual design. Pavilions, arcades, potted plants and background masses of trees contributed to its charm.

These designs were recreated near the west entrance of the exposition grounds in an area previously known as the Montezuma Garden. Requa wrote:

> Not far distant rose the beautiful California tower, suggesting without too great a stretch of the imagination, the famed Giralda tower of Seville ... All the identifying characteristics of a section of the famous Alcazar gardens in Seville are there, the archways, fountains and seats, all faithfully reproduced, even to the design and color of the tile.

The grand buildings of the original exposition were adapted for exhibits and various other uses. In the central plaza, at the intersection of the main and cross axis of the original exposition plan, a temporary arched structure was erected to house elevated colored lights and loudspeakers. On each side in the center areas of the plaza were two temporary reflecting pools.

New structures which were to remain as community assets were the Old Globe Shakespearean theater, a Spanish Village designed to reflect ordinary Spanish-Colonial life, and a House of Pacific Relations, a series of cottages which primarily housed representatives of Latin American countries.

With the opening day approaching, between 2000 and 3000 persons had taken up residence in San Diego, in connection with the fair, and more than 3000 workmen were putting the finishing touches on buildings and grounds. Sale of concessions and advance tickets helped to keep the work progressing. State and federal relief agencies had made available additional funds and Mexico had contributed an exhibit costing $350,000. In all, twenty-three different countries were represented among the 400 exhibitors.

The day before the opening it was estimated that 60,000 visitors had arrived by train, plane, ship and auto, though, oddly, seven downtown hotels reported they were only ninety percent full.

At 11 o'clock on the morning of May 29, 1935, a color guard of the United States Marines led a parade across Cabrillo Bridge to Plaza del Pacifico, where the national flag was raised to officially open the exposition. At 8 o'clock in the evening, President Roosevelt spoke by telephone and designated two selected orphans, unknown to him, to press the buttons turning on the lights which

186

For the second exposition lighting gave a new charm to the original exposition buildings.
The lighting may have been Hollywood-conceived but it united the new and old buildings into a pattern which at night had the atmosphere of a painting by Maxfield Parrish.
This scene shows the temporary tower and reflecting pools specially placed in the central plaza.

bathed the grounds in color. In his remarks, heard over the loud-speaker system, Roosevelt said:

The decision of the people of San Diego thus to dedicate the California Pacific International Exposition is, I believe, worthy of the courage and confidence with which our people now look to the future. No one can deny that we have passed through troubled years. No one can fail to feel the inspiration of your high purpose. I wish you great success.

It was the lighting effects, installed by an expert from the Hollywood film industry, that at night transformed the park and its buildings into what exposition press agents described as a land of fantasy in the manner of the mystical painter Maxfield Parrish.

The first day's attendance was 60,000, which, however, was less than expected. The second day it was 56,000. The average for the first five days was about 44,000. Within a few weeks fair directors became aware that much more money had been spent in preparing the exposition than had been planned and operating expenses were running higher than anticipated. In his memoirs, Julius Wangenheim, of the finance committee, traced some of the blame to the inexperience of the young president, Belcher, but most of it to Zack Farmer, the managing director, and his staff:

187

EXPOSITION GARDENS

The 1935-1936 exposition left San Diego a heritage of beautiful gardens. This garden adjoins Casa del Rey Moro. It was inspired by one at the House of Moorish Kings in Ronda in southern Spain.

This inner garden courtyard, or patio, was copied after one in Guadalajara, Mexico, and is part of the House of Hospitality. The statue is by Donal Hord.

*The Alcazar Garden was duplicated for the exposition from the one adjoining the
Alcazar in Seville, Spain. It has been restored since the exposition after being allowed to deteriorate.*

It was soon evident that we could not survive the expensive setup, yet, in the face of the dominating personality of Farmer, there was little we could do about it. I was convinced that unless we could get rid of him, we were bound for the rocks.

An issue was raised, and Farmer, following his own strategy, one day handed us the resignation of the heads of all departments, figuring that we could not get along without all of them at once, and would be forced to come to terms. But it didn't work that way. Instead, we were able to get rid of Farmer and the whole extravagant organization at once, for we accepted all the resignations. And there was great rejoicing, and without much difficulty we made the necessary adjustments.

Julius Wangenheim

The fair had been planned by professionals; now it was necessary to make it pay. Philip L. Gildred, the financier who had come to San Diego from Peru and erected one of the town's large buildings, was appointed managing director and two other businessmen, Hal G. Hotchkiss and Douglas Young, were named to serve as a management committee. Wayne Dailard, with a background of theatrical experience and theater operation, was retained as Gildred's assistant. Advertising was concentrated in California, and particularly in Los Angeles, and in the Southwest region within relatively easy driving distance of San Diego.

The exposition settled into a successful run. The exhibits were supplemented by a large midway, a so-called "nudist" colony and a Western mining town situated in a canyon and named the Gold Gulch. The police, in an unusual burst of activity, harrassed attempts to maintain illegal gambling games in the gulch.

There was Latin music by strolling musicians and Spanish dancing in the gardens, patios and plazas. The West's best symphony orchestras imported by the Ford company were heard daily through the summer and early Fall. The renovated buildings of the 1915 fair once again were filled with life and excitement.

A trip to see the exposition was an excuse for thousands of persons in the Midwest or East to visit relatives who had left their homes to settle in Southern California. The fame of the area's climate had been a lure that had never grown dim. The Santa Fe Railroad, which once had promised to make San Diego its principal terminal, and then had moved out and left the city at the end of a branch line, placed advertisements of the exposition all over the country and operated excursion special trains.

Rear Admiral Joseph M. Reeves

In "Fleet Week" in June 114 warships and 400 military planes arrived under command of Admiral Joseph M. Reeves, Commander-in-chief of the United States Fleet. It was described as the mightiest fleet ever assembled under the United States flag. It included forty-eight battleships, cruisers and carriers, with more

The Spanish atmosphere was retained for the later San Diego exposition. Here Spanish dancers and musicians are shown by one of Balboa Park's original ponds which was known as Laguna de Espejo, or the mirror, or reflecting pool.

In later years Southern California pushed aside its Spanish and Mexican inheritances. The pool became popularly known as the lily pond.

191

than 3000 commissioned officers and 55,000 enlisted men. Most of them visited the fair, and in turn, thousands of San Diegans and fair visitors were guests on the various ships.

Two months later 115 warships returning from a summer cruise in Alaskan waters, passed in review between La Jolla and Point Loma, forming a column fifteen miles long. The review was dedicated to the children of the nation and 15,000 school children were assembled on Ballast Point to watch the ships as they steamed into the harbor.

The comings and goings of Navy ships always had a great effect on the economy of San Diego.
When the fleet was out, business was bad; when it returned, business picked up. In those days fleet reviews demonstrated to the world the might of a Navy still dependent to a great extent on its battleships.
In honor of thousands of school children assembled from all over Southern California, the fleet, upon its return from Alaskan waters and led by its battleships, passed in review off San Diego in a column fifteen miles long.

The exposition recreated some of the atmosphere of the boom of the 1920's. Joseph E. Dryer, who had come to San Diego from Minneapolis to retire, when he was only thirty-eight years of age, but had gone back into business, was walking through the fair grounds. He thought of the attractions that had brought him to San Diego, and which were luring thousands more settlers and tourists, and said to himself, "truly, this is heaven on earth." With that thought, he organized the Heaven-on-Earth Club which issued promotion literature and distributed "Million Dollar Bonds" and a "Table of Sunshine" around the world.

As a result of the exposition, economic conditions in San Diego were more favorable than they might have been.

However, the end of one of the area's most important attractions came on July 21, 1935. The new president of Mexico, Lazaro Cardenas, issued a decree banning gambling and on Sunday evening all of the games at the Agua Caliente resort came to a halt. The hotel was emptied of its visitors and the horses removed from the race track. A resort estimated then to be worth $10,000,000, and with 1500 employes and 500 stockholders, was taken from the scene with the stroke of a pen.

The early New Deal emergency measures had failed to substantially reduce unemployment nationally, and though business had been stabilized a rising production curve had not kept pace with the increase in population and costs. In the summer of 1935 President Roosevelt inaugurated the Works Progress Administration with its massive construction projects.

The fair's most important visitor came in the Fall. President Roosevelt arrived by train, stayed at Hotel del Coronado overnight, and the next day, October 2, traveled by auto along a thirty-mile route lined with thousands of spectators. It was the second time he had seen a San Diego exposition. In the stadium he said the exposition was a sign that the economic clouds were leaving the country. Continuing, he remarked:

Individual effort is the glory of America. The country has a right to look forward to a brighter future, being mindful of the mistakes of the past. As the burden lifts, the federal government can and will divest itself of its emergency responsibility, but at the same time it cannot ignore the imperfections of the former order.

It was not the exposition so much as a building on Lindbergh Field which altered the development of San Diego.
In 1935 the plant of Consolidated Aircraft Corporation was dedicated at Lindbergh Field. The original building was 900 feet long and 300 feet wide. Bay water lapped at its foundation, as shown in this 1936 photograph, and dredging to enlarge the field was continuing.
In a few years Consolidated would play a significant role not only in the history of San Diego but the history of the country as well.

The report in *The San Diego Union* said that the President assured the crowd that America's policy was to keep out of foreign entanglements and remain at peace with the world even though Europe's clanking swords threatened disaster to civilization:

We intend to remain at peace with the world . . . Despite what happens in continents overseas, the United States of America shall and must remain—as long ago the fathers of our country prayed that it might remain—unentangled and free.

At San Diego he boarded the cruiser *Houston* to review the fleet at sea and returned to Washington by way of the Panama Canal.

Three weeks later Major Rueben H. Fleet dedicated the new plant of Consolidated Aircraft Corporation at Lindbergh Field. The building was 300 by 900 feet. More than 300 selected employes had come with the company. The payroll at the time was 874, and the company expected it to rise to 2000 within six months and 3000 by the next summer. In his dedication address Fleet said that when engines of sufficient power were made available, gigantic flying ships carrying a hundred passengers to Honolulu would cross the Pacific in twelve hours with greater comfort and safety than surface ships. He continued:

Aviation will become the greatest boon to humanity because it promotes and can guarantee world peace. It looks as though world peace will come only when forced, and that force backs all agreements that stand the test of time . . . just as the airplane has become man's greatest means of making neighbors of all nations, will it surely become the instrumentality to guarantee world peace by force until the temperament of mankind changes.

An eventful year closed with another dedication at the site of the Civic Center. George W. Marston, G. Aubrey Davidson, Julius Wangenheim, and others, had been successful in obtaining federal relief financing for construction of the combined city and county building on the tidelands that had four times failed to win sufficient support from the voters. Through the intervention of Ralph E. Jenney, a San Diegan who was director of the California Relief Commission, about $300,000 in federal funds was made available for an immediate start with an assurance of more to come. San Diegans were certain, however, that somewhere along the bureaucratic line the influence of President Roosevelt had been exerted in their behalf.

In turning over the first spadeful of dirt for the first unit for a grouping of public buildings on the waterfront that had been talked about for thirty years, Marston said:

Reuben H. Fleet

Here will rise an impressive group of buildings in fulfillment of our long-time hope of a noble civic center. Here will be the seat of our community government, the physical center of the laws and rights of the people. Therefore, my fellow citizens, let us think of the dignity and surpassing value of this great enterprise.

It had been five years since the full effects of the depression were first felt. Despite conditions, the population had continued to increase. The city had gained an average of 4000 persons a year, growing from 148,000 in 1930 to an estimated 168,000 in 1935. In the county the population had increased from a little less than 210,000 to about 246,000. Because of the exposition more than $6,000,000 had been expended for WPA projects. The value of building permits almost doubled in 1935 and tourist income rose more than $5,000,000. The value of manufactured products nearly doubled, and the value of agricultural products went up $2,500,000.

Southern California provided a chance for many to start over again, in different pursuits, or to reinvest in an area certain to grow and prosper with time, or to enter new and challenging opportunities appearing with the scientific age. In the border states clouds of dust were beginning to darken the skies and force farmers onto the roads west.

East of San Diego in the Imperial Valley a giant "walking crane" was chewing its way through "America's Sahara" for the All-American Canal, and to the northwest a tunnel thirteen miles long was being dug under Mount San Jacinto to bring water to the coast—and eventually to save a city which had voted to deny its future.

CHAPTER NINE

Boulder Dam, later to be renamed Hoover Dam, was completed in 1935.
This photograph shows Lake Meade still rising behind the dam and Colorado
River water falling from twelve outlet valves.
This marked a turning point in the development of the Southwest. Besides
the opening of new agricultural empires, it helped to make possible an
industrial expansion that was to rush upon California within a few years.

MAKING A RIVER

The giant dam on the Colorado River was completed in 1935. The river was at last brought under control and placed at the service of an ever-widening empire of the West.

First called Boulder and later to be named Hoover Dam, it differed from other river development projects in the United States in that it was not built at the expense of the general taxpayer. The electricity generated by the release of water stored in its reservoir, and sold to private as well as public power companies, would repay its cost.

California's share of the annual flow of the Colorado had been apportioned among various agencies, all of them in Southern California, both as to amounts and priorities. San Diego, next to last on a list of six, was allotted the 112,000 acre feet on which it had filed.

The total for Southern California, of 5,362,000 acre feet annually, would soon be challenged and water experts were well aware that even with the Colorado River, it would not be possible to put water on more than nine percent of Southern California's 50,000 square miles.

While the citizens of San Diego still hesitated in accepting the idea of going as far as the Colorado River for water to drink, no matter the warnings of Phil Swing, Hiram Savage and Fred Heilbron, the Metropolitan Water District had gone ahead with an aqueduct system across some of the most desolate country of the Southwest. No other water in the world was carried as far or lifted as high.

In those days the California Desert was just beginning to become a winter playground. Much of it had not been surveyed and the first task was the contour mapping of 25,000 square miles. The few roads that existed were merely trails, and water was available only in a few widely separated wells drilled deep into the sand. Selection of a route had been a process of many years. In one of its reports, the Metropolitan Water District recalled:

By the end of 1930 surveys had been made and estimates prepared for literally hundreds of lines. These lines covered most of Southern California, not in a symmetrical or uniform manner but as sort of irregular network, knotted together by controlling geographical features.

Unlike the wagon trails of the pioneers, these lines headed for mountain passes to avoid the long and hazardous tunnels required by more direct alignment. Where the wagon trails went over the top of passes, the aqueduct could not follow because of limiting grades or the excessive cost of pumping. Controlling divides must be penetrated by tunnels, and mountain passes . . . usually represent weak spots in the mountain barrier where the rock is broken, easily eroded, and subject to caving. Some of the passages into the coastal area are traversed by earthquake faults which are a hazard to any kind of underground construction. Some were waterlogged.

After years of study, a route known as the "Parker Route" was chosen for an aqueduct that would bring Colorado River water to the coastal lands of Southern California.

This map shows how the water was taken from the river and lifted five times to reach levels from which it could finally flow through the San Jacinto Mountains to a distributing reservoir.

The $200,000,000 project of the Metropolitan Water District was an undertaking, not of government, but of water users, or potential users, united in a common effort.

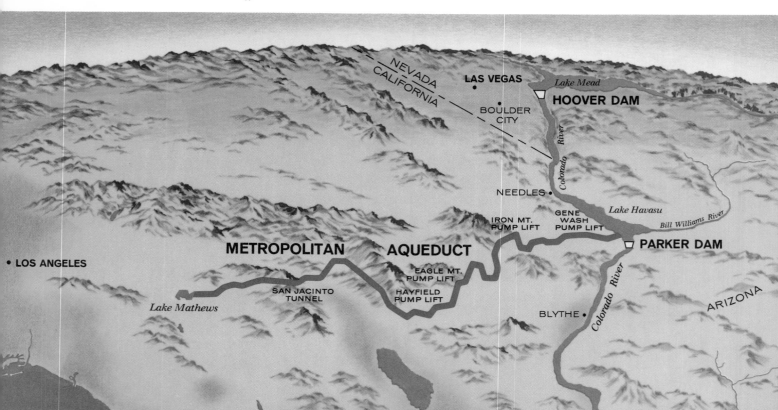

A route known as the Parker route was selected, as the safest and most economical, to ultimately deliver 1,212,000 acre feet of water, or a billion gallons daily, to the coastal population. In 1931 the voters of the district, which by then comprised thirteen cities, approved a bond issue of $220,000,000 by a ratio of five-to-one. Even before Boulder Dam was finished, work was started on a second dam 155 miles downstream, which would re-store water released from the lake behind Boulder Dam to provide a pool for diversion for the Metropolitan system. It was from here that the water would start its long journey to the coastal plain of Southern California.

While Parker Dam was built by the federal government with $13,000,000 furnished by the Metropolitan District, it also would serve to regulate the flow of the river below Boulder for the benefit of all downstream users. Anchored in a red canyon of the Whipple Mountains, it was called the deepest dam in the world. Engineers had to go 240 feet below the level of the stream, through silt deposited by ages of time, to reach bedrock, while its height above the stream was about seventy feet.

The water for thirsty Southern California was to be taken at an elevation of 450 feet above sea level. But on its course westward it would have to pass a desert basin dropping below sea level and confront a mountain range with a peak of more than 10,000 feet.

Even before the water could begin its journey it had to be lifted from the lake to be formed behind Parker Dam and taken up the side of the Whipple Mountains, in order to provide for a gravity flow until the next hilly barrier was reached. Through the release of water at Boulder Dam the river was made to provide its own lifting power, in the generating of electricity.

Pumps were designed to lift the water 291 feet, almost straight up, and send it through a short tunnel where it was again lifted 303 feet. Then at an elevation of more than a thousand feet, it entered another tunnel and emerged on the other side of the mountains, to flow sixty miles through siphons and open canals in a barren and arid country.

At Iron Mountain where it met its second barrier of hills the water was lifted 144 more feet and sent through another tunnel ten miles long, from where it could be turned to the southwest. A dozen miles beyond rose the Coxcomb Mountains, which in the brightness of the day look as if they had been scorched by a flame from the sun. This necessitated another tunnel of four miles in length.

In the next thirty-five miles the water had to be lifted twice in the Eagle Mountains. First it was lifted 438 feet to an elevation of

Engineering was a trail-breaking job

Mojave Indians watch the penetration of their desert home

more than 1400 feet. The next and last lift on the long run to the coast was at a place identified as Hayfield. This was a lift of 441 feet to 1800 feet above seal level and a total lift of 1617 feet. From there it was all downhill. But that did not mean that the worst was over.

The aqueduct was now nearing the most historic pass of Southern California, San Gorgonio, lying between the San Bernardino Mountains to the northeast and the San Jacinto Mountains to the southwest. The pass provided a gentle rise, from sea level to 2500 feet, through the coastal mountain barrier that had so frustrated the earliest explorers and pioneers. It was a natural railroad pass, and when the Southern Pacific chose this route to reach the coast, San Diego lost its race for commercial equality with the rising cities of the West.

The water would run at an elevation 1800 feet higher than the low point of the upper portion of the desert's Coachella Valley. It would have about sixty miles to go before entering a tunnel the engineers were driving through the San Jacinto Mountains. The water could not be dropped down to the desert floor to be pumped up again, nor supported at such a height and length by a Roman-type aqueduct. But there was a natural aqueduct system in the San Bernardino Mountains.

Almost forty miles of continuous tunnel were dug along the dry slopes of the desert side of the mountains, so the water could be made to run gently downhill to meet the land as it rose in the upper part of San Gorgonio Pass. At a place called Cabazon above Palm Springs the aqueduct was taken underground across the pass to reach the base of the San Jacinto Mountains at an elevation of 1536 feet.

The base of the mountains was thirteen miles thick. And it was one of the strange features of Southern California that the green valley lying beyond the mountains was at a lower elevation than the desert on the inland side. The San Jacinto Mountains stood between the coastal plain and the desert, and the western slopes caught the rain and the east side did not.

J. L. Burkholder, who was assistant general manager of the Metropolitan District, later recalled that at the time they heard of Indian legends of fish inside the mountains. Shafts for the tunnel started from both directions. In July of 1934 miners working eastward from the west portal encountered an earthquake fault which loosened a reservoir of water that had been locked within the mountains. Three times water was pumped out, but the flow never ended. The tunnel had been started in May of 1933 and a year and

Surveyors at
Mount San Jacinto

The main aqueduct of the Metropolitan system is 242 miles long and extends
across the state of California. It is one of the giant water lines of the world.
Tunnel and conduit sections are sixteen feet in diameter, large enough to
accommodate a railway locomotive.

This construction photograph shows a pipeline section as it was being laid
across a desert area.

The system was designed to deliver more than a billion gallons of water a day.

a half had been required to dig two miles. The contractors gave up.

The engineers of the Metropolitan District took over. They advanced by pumping liquid cement against the flow of the water at tremendous pressures, thus stopping up the fissures through which the water was pouring. When they reached the main faults they pushed through with the aid of powerful pumps, temporary supports and other special methods. At one time the flow of water reached eighty-eight cubic feet a second.

The tunnel was completed November 19, 1938. Its two shafts

The aqueduct that was to bring Colorado River water to Southern California finally came up against its last barrier—the San Jacinto Mountains.
Here there was a summit 10,000 feet high. The water had to be taken through the mountains in a tunnel thirteen miles long.
Inside the mountains was a "lake" which for a time threatened to bring the project to a dead end.
But this problem, too, was conquered, even as the desert had been conquered.

came together with only a tenth of an inch difference in elevation and none laterally. The point where the water would emerge on the cooler side of the mountains was forty-four feet lower than the entrance to the tunnel. Its point of destination was the terminal reservoir ten miles southwest of Riverside at an elevation of about 1400 feet. From the reservoir, 242 miles from the Colorado, the water would be distributed to the district cities, and to the communities and agricultural areas to be added in the future. After coasting downhill for 115 miles, at this point the water would still be almost a thousand feet higher than when it had started its journey.

From there it was only seventy miles by gravity flow to possible storage basins in San Diego. But the interest there in becoming a member of the Metropolitan District was not very high; for that matter, there was little concern over a crisis that might arise in some distant future.

The capacity of San Diego's existing system of dams and impounding reservoirs in the higher country and the pumping plants taking water from sands in the lower valleys had been built up to a net safe yield of 26.6 million gallons a day. This was considered adequate to serve a population of 200,000. The addition of the proposed San Vicente Dam and reservoir would add enough for a population, it was thought, of 260,000.

When the time came that San Diego had to reach to the Colorado for water, it was felt that the city should build its own aqueduct and pumping system and be the undisputed master of its future. The key to this sense of security was the All-American Canal. Nothing like it had been attempted in the United States and it was designed to serve the largest single irrigated acreage in the Western Hemisphere.

This is the route of the All-American Canal and its principal branch, the Coachella Valley line.
The All-American Canal route was selected to provide a gravity flow for its length of eighty miles, and its rate of descent allowed provision for generating electric power.
The canal freed the rich Imperial Valley from dependence on water that had to reach the valley by way of Mexico.
San Diego also hoped to tap the canal and lift Colorado River water through the coastal mountains directly into its own reservoirs.

More than 4,000,000 acre feet of water would be required every year to irrigate the desert lands already broken to the plow, or soon to be. This meant enough water to cover 4,000,000 acres to a depth of one foot. The total cost of the project, with the Imperial diversion dam and the All-American Canal and its Coachella branch, was put at $38,000,000. The Imperial Valley Irrigation District committed itself to repay its proportionate share, $25,000,000, over a period of forty years.

There were some indications, however faint, that the farmers of the valley were not to be independent as they had believed. The canal was to be designed to also assist Mexico and federal participation carried with it the shadow of future influence.

The task confronting engineers was to bring into being a river in a desert, half a city block wide at its surface and twenty-two feet deep, that would carry almost nine times as much water as the Metropolitan Aqueduct. The capacity of the canal was to be 15,155 cubic feet of water per second, the 155 representing the allotment for San Diego of 112,000 acre feet annually.

North of Yuma the Colorado ran 150 feet above sea level in a bed of silt it had built up over thousands of years, and thus higher than the low land it was to water in the Imperial Valley. But between the river and the farms was a high and stubborn mesa and a five-mile wide ridge of sand hills which stretched in a north-south direction for thirty miles before dying out in Mexico. It was these two barriers which had forced the farmers of the valley to divert their water near the border and route it through Mexico.

Before a spadeful of earth was turned, the canal began to take form in models and drawings. In an outdoor laboratory experimenters made miniature canals, heaping up samples of materials, sprinkling and tamping them with rollers, and creating model embankments with varying degrees of slopes. With instruments they gauged the density of the banks, measured the percolation when exposed to water, and learned exactly how steep the banks should be made. In a report on the planning and early construction, the *Popular Science Monthly* in 1936 added:

How the sand hills were first crossed

But the most serious problem of all was that of crossing the valley of walking sand dunes, a Sahara-like waste of towering sand hills that slowly migrate under the influence of the wind. Reckless indeed seemed the engineers who dared to undertake the job, but careful observations of the dunes dispelled some of their terrors. The migration, though constant, was quite slow. A high embankment thrown up of the material excavated from the canal would adequately guard against encroachment by the walking sand hills.

206

It was because of these same hills that the early immigrant trails and later the Butterfield Overland Stage route had followed a circuitous course passing through Mexico for more than fifty miles.

The digging of the canal and construction of its diversion works began a year and a half after the start of the Metropolitan Aqueduct. As with the aqueduct, the All-American Canal needed its own system for diverting water from the river. The point selected was in the lower hills of the stark Chocolate Mountains, 148 miles below Parker Dam and 180 feet in elevation. The river valley is wide here and the diversion dam of the Bureau of Reclamation was 3485 feet long with one end resting in California and the other in Arizona.

After being drawn from the river at Imperial Dam, the water for the All-American Canal was to be taken in a new bed, one higher than the river, and directed toward the first range of rocky hills.
A huge canal was sliced through the low hills of the Chocolate Mountains and it became known as the Laguna Cut.
This downstream view shows work in progress at the point where the canal was turned away from the river and headed in a southwesterly direction along the base of the hills.

This was a multi-purpose project, diverting water for domestic and agricultural users in the Bard, Imperial and Coachella valleys of California, and for the Wellton-Mohawk, Gila and Yuma valleys and the Yuma Mesa in Arizona. For the All-American Canal the dam lifted the level of the river thirty-one feet to enable the water to be diverted into a man-made channel above the flood plain of the river.

There was more to the problem of diversion than merely providing a new and convenient channel. The Colorado was ladened with vast amounts of silt which choked up the Alamo Canal in Mexico and was carried to the fields of Imperial Valley. Farmers constantly had to relevel their land and between 1923 and 1930 the district had spent an average of more than three-quarters of a million dollars annually for silt control.

The reservoirs higher on the river would retain much of the silt, but still sand and dirt picked up on the lower river were expected to be a costly nuisance and it was considered necessary to build a system of desilting basins below Imperial Dam where the water could be "laundered" and cleansed of its unwanted material.

The new channel, or canal, built up with the silt of the plain paralleled the course of the river southward, until it met the low

This is how the All-American Canal appeared as the man-made cut approached the area of Winterhaven and Yuma and once again swung near the Colorado River.
This section is five miles northwest of Winterhaven and along the low sandy terraces which are part of the Pilot Knob Mesa.
The canal cut was half a city block wide at its rim and twenty-two feet deep.

hills and gravelly terraces extending from the foothills of the Chocolate and Cargo Muchacho mountains, and form the Pilot Knob mesa. Here, as with the Metropolitan Aqueduct, the water was to flow through an excavated canal cut through the hills above the old Laguna diversion dam, and, avoiding a direct challenge of the sand hills and the East Mesa, it would head for the international border and Pilot Knob.

Pilot Knob is a rocky eminence which got its name from the days when shallow-draft steamboats plied the Colorado River. At Pilot Knob the canal was in the approximate area of the original Hanlon Heading which had diverted water into the Alamo Canal. By following this route it would be possible to supply water to Mexico,

Near the international border the canal reached Pilot Knob, a landmark for the river boats which once had plied the Colorado to supply the Army and mining camps.

The canal was taken as far south as Pilot Knob so that Mexico could be served with Colorado River water, even though the Imperial Valley farmers had hoped to free themselves from any obligations to landowners below the border.

To keep it within the United States, the ditch had to be taken right through Pilot Knob. This shovel is making the last lift of the big rock cut.

either by a return flow to the river or by a direct discharge into the Alamo Canal.

In twenty miles the drop in water elevation had been about twelve feet. Yet the water level in the canal still would be fifty-seven feet above the river, enough to permit the development of hydro-electric power in the diversions to Mexico. The elevation above sea level was 167 feet.

To go around Pilot Knob would have taken the canal into Mexico. So the engineers went through it, blasting out a curving channel in its shoulders. On the other side, the canal turned along the border, once again riding thirty-three feet above the valley and little Mexican settlements just to the south.

The canal then was diverted in a northwesterly direction and cut across Pilot Knob mesa and taken up through the east edge of the sand hills. At a low point in the yellow hills the canal turned abruptly and sliced through them in a southwesterly direction toward the international border, passing through a gap in the hills known as Buttercup Valley. The depth of the cut through the sand hills varied from approximately fifteen feet to ninety feet and averaged about forty-five feet.

At the border it was swung westward in almost a straight line for fifty miles and a downhill slide of 174 feet across the East Mesa and into the garden lands. The elevation at the edge of the mesa at the sand hills is 160 feet above sea level. The mesa slopes westward at the rate of five feet a mile, but at its western edge, it falls off forty-five feet in five miles.

The flow was by gravity and at three different places a sharp drop was provided to supply falling water for generating electric power. Just beyond Calexico it reached its end at minus 6.65 feet. On the eighty-mile course the total drop was about 186 feet. The Imperial Valley stretched away in the distance, to the north, with all of its irrigated acreage lying below the level of the sea.

The All-American Canal was dug at a time when machines were replacing mules and horses in construction work. As the depression had made marginal farming uncertain, farmers of the valley were invited to bring their horses and "fresnoes" and help in building what they thought would be their own canal. More than 1000 animals competed with what *Popular Science* described as "herds of mechanical mastadons":

Ahead of the construction crews came surveyors and rodmen with transit and chain, staking out a path through the sage brush and cactus. Behind them followed gangs of Indians, who cut away harsh brush with hooked, sharp instruments resembling medieval battle axes. Tractors broke the virgin

210

soil, loosening the earth and picking up heavy material. Where the surface was low, farmers drove four-horse teams pulling "fresnoes," or scrapers, to cut and fill ... in their wake came big machines. Steam shovels, diesel tractors and bulldozers puffed and snorted. Trucks, by the hundred, piled high with excavated material, began to thunder over crude highways.

New marvels of the beginning of a technical age were used to do most of the major digging, particularly through the sand hills. They were drag-line excavators:

No larger digging machines ever walked the earth than the drag-lines that scoop out the main contours of the canal. Twenty freight cars are required to carry the dismantled parts of such machines. A 100-car train was needed to bring in the equipment used in digging a single thirty-mile stretch.

Construction of the All-American Canal was begun as an emergency project during the depression, though it had been long planned.
While new big machines of a mechanical age did the major share of digging, jobs were provided for Imperial Valley farmers hurt by low prices.
Farmers were invited to bring their horses and old "fresnoes" to help excavate the canal bed in the area west of Calexico.

When the 650-ton machine was ready to travel, it literally walked ahead on its own feet. Two shoes, each weighing some 42,000 pounds, were mounted eccentrically on an axle forty-five feet long. As the axle turned, first one shoe and then the other moved to propel the drag-line ahead, at seven feet a step.

The man who had conceived the idea of the All-American Canal, Mark Rose, and many of the other original pioneers were still alive. In the closing years of their lives, they were able to witness the triumph over nature that climaxed a struggle begun at the turn of the century:

Under the scorching noonday sun, under the huge, desert moon, through summer heat and blinding sand storms, the work will go on. At night, the powerful glare of floodlights attached to the booms makes daylight where they work. Before water can flow, sixty million cubic yards of material must be excavated and hauled to its proper place—enough, loaded upon standard forty-foot gravel cars, to make a trainload 2235 miles long, stretching from Chicago to Los Angeles.

But more than a colossal job of earth-moving, more than the biggest irrigation ditch ever built, is this huge gash engineers are cutting in the southern desert. In combination with Boulder Dam, it not only will bring life-giving water to parched desert lands, but will permanently end the menace of the millions of tons of water that thunder down the Colorado's steep-walled chasm.

When the All-American Canal was in the planning stage no one was sure that it could be driven through the shifting sand hills west of Yuma.
Tests, however, showed the drift of sand was less than believed. Giant drag-line machines walked by means of their own power across the hills, scooping up sand, and creating a river in the desert.
This scene looking north is at the east edge of the sand hills, about two and one half miles downstream from the Highway No. 8 bridge.

In a few years, with the completion of the canal, farmers would be relieved of the dread of recurring floods and periods of low or little water.

A second and smaller though longer branch canal was to water the Coachella Valley. Eventually it would be 123 miles long and curve around the upper end of the Salton Sea. In the future were to be other canals, to water the East Mesa and the 125,000 acres of the West Mesa lying between the Imperial Valley and the foot-hills of the Coastal Mountains.

The decision for San Diego was whether, when the time was

212

right, to join the Metropolitan District or connect with the proposed West Mesa canal and lift the water over the mountains with its own pumps, canals and tunnels. The city's hydraulic engineer, Hiram Savage, who had pressed for studies on bringing Colorado River water to San Diego, had died in 1934. In 1936 the city retained three consulting engineers to study the problem and make recommendations.

Their report became known as the Ready, Hill and Buwalda report and it was submitted the following year. It concluded that though the future rate of growth of San Diego would be less than

The sand hills had lost their terror.
Light and shadows play across the yellow sands along the sides of the open ditch of the All-American Canal.
Since the days of exploration the sand hills had been a barrier to the crossing of the low desert between the Colorado River and the coastal mountains.
Even the Butterfield Overland Stage had gone around them, through Mexican territory, but a plank road later proved that they could be traversed.

the rate for the decade of 1920 to 1930, it would continue at a fairly high level as the Pacific Coast and Southern California areas developed. It estimated that in 1960 there would be 320,000 persons in San Diego and about 370,000 in the metropolitan area. By the year 2000, it was predicted the population of the city would exceed 500,000.

While full development of all local resources was recommended, the report said that additional water would be needed from the Colorado between the years 1950 and 1960, and the most economical way to get a supply of twenty-five million gallons daily would be by the All-American Canal. The cost of building its own facilities was given as about half that of joining the Metropolitan District and assuming a fair share of the cost of its aqueduct and distribution system.

The West Mesa Canal would require two lifts, one of fifty feet and another of 112 feet. Water would be conveyed for a distance of fifty-four miles to a point in Borrego Valley east of Julian. It generally would follow the course of San Felipe Creek, which ambled down from the mountains across the desert to the Salton Sea. To get through the mountains at an elevation of 1000 feet would require a tunnel twenty-seven miles long. Instead, the report recommended that the water be carried twenty-six miles up the east slopes. This would require a tremendous lift of 2700 feet, 1100 feet more than the combined lifts of the Metropolitan Aqueduct. Again San Diegans were reminded of the high barrier and the absence of low, straight passes that had made road building so difficult and costly, and railroads virtually impossible.

At a point near Banner, a tunnel more than seven miles long would be dug through the mountains, passing just south of Julian. On the west side the water would be dropped 1800 feet and delivered to El Capitan Reservoir. The location of the tunnel was chosen because it was outside of known active earthquake faults.

Oddly, during the boom of the 1880's a promotional syndicate interested in selling land had proposed taking water in the opposite direction. It suggested a reservoir in Banner Canyon and drilling a tunnel 3000 feet long up into the Cuyamaca Mountains, to tap the melting snow and bring life to the "rich empire plains known as the Colorado Desert."

While the Ready, Hill and Buwalda plan was considered practical it was not known when the proposed West Mesa Canal, so important to the project, would be built. No money had been appropriated and no plans drawn. If San Diego experienced another prolonged drought, it was thought an emergency pipeline could be laid in the open over the mountains and down to one of the laterals of the All-American Canal.

There was no use thinking about the Colorado River if the voters did not proceed with ratifying an agreement with the federal government providing for capacity in the All-American Canal to carry water for San Diego. This had not yet been done. And the engineers suggested that as an initial step, in providing both a permanent and emergency supply ahead of actual need, it might be possible to justify construction of the San Felipe Tunnel with federal aid. It would require four years to complete it. Until these things were done, the report concluded that formation of a Metropolitan District for San Diego County, along the lines of the one serving the communities surrounding Los Angeles, was not necessary.

The report was read and it was generally agreed that it ably charted the future course for San Diego. But the local reservoirs were rich with water and the winters had been kind, and unlike the people of Imperial Valley, San Diegans had forgotten how it was to live on the edge of disaster.

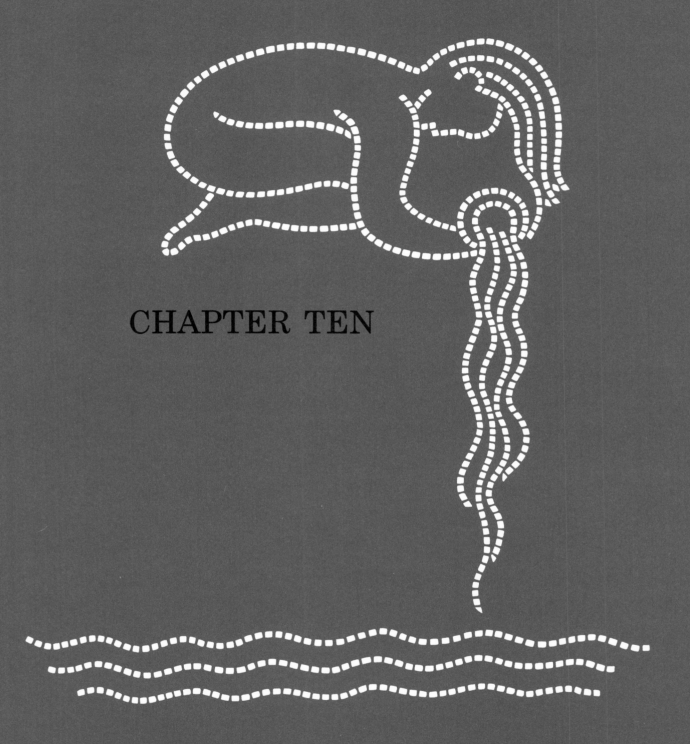

CHAPTER TEN

Life-giving water at last was beginning to flow in man-made rivers just as demand was about to explode with a war.
This is a view of the All-American Canal, looking in a southeasterly direction, from seven or eight miles upstream from the east edge of the sand dunes.
In the background is the tip of Mexicali Valley in Baja California.
The canal would enrich an agricultural empire. To the north, the Metropolitan Aqueduct provided the water that was to save a city in the south.
It was a region no longer watered by tears.

CHANGES OF WAR

No one could have foreseen all that happened as the Thirties drew to their close. The last five years began simply enough.

At San Diego one of the largest crowds of the exposition rose and cheered as a tall, slender figure stepped to the stage of the Ford Bowl. He was Dr. Francis E. Townsend, the retired physician and promoter of a pension plan to end poverty and unemployment.

Another seemingly harmless emotional movement had grown, as had Upton Sinclair's EPIC campaign, into a political force. It had been endorsed by Governor Merriam. The State Legislature had memorialized Congress to put it into effect. Mayor Benbough, owner of a number of mortuaries, had prudently joined in supporting a plan that was so appealing to the elderly.

Now with his movement spreading across the country, Townsend told thousands of persons gathered in the bowl and on the adjoining plaza and hillsides that:

We may have to shove aside a legislature or two and maybe a congress before we complete our job—but it will be finished ... The twenty million persons on the dole are doomed to chronic pauperism under our present system ... let us wipe out the great curse of the world—poverty.

Townsend proposed to give everybody over sixty years of age a pension of $200 a month, to be raised by a transaction tax. The money would have to be spent within a month in order to keep business rolling and producing more taxes.

Though the movement had originated in Long Beach, where Townsend resided, San Diego, with its many pensioners and a population more than average in age, soon found itself a center of the storm. Townsend Clubs sprang up in every community area and drew in the old folks who formerly had centered much of their social life in state societies. But Townsend said San Diego had no monopoly in the enthusiasm for the plan and "it is just as good in other parts of the country."

In Sacramento a state senator by the name of Culbert L. Olson had emerged as leader of the Democrats and the remnants of Sinclair's EPIC forces in the State Legislature. In Los Angeles a new movement called the California Pension Plan was promising $25 every Monday morning to everybody over fifty years of age. It was an intricate and supposedly self-liquidating scheme which few understood, providing for the issuance of state warrants redeemable at the end of the year and when weekly tax stamps of two percent had been affixed.

Whereas Dr. Townsend represented a new and delayed concern over the plight of the aged and he made his movement a national

A new type of California "pioneer" pushed into the state.
They came from the Dust Bowl of the mid-country in larger numbers than in the days of the Gold Rush.
The auto made possible a mass migration of families. They packed everything they had left, after the tragedy of losing their farms and animals, and headed for new land.
But they found the best land already taken up and they took to the fields as transient workers. A war soon would draw them into industry and new ways of life.

one, the leaders of the new pension group were primarily concerned with political power in California. They soon rode over the Townsend plan and came within grasp of success.

Also added to a depression that would not recede was the tragedy of the Dust Bowl. The top soil of much of the Great Plains was being blown into the air and with it went the hopes of a generation which had misused the land opened in the rush to the West.

Francis E. Townsend

California was the goal of a stream of destitute migrants, from Texas and Oklahoma, from Nebraska and Kansas, and from as far north as the Dakotas. In the last six months of 1935 more than 43,000 of them entered the state, but they found that all of the open land long since had been taken up. So they followed the crops as temporary workers from Imperial Valley north to the Central Valleys.

The flood of migrants became so large and the problem of providing relief and temporary housing so serious that the Los Angeles Police Department placed border "blockades" at sixteen points, including Yuma and Blythe, on the principal highways into California. The one at Yuma was at Winterhaven, within California, and on highways leading to San Diego as well as Los Angeles. The pretext was to prevent an influx of a criminal element, but a State Relief Administration report claimed that of 7984 persons checked at one point only 272 had police records.

San Diego authorities refused to participate in the blockades. The Mexican nationals who had done most of the farm work in San Diego County had begun a return to their homeland, because of the depression and labor troubles, and were being replaced by transient workers. In San Diego representatives of twenty governmental and private organizations combined to offer assistance to transients, and in one month 696 of them applied for help. In all of California help was given to 77,118 transients in the same time. By 1937 the number of migrants into the state had surpassed that of the Gold Rush of 1849-1850.

It was in the Imperial Valley where much suffering was experienced and the number of transients almost overwhelming. One family, with a blind baby and a tubercular mother, was unable to go any farther. Their auto was out of gas and one tire was flat. A State Relief Administration report described one of the migrant camps:

... many families were found camping out by the side of the irrigation ditches, with little or no shelter. One such family consisted of the father, mother, and eight children. The father hoped there would be some work in the valley later in the year ... the family had no home but a 1921 Ford. The mother was trying to chop some wood for the fire ... a meat and vegetable stew was being cooked in a large, rusty tin can over a grate supported by four other cans.

However, most of the transient families were able and willing to work and merely unfortunate victims of events beyond their control and public disapproval caused the removal of the blockades after about three months.

Transient laborers kept the relief rolls high but with the approach of war they began to melt into the New California. In San Diego in 1935 there were still 15,000 persons registered as unemployed at the federal-state employment service and the labor movement had drifted into disorganization. Harry Steinmetz, the teacher who had run unsuccessfully for mayor, led a group of radical candidates which seized control of the San Diego Labor Council of the American Federation of Labor. Accusing old-line members of being more interested in buying beer than in paying dues, he called for a new goal for organized labor in San Diego. He was quoted in the union newspapers as saying:

It must lie beyond bread and butter; the goal must be social. We must be welders of a new and better social order, even of a new civilization based upon production for use, competition of ideas, devotion to classless society, peace.

Charges of association of the new leaders with Communist front organizations led to intervention of the parent AFL organization. William Green, AFL president, appointed a representative from San Francisco to take charge of the San Diego council and he declared all offices vacant. What was happening in San Diego was happening elsewhere. The unemployed would be formed into separate militant unions and organized labor itself would be split into two major divisions and years of turmoil would follow.

Oddly enough, and despite the number of workers on relief, vacant housing was disappearing. The arrival of new settlers and the attraction to San Diego of a new class of industrial workers required by Consolidated Aircraft brought about a revival of home building, with 840 new homes constructed in 1935. The value of building permits doubled to five million dollars. Apartments and hotels enjoyed a measure of prosperity and revenue from tourists rose from fourteen to twenty million dollars.

Exceeding promises of its president, Major Fleet, Consolidated Aircraft had more than 2000 employes by December when the first pursuit plane under a $2,300,000 Army contract was completed. Six were to be delivered by February 17, and six more each month until the contract for fifty had been fulfilled. In his speech dedicating the new plant on Lindbergh Field, Fleet had said that he would have 3000 employes by the summer of 1936.

More significant than the producing of the first Army pursuit plane in the San Diego plant were the records being set by seaplanes developed and improved in subsequent models by Consolidated Aircraft under a military program to build a flying Navy of 1000 planes.

The aircraft industry which had persisted in Southern California introduced an era of advanced technology.
At San Diego in the middle 1930's Consolidated Aircraft was producing the "flying boats" which were helping to put the Navy into the air.
Here are PBYs. The famed war-time Catalina *evolved from the earlier models which set overseas flight records for the United States.*

In 1933 the Navy flew six P2Ys to Coco Solo in the Panama Canal Zone, a distance of 2059 miles, in twenty-five hours and twenty minutes. Early in 1934 a squadron of six P2Ys flew 1667 miles from Coco Solo to Acapulco, and then 1616 miles to San Diego. Several days later they went on to San Francisco and then headed across the ocean on a 2408-mile non-stop flight to Honolulu. They arrived at Pearl Harbor twenty-four hours and thirty-five minutes later, for another world record. President Roosevelt called the flight the "greatest undertaking of its kind in the history of aviation."

In October of 1935 an advanced version of the P2Y flew nonstop from the Canal Zone to San Francisco, 3281 miles, setting a new record for seaplanes. A new competition produced another version which was designated the PBY, or a patrol bomber. It was the famed *Catalina*.

An expansion of the Consolidated plant was begun in May of 1936 and two months later it received another Navy order, this time for fifty more patrol bombers to cost more than five million dollars. Another contract for more than six million was received in November, raising the total of patrol planes on order to 176 and contracts to more than eighteen million dollars. The number of employes rose to 3000.

The new *Catalinas* quickly demonstrated their capabilities in the Pacific early in 1937. A squadron of twelve flew non-stop from San Diego to Pearl Harbor and another squadron of twelve from San Diego to the Panama Canal.

Ryan Aeronautical Company's orders for its all-metal monoplane tripled in 1937 to $420,000 and Solar Aircraft Company reported sales of about $400,000 for exhaust manifolds and other airplane parts.

The threat of war was rising in Europe and military orders for airplanes were going to other aviation companies which had concentrated in the Los Angeles area, Douglas, Lockheed and North American. Adolf Hitler had defied the Versailles treaty of World War I and sent his army into the Rhineland. General Francisco Franco led a military revolt that brought civil war to Spain.

Because of the dominant position of the Navy in San Diego it was inevitable that North Island would pass entirely under its control. On October 25, 1935, the Army moved the last group of planes from Rockwell Field, to March Field near Riverside. It would take several years to close out all its operations there, however.

It was not a happy hour for the Army. In its record books for Rockwell Field were some of the most significant flights in the history of aviation. Most of the pilots who were reaching positions of command, just before the outbreak of the greatest of all the wars, had learned to fly at Rockwell Field, or had received much of their early training there.

When the exposition drew toward its scheduled close, there was a dispute as to whether it should be continued for another year or replaced by an annual fair of one month. The decision was to re-open for another season. The 1935 fair closed on November 11. The exposition corporation had spent $1,250,000 of its own money, of which $650,000 had come from paid-in subscriptions, $300,000 from advance ticket sales and $300,000 from the sale of exhibit space. The books were closed with $315,833 in the bank, enough to return half of what had been advanced and $75,000 in reserve to restore park areas to their former condition.

Total attendance was 4,784,811, but no effort had been made to determine how many of them had been out-of-town visitors or how much new money had been brought into the community. However, everyone was more than happy with the attendance and financial report.

The re-opening was scheduled for February 12. That day it rained. The fair never reached the attendance or revenue of 1935. Too many of the exhibits were no longer new and there was competition from fairs in other sections of the country. The Ford company along with other major exhibitors reduced or changed their exhibits. The magic had faded. The fair would stagger on until midnight on September 9, 1936, but the number of visitors to both runs of the fair would reach 7,220,000. While there was no large sum of cash to distribute at the end, the exposition did restore the community's confidence that its future must lie with its climatic and geographical advantages, and that there was "gold in the sun." It also left a series of buildings and an open air bowl which became permanent assets for residents as well as visitors.

The general success of the exposition also gave the business community renewed confidence in its own initiative. The depression was not the end of everything. In October of 1936, for example, one of the city's most spectacular fires destroyed the Whitney department store in the south half of the block bounded by Broadway and E and Fifth and Sixth streets. Within twenty-five working days, its owner, Guilford Whitney, had the store rebuilt, refurnished, restocked and reopened for business.

Even though the exposition was attracting money into the community in 1936 and there were many substantial federal works programs, the San Diego County delinquent tax list grew to 106 newspaper pages of fine print. Much of it represented property within the Mattoon districts and other large acreages on which owners simply chose not to pay taxes and to wait out the period of grace before forfeiture to the state.

Guilford H. Whitney

At long last the civic as well as official leadership in the city and county moved to lift the blight of the Mattoon Act which had removed so much property from the taxrolls and had limited its sale and development. A $2,600,000 county-wide bond issue was proposed to purchase more than $14,000,000 in outstanding improvement bonds. The assessments on the properties would be reduced to $1,381,000, which, when collected by the county, would go to help retire any remaining bonds.

E. G. Merrill Jr. was named chairman of a settlement campaign committee and James B. Abbey was selected to handle legal matters. The bond issue was approved by the voters on October 29, 1935. The major share of the bonds was bought up in four or five years at prices varying from fifteen cents to fifty cents on the dollar. Some bond holders held out, however, hoping that eventual increase in land prices would re-establish the value of their bonds. The last settlement was not made until thirteen years after the election.

The War Department had completed widening the bay channel and the WPA was contributing $2,500,000 for harbor and tidelands improvements. More than 200 acres were reclaimed by dredging, the airport enlarged, a seaplane landing area created and a taxi strip added. A baseball park was constructed at the foot of Broadway. Large areas of mud flats disappeared and in their place appeared paved streets lined with palm trees. The Harbor Drive so enthusiastically supported by the planner Nolen was beginning to take shape.

The deepening of the harbor kept alive San Diego's hopes of becoming a trading center of a region described as a "vast Western Empire" embracing Southern California, Arizona, New Mexico and northern Old Mexico.

Joseph Brennan

The voters of San Diego had committed themselves to six million dollars in port developments exclusive of more than five million expended, or to be expended, by the federal government. Yet, as the port authorities themselves said, "within the territory served by the port of San Diego lies a region practically unscratched."

Over the years dozens of citizens had given of their time without pay to serve as Harbor Commissioners, among them, Captain W. P. Cronan, U.S.N. retired; Major General R. H. Van Deman, U.S.A. retired; Rufus Choate and Emil Klicka, who worked with their port director, Joseph Brennan, to bring about the development of the harbor as one of the major ports of the Pacific.

*Major General
R. H. Van Deman*

There was a disappointment that the port had not produced the commerce so many had anticipated with the completion of the Panama Canal, which San Diego had celebrated with the staging of an exposition, and with the rapid growth of the West. Coastal shipping was beginning to decline in favor of trucking. After 1925 cargo tonnage had leveled off. The bulk of it was in military supplies, fish and petroleum products, very little of it representing goods in domestic and foreign trade.

San Diego liked to think of itself as the terminus of two great railroad systems, the Santa Fe and the Southern Pacific, when, in fact, it was at the end of branch lines. But the development of

The expansionist maneuvers of Japan brought a growing concentration of
United States naval forces in the Pacific.
The Navy was being enlarged by President Franklin D. Roosevelt and its light
forces were gathering in increasing numbers in the harbor of San Diego.
Many San Diegans always had believed that the city's future was in the
development of its harbor. Though they had seen this in terms of commercial
shipping, it was the Navy that fulfilled the port's promise.

trucking gave some promise of further penetrating the inland citrus growing areas, the farm lands of Imperial Valley, and the mining, cotton and cattle country of Arizona and New Mexico.

The attention that had been given to the harbor, and to keeping it relatively free of politics, however, did prepare it for war that was now approaching. And then another generation would find that those who had believed so much in the future possibilities of the port had been right all along.

Though San Diego was an "Air Capital" in the sense of military flying and in the production of airplanes, and though it was being served by the United Air Transport and Western Air Express, it remained, as in the case of the railroads, a branch-line town.

To almost everyone's surprise, Tijuana had surmounted the end of prohibition in the United States and the end of gambling in Mexico. It had become a prosperous town as well as a mecca for tourists who could visit a foreign country by day and return by

This is the site on which so many people had believed San Diego should group all public buildings.
The city lay at its back; the bay at its door.
After many years of disappointments, a Civic Center was created and one building started.
In a short time, however, the city became embroiled in a dispute over whether a new city jail and police station should be included in the Civic Center or on another waterfront site.

night. Betting at the Agua Caliente race track was not included in the ban on gambling and it continued to operate intermittently under various managements. Several attempts were made to re-open the hotel and resort without gambling but they failed, and President Cardenas ordered its expropriation under his land reform program on December 28, 1937. Hundreds of Tijuana's poor streamed into the golden rooms and bedded down, and it required a force of soldiers to evict them. It became a military school. The gambling hotel in Ensenada had been a failure from the beginning and the town remained off the tourist path.

In an unusual venture, the WPA also advanced a half million to the 22nd Agricultural District for new county fair grounds north of Del Mar, which was to include a grandstand and race track. In the summer of 1936 a franchise to conduct racing was granted to a combined Hollywood and San Diego group led by the singer Harry "Bing" Crosby. When money ran low Crosby and his associates advanced cash and the track was ready for racing on July 3, 1937.

At the City Hall Mayor Benbough chafed under the restraints the City Charter imposed on the power of the mayor and angrily protested that thousands of dollars were being paid to "fixers" to allow the operation of illegal enterprises and that prisoners were being inhumanely treated in the city jail.

Robert W. Flack

In the summer of 1935, after a long search, the City Council appointed a new city manager, the fifth in three years, to succeed George L. Buck. He was Robert W. Flack, forty-seven years of age, with eleven years of experience as a city manager in Durham, North Carolina, and Springfield, Ohio. His salary was set at $15,000 annually and he assumed his post on August 1.

One of the first tasks facing him was the problem of police administration and the need for new jail facilities. A year passed, with the mayor still unsatisfied regarding the police department, but Flack had the confidence of a majority of the City Council. In the summer of 1936 Flack recommended that a new police station and jail be constructed on a tidelands block facing Harbor Drive between F and G streets.

The recommendation came while the first building projected for the Civic Center was under construction ten blocks to the north at the foot of Cedar Street and future plans contemplated an adjoining Hall of Justice. Beyond the Civic Center site the Navy and Marines were maintaining the buildings and landscaping of the Marine Recruit Depot and Training Station in harmony with the development of the waterfront as envisioned by Nolen. The reaction was quick and sharp. One of the first protests came from Rufus Choate, a member of the Harbor Commission, who wrote to the City Council:

> I'm unalterably opposed to Flack's plan for a city jail on the waterfront because it violates all the precepts of the regulations governing the use of the harbor and tidelands for commerce, fisheries and navigation; it is a direct contravention of the policies of the Nolen Plan; and undoubtedly will be a constant source of derisive comment from the countless numbers of travelers who arrive in our beautiful harbor by the sea.

A former mayor, Harry C. Clark, appeared on the scene as head of a Citizens' Nolen Plan Committee. He was joined by Phil Swing, the former congressman, and Joseph Sefton Jr., the banker. Two other members of the Harbor Commission, Emil Klicka and General Van Deman, said they had not been aware that a Civic Center site was available and rather regretted having granted the city the right to use tidelands.

While Flack said he favored a Hall of Justice, he thought it should be restricted to courts and produced a telegram from Nolen which he interpreted as expressing opposition to the inclusion of a jail within the Civic Center. At the same time, Flack abandoned the F Street site when the Navy indicated it had its own plans for that area, and instead proposed a new site a block away on the south side of Market Street between Kettner Boulevard and

Pacific Highway. This adjoined the tidelands area being developed as Battery Park in accordance with the Nolen Plan.

The site was approved by the Council with only Mayor Benbough dissenting. This issue now was whether San Diego really wanted a planned, orderly development and a grouping of its public buildings, as had been the hope of so many for a generation. Edgar Hastings, chairman of the Board of Supervisors, said:

> The people have adopted a plan. Now we have a new council and a stranger as city manager, and they would forget the plan. I think they are in error. I'd like to build the complete Hall of Justice. If the city can start it, I'm for it.

The threat of legal action, indecision regarding plans and costs, and the uncertainty of a WPA grant, prolonged the dispute for more than a year.

Meanwhile, the Civic Affairs Conference, which had been organized to select candidates for the City Council who would pledge full support of the City Charter and the city manager form of government, elected three more councilmen in the Spring of 1937. All six members now owed their election to the volunteer organization.

Ignoring warnings from the mayor and the Chamber of Commerce, the Council proceeded to give final approval to manager Flack's plan to split the new police station and jail from the Civic Center site and brought about the removal from the Harbor Commission of Rufus Choate who had opposed the tidelands site. Supporters of the original Civic Center plan were divided on the jail issue. George Marston did not enter openly into the public controversy but along with Julius Wangenheim thought it would be a mistake to combine a jail, with all of its noise and confusion, with a Hall of Justice at the Civic Center.

There were others who always had opposed use of tidelands for anything but commerce. Two successive grand juries, however, urged a Hall of Justice adjoining the main Civic Center building and housing the jail and police station as well as courts. Directors of the Chamber of Commerce placed the blame for the controversy on the city manager personally.

The politically isolated mayor began a rear-guard fight against the Police Department and was aided by the *San Diego Sun* which jumped with fatal enthusiasm into a campaign against civic corruption. No suspicion of wrong-doing attached to Council members elected by the Civic Affairs Conference but they supported the manager and chief of police in a policy of an "open town" because of San Diego's status as a tourist city and as a military center.

*These three sketches show the "evolution" of a Civic Center—or, perhaps,
record the decline of a larger idea.*

*The sketch at the top is how the city and county administration building on
the tidelands was first conceived. The second shows how it was scaled down
to a more immediately practical concept. The third shows how the high
tower was sacrificed to the demands of aviation. The two bayside wings were
later eliminated.*

*This one building was the first and last of the ones originally planned for
the Civic Center.*

The discharge of a police officer, who complained of being punished for trying to suppress gambling on his beat, led to a Civil Service Commission hearing. Under the influence of one of its members, a woman attorney, Marie Herney, the commission subpoenaed ranking officers and members of the police vice squad and provided citizens with a close-up view of the regulation of vice. Gambling establishments were being opened only a few steps off Broadway in a manner reminiscent of the boom of the 1880's. The question of who decided what place was to operate, or not to operate, was not made clear, though Mayor Benbough had kept

President Franklin D. Roosevelt visited San Diego in 1938 to dedicate the administration building at the Civic Center.
The row over what other buildings should be erected there was laid aside while the President called attention to the motto above the entrance, that "The Noblest Motive is the Public Good."
That, he said, would ensure democracy. After the ceremony he boarded the U.S.S. Houston *for an equatorial cruise.*

insisting that $2000 a month was going somewhere or to someone for "protection."

While the arguments continued the Civic Center building was being completed without its tower, or campanile, which had to be sacrificed upon the insistance of airport authorities that it would be an obstruction to aviation. The $2,000,000 structure was dedicated on July 16, 1938, by the President of the United States. Roosevelt arrived at Los Angeles aboard a presidential train and then was driven to San Diego. While in his car, he looked up at the stately building and remarked that he was proud of San Diego and that the motto across its portal, "The Noblest Motive is the Public Good," insured eternal democracy. That afternoon he boarded the cruiser *Houston* for an equatorial cruise.

The civic armistice that had been declared for his visit came to an end. The WPA granted $166,500 toward construction of the $350,000 jail and police station. Petitions for a referendum and the filing of legal obstructions failed to halt the award of a contract to begin construction. In a sudden move, Flack resigned as city manager. While a search was under way for a successor the resignation was withdrawn and the Council voted six-to-one for his reinstatement.

Ham and Eggs agitates California

The civic controversy, however, was overshadowed by the Townsend movement and then by the rival "life warrants" pension plan which had been converted from "$25-Every-Monday-Morning" to "$30-Every-Thursday," and then became known simply as "Ham and Eggs."

On July 25, 1938, Archie Price, a sixty-four-year old man who had been on relief, committed suicide in Balboa Park. Some time before he had walked into a newspaper office and threatened to commit suicide. On his body were found notes in which he had written that he was "too young to receive an old-age pension and too old to find work." He was buried in a pauper's grave.

A month later promoters of the Ham and Eggs movement heard of Price and had his body exhumed. They led a caravan of 150 autos to San Diego where a second burial was conducted in a well-kept cemetery. Ham and Eggs was now so powerful that two leading Democrats, Culbert L. Olson, candidate for governor, and Sheridan Downey, candidate for the United States Senate, appeared at the ceremony before a crowd of 5000 to 6000 persons and expressed their feelings about the fate of Archie Price. His death was dramatized throughout the state and more than 750,000 persons signed petitions which qualified $30-Every-Thursday on the November ballot as an initiative measure.

Promoters try to capture the state

While Olson did not endorse Ham and Eggs, he did not directly oppose it. Downey, however, gave it his endorsement. Both were elected, Olson defeating the incumbent Republican governor, Frank Merriam, by about 220,000 votes. Ham and Eggs polled more than a million votes but fell short of winning by 255,000.

In San Diego County, the story was a different one. Olson led Merriam by a fairly wide margin of 9000 votes and Ham and Eggs had a majority of more than 3000.

The prevailing political discontent in San Diego had been accompanied by a slow but persistent decline in the fortunes of its biggest manufacturing plant, Consolidated Aircraft. New orders had not materialized and the company was coming to the end of production contracts for its Navy patrol bombers. The number of workers dropped from about 3000 to 1400.

Events in Europe and Asia had not yet alarmed the country. The promise of "peace in our time" followed British and French acceptance of the German dismemberment of Czechoslovakia. Then in Asia Japanese airplanes sank the U.S. gunboat *Panay* in the Yangtze River.

The situation changed in the Spring of 1939. Consolidated received seven and a half million dollar contracts to begin production of a four-engine "flying battleship" for the Navy and the first of 1000 four-engine attack bombers for the Army Air Corps. The Ryan Aeronautical Company's S-T trainer was adopted by the Army Air Corps and Ryan also introduced a new observation plane called the *Dragon Fly*.

The city election in the Spring gave Mayor Benbough the opportunity for which he had been waiting for two years. He announced for re-election and put up two Council candidates of his own to oppose those supported by the Civic Affairs Conference. Benbough vowed to "mow 'em down" and he did. He was overwhelmingly returned to office and his two Council candidates were elected. A third candidate who ran independently, Harley Knox, also won and the conference had lost its majority.

The city manager resigned. He had served four years, longer than any of his predecessors. Under the influence of the Civic Affairs Conference, the Council had become a policy body, as intended under the Charter; city government largely had been withdrawn from the political arena, and the authority of a city manager defined. The defeat of the city administration was a matter of policy. The people wanted a different kind of a city. The concept of an "open town" was gradually abandoned, as was being done in many other areas, and the police department reorganized along more professional lines.

But with the new police and jail building ready for occupancy, the plan of grouping public buildings on a landscaped waterfront site was dead, though there was no one to fully acknowledge it as yet. It had met the same fate as the original Nolen Plan for raising a "city beautiful" around the habor in the manner of the more famous Latin American and European port cities. Though the Nolen Plan would disappear from public attention, its recommendations would in a general way continue to influence the

Culbert L. Olson

Sheridan Downey

Harley Knox

235

planning and development of San Diego, and its orientation toward the bay, for recreation as well as commerce.

Flack's successor was Fred Rhodes, who had served as city manager of operation before the adoption of the City Charter and had been fired in the quarrels over development of water resources.

The Metropolitan Aqueduct had been completed and the first Colorado River water had arrived on the coastal plain. The All-American Canal was being readied for use and voters at last ratified the agreement that would enable San Diego to have its share of water delivered to the base of the mountains. The city agreed to pay an average of $15,000 a year for thirty-eight years to help defray operating costs and for the extra capacity built into the canal.

There had been successive wet years. In the 1936-1937 season there were sixteen inches of rain. El Capitan reservoir began to fill with the water coming down the San Diego River from the mountains. But below the dam the runoff from the surrounding hills caused a near-flood condition, with 14,200 cubic feet of water a second rushing to the sea. Without the dam there might have been heavy flood damage. In the 1916 flood, the flow had reached 70,200 cubic feet a second. In the Spring of 1938 water was going over the El Capitan Dam spillway. With the reservoirs brimming with water, and with acceptance of the All-American Canal contract, a bond issue to construct another dam on San Vicente creek of the San Diego River system was rejected.

On September 1 the German army invaded Poland. On September 3 Great Britain and France declared war. War still seemed remote to Californians, and the business community in San Diego as well as the state turned its attention to defeating a second attempt to force the Ham and Eggs scheme upon the state. The threat to the future of the state was clearly drawn. Among others, the president of Solar Aircraft, Edmund T. Price, warned that if the plan was adopted he would seek an East Coast site as "we feel we could not operate under the chaos which would undoubtedly follow."

The fever of social change was running down, however, and in November Ham and Eggs was defeated easily and even in San Diego County it lost by a margin of more than two-to-one.

A casualty of the times was the *San Diego Sun*. The death of E. W. Scripps had been followed by that of his son and the newspaper was of little interest to the men then in command of the Scripps-Howard chain. The days of the crusading newspaper and of poorly nourished multiple newspapers were drawing to a close. The *Sun*,

Voters got the message

with its excess of reformist zeal and its occasional support of socialistic causes, had lost much of the confidence of the community. It was offered to Colonel Copley and absorbed into his *Evening Tribune*.

Though Scripps-Howard may have had little faith in the future of San Diego, the city's population reached an estimated 182,000 by the end of 1939 and in addition there were 27,000 men in uniform. Some of the city's growth in population after 1936 could be attributed to annexations of subdivisions northeast of the city resulting from San Diego's refusal to increase water services and their prospect of having to construct their own sewage facilities.

The eight Navy and Marine establishments in San Diego County—the Naval Hospital, Marine Corps Base, Naval Training Station, Destroyer Base, Naval Air Station, Naval Fuel Depot, Naval Supply Depot and the Radio Station—embraced nearly 4000 acres and 634 buildings representing an investment of $51,000,000. The cost of development programs under way or soon to be under way was estimated at $29,000,000.

In May of 1940 the Nazis invaded Belgium and The Netherlands and on May 10 they crossed the French frontier and reached Paris two days later.

In September Consolidated Aircraft dedicated an addition to its plant and Major Fleet, the president, told a crowd of 5000 persons that "we came here with $6,000,000 worth of business . . . Today our backlog is $132,000,000." More than 9000 persons now were employed in the production of war planes.

The city's airport had been expanded to meet the demands placed upon it. Various dredging projects and exchanges of tideland properties with the Navy and Marines had enlarged the airport to 455 acres. In one of the last exchanges the city acquired sixty acres of tidelands in trade for 544 acres of city pueblo lands north of La Jolla for a Marine rifle range, Camp Mathews.

The Ryan company was training large numbers of flying cadets for the Army Air Corps. The number of employes at Solar rose to 700 and the backlog of orders to more than three million dollars. Fred H. Rohr, who had worked on Lindbergh's *Spirit of St. Louis*, resigned as factory manager for Ryan and set up his own company to provide special components for the aircraft industry. His operations started in a garage and were soon moved to a warehouse, and from there to a new plant of his own in Chula Vista.

The fleet of tuna clippers had grown in value to $10,000,000 and for a decade San Diego had been the leading tuna port of the Pacific. New "queens" of the sea had supplanted the *Atlantic*, the

Fred H. Rohr

The tuna clippers had covered many millions of square miles since the disappearance of the albacore and they had changed into small liners.
The Normandie *was 150 feet in length, equipped for handling 400 tons of tuna on a long voyage home.*
The fleet was valued at more than ten million dollars.
So improved were the clippers that in a few years two-thirds of them would serve their country, not as gatherers of food, but as fighting ships.

first of the tuna clippers, and ranged over an ocean area of more than two million square miles. The *Normandie*, 150 feet in length, and the *Queen Mary*, 149 feet, were equipped with brine refrigeration systems capable of handling 400 tons of tuna. Soon the redoubtable clippers would be offered to the government and two-thirds of them would see duty in war.

The rapid growth in population and in industrial and military facilities foreshadowed a crisis in water. But it was asking too much of San Diegans to anticipate what might happen almost overnight. And there was some comfort in the knowledge that they had the right to tap the All-American Canal whenever necessary. The first water had been turned into the canal the year before at a ceremony at Imperial Dam. At that time the water was not destined for the valley's farms but for seasoning the canal. The principal speaker was the Secretary of the Interior Harold Ickes. An interested spectator was Phil Swing, the former Republican congressman and principal author of the bill which made the canal as well as Boulder Dam possible. Democrats in charge of the program did not call upon him to speak. Swing was content, however, and told reporters, "I only took up the work of others and did my best ... let us all feel joyful."

A sharp earthquake occurred in Imperial Valley on May 18, 1940. There was a pronounced horizontal movement along forty miles of the Imperial fault which runs through the Imperial-Mexicali Valley. The epicenter was near the town of Imperial, where fifty percent of the buildings on the main street were damaged to a point of condemnation. Eight persons in the valley lost their lives.

Irrigation facilities were extensively damaged and a section of the All-American Canal had to be put into use before anticipated. Water was diverted from the old Alamo channel in Mexico into the new canal. East of Calexico the north embankment of a section of the canal was displaced more than fourteen feet and had to be rebuilt. It could not be placed in service until 1941. The formal dedication of the canal took place on October 12, 1940, and this time Swing was an honored guest and speaker.

Orders for water would be placed with the Bureau of Reclamation, for release at Boulder Dam 303 miles upstream from the Imperial diversion works. In 146 hours it would arrive at the farmer's

Riches were never taken from the soil of Imperial Valley without a struggle.
Water by "controlled" rain was applied with great difficulty and expense.
In 1940, before the All-American Canal was put into service, an earthquake ripped the valley.
This photograph shows the power and extent of the movement along the Imperial fault. On one side of the fault the secondary Yule Canal was abruptly moved sideways. A section of the north bank of the All-American Canal was moved fourteen feet.

For decades an argument had raged about whether San Diego should be
a city of smokestacks or geraniums.
World War II put an end to the debate. The little meager aviation industry
became a giant.
This photo shows a production line for B-24 bombers at Consolidated Aircraft
Corporation. Where once the aviation plants in San Diego had employed
several hundred, at the beginning of the war 20,000 were at work and more
thousands were to be hired.

240

control gate after having traveled 410 miles under controlled conditions through the main canal and its branch lines.

In 1938 the Mexican government had expropriated 287,000 acres of the Chandler lands in Lower California which had been dependent on Colorado River water for irrigation. But time would prove that this did not free the users on the United States side of the border from the threat of increasing appropriations in Mexico. New land owners took over and maintained and built up rights in a river that would never have enough water to meet all demands upon it.

The federal census of 1940 gave San Diego City a population of 203,341 and the county 289,348. The city had begun the Twenties with only 74,361. Los Angeles City had expanded to a million and a half. More than three million persons now resided in Southern California. Since 1930 the rate of growth of San Diego County had been more rapid than either Southern California or California as a whole.

When the figures were announced the San Diego Chamber of Commerce estimated that 30,000 new residents had arrived in San Diego since the census had been taken and by the summer of 1941 the city would have to absorb and house perhaps 45,000 more. In 1928 in San Diego there were only 232 persons in the aviation industry. Now there were 20,000. Consolidated's four-engine land bomber was designated the B-24 *Liberator* and was being produced at a record pace of one a day. On December 7, 1941, the Japanese bombed Pearl Harbor.

Gone forever was the peaceful harbor which Alfred Mitchell had painted in the early 1920's. This water color by Arthur Beaumont shows the cruiser San Diego returning to the harbor from war duty and the feverish activities which had come with the rapid expansion of the Navy and its many shore establishments. But nothing really had changed. The climate was still the same, the hills were still blue, and the bays and the ocean were alluring the year around. The issue of "geraniums vs. smokestacks" had a surprising answer.

EPILOGUE

When World War II began, the population of San Diego City had reached the predictions of what it would be in 1950. San Diego had been warned that when the population reached 260,000 and all its local sources had been developed, it should begin the long undertaking of going to the Colorado River for additional water. By 1944 the city's population was estimated to be 286,000 and it was expected to go over 320,000 in another year.

War-oriented companies operated around the clock. Consolidated's production of B-24 bombers jumped to a peak of 253 a month and a total of 6724 of them were to come off the lines at two San Diego plants. San Diego, which for so long had resented living in the shadow of Los Angeles, had become a city with industry but it was in an advancing technology that would continue to contribute to a different and individual course of development.

All military establishments in San Diego were expanded. The Navy spread out to Camp Elliott on Kearny Mesa north of San Diego, developed an Amphibious Base on the Coronado Strand, and took over some of the exposition buildings in Balboa Park. The Marines acquired more than 123,000 acres of historic Rancho Margarita in northern San Diego County. The Army established Camp Callan on Torrey Pines Mesa.

A county-wide shortage of water was imminent. As it was a center of the war effort, a lack of water could prove disastrous. The

Navy became alarmed. In 1943 the federal government entered into an agreement with the city and county to determine the most feasible method of obtaining additional water, whether by a connection with the Metropolitan Aqueduct or by way of the All-American Canal.

Little attention had been paid at the time to the fact that when the city filed for Colorado River water it also had included the "county of San Diego." This enabled the inclusion of the entire county in a County Water Authority organized in 1944. That same year President Roosevelt appointed a committee on San Diego water problems, which included Phil Swing, general counsel for the San Diego County Water Authority.

It soon became apparent that it was too late to consider the massive pumping system that would be needed to raise the water over or through the mountains from the All-American Canal to San Diego, or to build additional reservoirs entirely dependent on rainfall and which could not be filled even by the runoff of a number of successive wet years.

Before the year had ended Roosevelt sent a message to the Senate asking that it approve the report of the Committee on San Diego Water Problems and announced that he had directed the immediate construction by the Navy Department of a pipeline connecting the San Diego water system with the Metropolitan Aqueduct. Hearings were held in the Senate by a committee headed by Senator Sheridan Downey of California. Downey had lived down his support of Ham and Eggs and was taking leadership of California's legislative fights for water from the failing hands of Senator Johnson.

The War Production Board, however, interposed objections on the grounds of material shortages and asked for a year's delay. Conference followed conference and finally it was agreed that work should begin within ninety days. The first construction contract was awarded by the Navy Department on May 18, 1945.

The city of San Diego entered into an agreement to assure completion of the line regardless of when the war might be terminated. In 1946 voters of the city and county approved the transfer of the San Diego-Navy contract to the San Diego County Water Authority and the merger of the authority with the Metropolitan Water District. On December 11, 1947, the new aqueduct was dedicated and put into operation. The population of the city was estimated to be 367,000 and that of the county, 575,000. Even though there had been an average of almost sixteen inches of rain in six seasons, almost six inches above normal, if it had not been for the aqueduct San Diego would have been entirely out of water in 1947.

Before the war was over, however, Senators Downey and Johnson had lost California's battle to reduce the claims Mexico was making on the water of the Colorado River. The United States Senate approved a treaty which granted Mexico 1,500,000 acre feet of water annually. It was agreed the nations should share the waters of the Cottonwood-Tia Juana river system. It soon became apparent that the "last water hole" of the West would not be able to assure the future of Southern California, and the reach for water turned to new sources in the rain country of the distant north.

The war brought about a revolution in many phases of the economic and social life in all of California. And what of San Diego, and the conflicting aspirations of several generations, as to what kind of a city it should become?

Thousands of men who passed through the various military establishments, or visited the harbor on Navy ships, could not forget the climate or the setting between the bays and promised themselves that someday they would return. In this they were no different from the seamen of the days of the sailing ships who had seen the port as otter fur hunters or hide traders. And the thousands who came for war-time jobs, over the railroads and highways that followed the trails of the covered wagons of earlier migrations, also were to remain, as the others had before them.

Industry also had come. Those who had favored smokestacks over geraniums had won out in a civic struggle that had lasted seventy-five years. But those who had favored geraniums had not lost either. As a few of its more foresighted people had known, smokestacks and geraniums could exist side by side.

CHRONOLOGY

1920 Edward, Prince of Wales, addresses crowd of 25,000 in the city stadium.

1920 William Kettner retires from Congress and is succeeded by Phil D. Swing of Imperial County.

1920 Federal Census sets San Diego's population at 74,683.

1921 Claim for right to water filed on Colorado River.

1922 Navy expansion includes completion of hospital in Balboa Park, units of the Supply Depot and Destroyer Base.

1922 Lieutenants Oakley Kelly and John Macready set a sustained flight record of 35 hours and 18 minutes.

1922 Lieutenant James H. Doolittle sets flight record from Jacksonville, Florida, to San Diego of 21 hours and 19 minutes.

1923 U.S. Naval Training Station commissioned.

1923 Navy takes first aerial photographs of eclipse of sun above San Diego.

1923 Lieutenants Kelly and Macready make first transcontinental non-stop flight from Mitchell Field, New York, to San Diego, in 26 hours and 50 minutes.

1923 First airplane refueling in air completed over San Diego.

1923 Boulder Dam Association formed by representatives of Southern California counties.

1923 Dedication of first southern all-weather transcontinental highway terminating at San Diego.

1924 New electric railway line opened to Mission Beach and La Jolla.

1924 U.S.S. *Shenandoah* moors at San Diego at end of first dirigible transcontinental flight.

1925 City agrees to buy San Dieguito water system.

1925 John D. Spreckels opens new $4,000,000 amusement center at Mission Beach.

1925 Ryan Airlines, Inc. establishes air passenger service between Los Angeles and San Diego, first in the United States.

1926 E. W. Scripps dies on his yacht off the coast of Liberia, Africa.

1926 City Council adopts Second Nolen Plan as a guide.

1926 John D. Spreckels, financial patriarch of San Diego, dies.

1926 Route from Savannah, Georgia, to San Diego designated Highway 80.

1927 City voters approve a Civic Center on the tidelands.

1927 Metropolitan Water District organized.

1927 Charles Lindbergh leaves for St. Louis in his San Diego-built plane, *Spirit of St. Louis.*

1927 Lindbergh makes the first non-stop flight from New York to Paris.

1927 Lindbergh returns to San Diego to receive ovation of 60,000 persons in City Stadium.

1928 Ira C. Copley purchases *The San Diego Union* and *Evening Tribune.*

1928 President Coolidge signs Boulder Dam Project Act.

1928 Agua Caliente Hotel and Casino open in Baja California.

1928 Lindbergh Field dedicated.

1929 Tuna clipper *Atlantic* leads four vessels to Galapagos Islands tuna fishing areas.

1929 Prudden Aircraft Co. becomes Solar Aircraft Co.

1929 State Supreme Court rules City of San Diego entitled to all water of the San Diego River.

1929 Presidio Park and museum dedicated on 160th anniversary of first California mission.

1929 Stock market collapse and beginning of the Great Depression.

1929 New $1,800,000 Fox Theatre building dedicated.

1930 Tuna catch for first time exceeds 100 million pounds.

1931 New City Charter adopted for city manager form of government.

1931 New San Diego State College dedicated.

1931 U.S.S. *Saratoga,* Navy's newest aircraft carrier, enters San Diego harbor.

1932 Franklin D. Roosevelt elected President.

1932 San Diego County has 16,000 persons unemployed and 4000 families on direct relief.

1932 Dirigible *Akron* arrives from New Jersey; two men killed in mooring.

1932 Planes in Army-Navy review total 420.

1933 Gov. James Rolph Jr. orders bank holiday.

1933 Southern California earthquake kills 121 persons.

1933 Transfer of 200,000 acres of federal land establishes Anza-Borrego Desert State Park.

1933 The Navy flies six Consolidated P2Ys to Coco Solo, Canal Zone, in 25 hours and 20 minutes.

1933 Hard liquor restored with repeal of 18th Amendment.

1933 All-American Canal approved as an emergency project and $6,000,000 allocated to start work.

1934 Socialist Upton Sinclair makes unsuccessful bid for governor with his EPIC Plan.

1935 California Pacific International Exposition opens.

1935 Gambling banned in Mexico; Agua Caliente closes.

1935 Boulder Dam completed.

1935 Consolidated Aircraft Corporation dedicates new plant at Lindbergh Field after moving from Buffalo, New York.

1935 Groundbreaking ceremonies held for the Civic Center.

1935 Rockwell Field and all of North Island comes under Navy jurisdiction.

1936 San Diego's exposition reopens for a second season.

1936 WPA advances a half million dollars for construction of County Fair and race track at Del Mar.

1937 Squadron of Consolidated *Catalinas* flies non-stop from San Diego to Pearl Harbor, and another squadron from San Diego to the Panama Canal.

1938 Civic Center dedicated by President Roosevelt.

1938 Ham and Eggs pension measure fails in California; San Diego County supports it by a majority of more than 3000.

1939 Hitler invades Poland; two days later Britain and France declare war.

1939 Ham and Eggs again defeated; San Diego County conforms with other sections of the state.

1939 Metropolitan Aqueduct completed to Lake Mathews, the terminal reservoir.

1940 Formal dedication of All-American Canal.

1940 Consolidated Aircraft Corporation employment rises to 9000.

1940 Federal census gives San Diego City a population of 203,321 and the county 289,348.

1941 Japanese bomb Pearl Harbor.

MAYORS

1917-1921	Louis J. Wilde
1921-1927	John L. Bacon
1927-1931	Harry C. Clark
1931-1932	Walter W. Austin
1932-1934	John F. Forward, Jr.
1934-1935	Rutherford B. Irones
1935-1942	Percy J. Benbough

CITY MANAGERS

May, 1932-July, 1932	Horace Hervey Esselstyn
July, 1932-May, 1933	A. V. Goedell
May, 1933-Aug., 1934	Fred Lockwood
Aug., 1934-Aug., 1935	George L. Buck
Aug., 1935-May, 1939	Robert W. Flack
May, 1939-Oct., 1940	Fred A. Rhodes

GOVERNORS

1917-1923	William D. Stephens (Rep.)
1923-1927	Friend W. Richardson (Rep.)
1927-1931	Clement C. Young (Rep.)
1931-1934	James Rolph, Jr. (Rep.)
1934-1939	Frank F. Merriam (Rep.)
1939-1943	Culbert L. Olson (Dem.)

POPULATION

	1920	1930	1940
CALIFORNIA	3,426,861	5,677,251	6,907,387
SOUTHERN CALIFORNIA	1,347,050	2,932,795	3,572,363
LOS ANGELES	576,673	1,238,048	1,504,277
SAN FRANCISCO	506,676	634,394	634,536
SAN DIEGO	74,683	147,897	203,341
SAN DIEGO COUNTY	112,248	209,659	289,348
IMPERIAL COUNTY	43,453	60,903	59,740

San Diego County Incorporated Towns:

CHULA VISTA	1,718	3,869	5,138
CORONADO	3,289	5,424	6,932
EL CAJON	469	1,050	1,471
ESCONDIDO	1,789	3,421	4,560
LA MESA	1,008	2,513	3,925
NATIONAL CITY	3,116	7,301	10,344
OCEANSIDE	1,161	3,508	4,651

BIBLIOGRAPHY

Adams, H. Austin
The Man John D. Spreckels. *San Diego: Frye & Smith, Ltd., 1924.*
The Story of Water in San Diego. *Chula Vista: Denrich Press, n.d.*

Adams, J. H. N.
A Modern Flying Carpet. *San Diego Business, 1925.*
New Municipal Pier Finest on the Pacific. *San Diego Business, April 1925.*

Adams, John R.
San Diego Authors. *San Diego State College Press, 1960.*

Ambrose, W. Wade
Tuna History in San Diego From First Big Catch. *San Diego Business, Jan. 1950.*

Anderson, E. Robert
San Diego's Record of Home Building. *San Diego Magazine, April 1928.*

Armstrong, T. G.
Mission Beach and Diamond Jubilee. *San Diego Business, May 1925.*

Arnold, Charles E.
Forecasting San Diego's Future. *San Diego Magazine, Oct. 1929.*

Athearn, Leigh
A Study of the California State Relief Administration from 1935-1939. *Los Angeles: 1939.*

Barlow, Alice
San Diego's Scientific Library. *San Diego Magazine, July 1928.*

Barnes, N. R.
The Rise of Solar. *Western Flying, Dec. 1938.*

Barrett, Marvin
The Years Between: A Dramatic View of the Twenties and Thirties. *Boston: Little, Brown and Company, 1962.*

Batman, Richard Dale
Great Cities Grow on Citrus Lands. *Journal of the West, Vol. IV, No. 4, Oct. 1965.*

Baur, John E.
Health Seekers of Southern California. *San Marino: Henry E. Huntington Library, 1959.*

Beckler, Marion F.
Palomar Mountain: Past and Present. *Palm Desert: Desert Magazine Pess, 1958.*

Beebe, James L.
A Business Man Examines the Ham and Eggs Amendment. *Los Angeles Chamber of Commerce, address, Sept. 15, 1939.*

Bellon, Walter, and Fred T. Lane
A Condensed History of San Diego County Park System. *San Diego Board of Supervisors, 1944.*

Benchley, Mrs. Belle
My Life in a Man-Made Jungle: Balboa Park Zoo. *Boston: Little Brown, 1940.*

Bigger, Richard, and James D. Kitchen
Metropolitan Coast: San Diego and Orange Counties, California. *Los Angeles: University of California, Bureau of Governmental Research, 1958.*

Biographical Family Files
O. W. Cotton, Ed Fletcher, F. G. Forward, G. W. Marston, E. B. Scripps, J. D. Spreckels. *San Diego Historical Society, Special Collection.*

Bohme, Frederick G.
The Portuguese in California. *California Historical Society Quarterly, Vol. 35, No. 3, Sept. 1956.*

Boulder Dam Association
The Colorado River Boulder Canyon Project and the All-American Canal. *Los Angeles: Burdett Moody, 1925.*
The Story of a Great Government Project for the Conquest of the Colorado River. *Los Angeles, 1925.*

Brisbane, Arthur
Today. *San Diego Magazine, April 1930.*

Britt, Albert
Ellen Browning Scripps: Journalist and Idealist. *Oxford: Scripps College University Press, 1960.*

Broell, Percy C.
Presidio Park and Old San Diego, 1905-1937. *San Diego Historical Society, typescript, n.d.*

Brotherton, William P.
Aviation in San Diego. *Ryan Aeronautical Company, typescript, 1946.*

Brown, Giles T.
Ships That Sail No More: Marine Transportation From San Diego To Puget Sound, 1910-1940. *Lexington: University of Kentucky Press, 1966.*

Brown, Walton
A Historical Study of the Portuguese in California, 1542-1940. *University of Southern California, thesis, 1944.*

Byers, Edgar B.
Where Rail Meets Water. *San Diego Business, Sept. 1926.*

Caidin, Martin
Golden Wings: History of the U.S. Navy and Marine Corps in the Air. *New York: Random House, Inc. 1960.*

California Department of Motor Vehicles
What is DMV? *Sacramento: State Printing Office, 1964.*

California Department of Natural Resources, Division of Beaches and Parks
Torrey Pines State Park. *Sacramento: State Printing Office, n.d.*

California Department of Natural Resources, Division of Fish and Game
Canned Fishery Products, San Diego District, 1920-1927. *Typescript, 1947.*
The High Seas Tuna Fishery of California. *Sacramento: State Printing Office, Bulletin 51, 1938 (see: Godsil).*

California Department of Public Works, Division of Water Resources
San Diego County Investigation. *Sacramento: State Printing Office, Bulletin No. 48, 1935.*

California Fisherman
Tiger of the Sea. *Jan. 1929.*

California Pacific International Exposition
Special Collection. *San Diego Historical Society.*
Special Collection. *San Diego Public Library, California Room.*

California State Chamber of Commerce
Economic Survey of California and its Counties, 1942. *San Francisco: 1943.*

California State Relief Administration
Special Collection, 1934-1936. *San Diego Historical Society.*
Migratory Labor in California. *Sacramento: State Printing Office, 1936.*
Transients in California. *Sacramento: State Printing Office, 1936.*

California Unemployment Commission
Abstract of Hearing on Unemployment Before the California Unemployment Commission. *Sacramento: State Printing Office, April-May, 1932.*
Report and Recommendations to the San Diego County Welfare Commission. *Sacramento: State Printing Office, Nov. 1932.*

Campbell, Roy
Cultivating an Industry (Aircraft companies in San Diego). *Western Flying, Oct. 1927.*

Carroll, Leo
The San Diego & Arizona Eastern Railway. *San Diego & Arizona Eastern Railway Company, typescript, 1947.*

Caughey, John Walton
California. *Englewood Cliffs: Prentice-Hall, Inc., 1953.*

Chute, George R.
Albacore, To Be or Not To Be, Is Question. *The West Coast Fisheries, Aug. 1929.*
Albacore Depart After Dismal Season Closes. *The West Coast Fisheries, Sept. 1929.*

Citizens Aqueduct Celebration Committee
San Diego's Quest for Water. *San Diego: 1947.*

Clark, Harry C.
The Mass Flight and Dedication in Retrospect. *San Diego Magazine, Aug. 1928.*

Clark, John G.
From 22 Cents to $3,600,000 in 62 Years: A Review of San Diego Business Property Values. *San Diego Magazine, Oct. 1929.*

Clarkson, Edward Dessau
Ellen Browning Scripps, A Biography. *San Diego State College, thesis, 1958.*

Clayton, William
Correspondence and Papers, 1900-1934. *University of California Library, Los Angeles, Special Collection.*

Cleland, Robert Glass
California In Our Time, 1900-1940. *New York: Alfred A. Knopf, 1947.*

Cleveland, Daniel
San Diego's Pueblo Lands: How City Acquired Title. *San Diego Union, March 14, 1926.*

Colorado River Association
California and the Colorado River. *Los Angeles: 1949.*

Convair
Historical Background of Convair, A Division of General Dynamics Coroporation. *Typescript, 1955.*

Corps of Engineers, U.S. Army and U.S. Maritime Commission
The Port of San Diego, California. *Washington: U.S. Government Printing Office, Port Series No. 27, 1947.*

Cotton, Oscar W.
The Good Old Days. *New York: Exposition Press Inc., 1962.*

Cross, Ira B.
A History of the Labor Movement in California. *Berkeley, University of California Press, 1935.*

Cumming, Larry G.
Arizona's Stand in the Colorado Controversy. *University of Southern California, thesis, 1963.*

Cunningham, Frank
Pots and Pans But No Airplanes. *Popular Aviation, Nov. 1939.*

Darnell, William Irvin
The Imperial Valley: Its Physical and Cultural Geography. *San Diego State College, thesis, 1959.*

Davidson, Ed
Let's Do Business With One Another. *San Diego Business, 1925.*

Davidson, G. A.
Backing a Judgment of San Diego. *San Diego Magazine, Nov. 1929.*

Davis, Edward J. P.
The United States Navy and U.S. Marine Corps at San Diego. *San Diego: Pioneer Printers, 1955.*

Davis, Kenneth S.
The Hero: Charles A. Lindbergh and the American Dream. *Garden City: Doubleday & Company, Inc., 1959.*

Degelman, John
Tuna Harvest of the Sea. *National Geographic, Sept. 1940.*

Deventer, John H. Van, Jr.
The Story of Mahoney Ryan. *Air Transportation, Dec. 15, 1928.*

Digges, Jeremiah
In Great Waters: The Story of the Portuguese Fishermen. *New York: The Macmillan Company, 1941.*

Dillane, Allan Perry
A Historical Geography of the El Cajon Valley, San Diego County, California. *San Diego State College, thesis, 1964.*

Dispatcher
General Files, 1956-1965. *La Mesa: Railway Historical Society of San Diego.*

Dodge, Richard V.
San Diego's "Impossible" Railroad. *Dispatcher, Railway Historical Society of San Diego, No. 6, June 1956.*
Rails of the Silver Gate: The Spreckels San Diego Empire. *Pacific Railway Journal, 1960.*

Donnelly, John Eugene
The Old Globe Theater at San Diego, California. *University of California Los Angeles, thesis, 1957.*

Duncan, Douglas Ian
Ride and Relax on a Fifty Cent Pass. *Dispatcher, June 1964.*

Eaton Manufacturing Company
A Chronicle of the Aviation Industry in America: 1903-1947. *Cleveland: 1947.*

Edwards, Paul
The Athens of America. *San Diego Magazine, July 1928.*

Erwine, Sam
The 1935 Expo: Sally Rand and Midget Men to the Rescue. *San Diego & Point Magazine, June 1965.*

Farmer, Malcolm
San Diego's Museums. *San Diego Historical Society, typescript, 1946.*

Federal Writers' Project
San Diego, a California City. *American Guide Series, San Diego Historical Society, 1937.* California, a Guide to the Golden State. *American Guide Series, New York: Hastings House, 1939.*

First National Trust & Savings Bank of San Diego
1883-1943: Sixty Years in the Service of San Diego. *San Diego: Raymert Press, 1943.*

Fisher, J. Donald
A Historical Study of the Migrant in California. *University of Southern California, thesis, 1945.*

Flack, R. W.
San Diego Affairs, 1936-37. *San Diego: Office of the City Manager, 1937.* Civic Affairs, 1937-1938. *San Diego: Office of the City Manager, 1938.*

Fleet, Dorothy
Our Flight to Destiny. *New York, Vantage Press, 1964.*

Fleet, Reuben
Consolidated Aircraft Corporation Dedication Address. *Typescript, 1935.*

Fletcher, Ed
San Diego's National Highway: A Dream Come True. *San Diego Magazine, April 1930.* U.S. 80: Savannah to San Diego. *San Diego Magazine, Feb-Mar. 1931.*

Memoirs of Ed Fletcher. *San Diego: Pioneer Printers, 1952.*

Fowler, Lloyd Charles
A History of the Dams and Water Supply of Western San Diego County. *University of California Los Angeles, thesis, 1953.*

Gabriel, S. (ed.)
Who's Who in San Diego. *San Diego: S. Gabriel, 1936.*

Galbraith, John Kenneth
The Great Crash, 1929. *Boston: Houghton Mifflin Company, 1954.*

Gardner, Gilson
Lusty Scripps: The Life of E. W. Scripps. *New York, The Vanguard Press, 1932.*

Gardner, Kenneth A.
City Planning. *San Diego Business, series of six articles, 1925.*

Geiger, Louise Jarratt (ed.)
Where We Live: Our Spanish-named Communities and Streets (San Diego County). *San Diego: Myra Bedel Cockran, 1965.*

George, Marcel
The Townsend Plan in California, 1933-1936. *University of Southern California, thesis, 1953.*

Gildred, Philip L., and Theodore Gildred
Why We Chose San Diego. *San Diego Magazine, Oct. 1929.*

Glasscock, Carl Burgess
The Gasoline Age. *New York: The Bobbs-Merrill Co., 1937.*

Gleason, Sterling
Digging the World's Biggest Ditch (All-American Canal), *Popular Science, Oct. 1936.*

Godsil, H. C.
High Seas Tuna Fishery of California. *Sacramento: California State Printing Office, Bureau of Marine Fisheries, Bulletin 51, 1938.* Preliminary Population Study of the Yellowfin Tuna and the Albacore. *Sacramento: California State Printing Office, Bulletin No. 70, 1948.*

Goldberg, Alfred (ed.)
A History of the United States Air Force. *Princeton: D. Van Nostrand Co., Inc., 1957.*

Golden, Morley
T. Claude Ryan and San Diego. *Grant Club, "Mr. San Diego" address, Nov. 29, 1965.*

Goodhue, Bertram G.
The Architecture and the Gardens of the San Diego Exposition, 1915. *San Francisco: Paul Elder and Co., 1916.*

Greenwalt, Emmett A.
The Point Loma Community in California, 1897-1942. *Berkeley and Los Angeles: University of California Press, 1955.*

Gregory, Robert M.
Opening Up the Gate—and a Bridge: New Torrey Grade, Rose Canyon Road, First Avenue Bridge. *San Diego Magazine, Jan. 1931.*

Gudde, Erwin G.
1000 California Place Names: Their Origin and Meaning. *Berkeley, University of California Press, 1962.*

Hall, Mary Harrington
The Phenomenal First National. *San Diego & Point Magazine, Jan. 1966.*

Hamill, Sam
Small House Architecture in Southern California. *San Diego Magazine, April 1928.*

Hanna, Phil Townsend
The Wheel and the Bell: The Story of the First Fifty Years of the Automobile Club of Southern California. *Los Angeles: The Pacific Press, 1950.*

Hansen, Esther (ed.)
The Official Guide and Descriptive Book of the Panama-California Exposition. *San Diego: 20th Century Press, 1916.*

Hanson, Virgil Raymon
Mission Valley, San Diego County, California: A Study in Changing Land Use, 1769-1960. *University of California Los Angeles, thesis, 1960.*

Harbor Department, City of San Diego
Port of San Diego: Industrial and Harbor Data. *San Diego: Harbor Commission, Fiscal years 1928 through 1945.*

Hardy, Edward L.
The New State College. *San Diego Magazine, Sept. 1929.*
San Diego State Dedication, May 1, 2, 3. *San Diego Magazine, April 1931.*

Harper, J. C. (ed.)
Ellen Browning Scripps. *La Jolla: 1936.*

Hawes, William T.
The Pioneer Devolpment of Aviation in San Diego. *San Diego State College, thesis, 1953.*

Heilbron, Carl H.
History of San Diego County. *San Diego: Press Club, 1936.*

Heilbron, Fred A.
Water Scrapbook. *Fred A. Heilbron Collection, San Diego.*

Hepner, Frances K.
Ellen Browning Scripps: Her Life and Times. *San Diego State College, Friends of the Library, 1966.*

Hevener, Harold Guy
The Pueblo Lands of the City of San Diego, 1769-1950. *San Diego State College, thesis, 1950.*

Hewett, Edgar Lee, and W. Templeton Johnson
Architecture of the Exposition. *Santa Fe: Papers of the School of American Archaelogy, Archaeological Institute of America, No. 32, 1916.*

Higgins, Shelley J.
A River as Birthright. *San Diego Magazine, Aug. 1929.*
This Fantastic City, San Diego. *City of San Diego, 1956.*

Hind, Roebrt R., and Margaret Carry (eds.)
The Struggle for Boulder Dam and Other Reminiscences of Phil D. Swing. *Stanford University, typescript, 1965.*

Hine, Robert V.
California's Utopian Colonies. *San Marino: Henry E. Huntington Library, 1953.*

Hobson, Hal
San Diego's National Highway Problem. *San Diego Magazine, March 1929.*

Hopkins, Harry C.
History of San Diego: Its Pueblo Lands and Water. *San Diego: City Printing Co., 1929.*

Horan, James D.
The Desperate Years. *New York: Crown Publishers, Inc., 1962.*

Hoyt, Roland S.
Landscaping Presidio Park. *San Diego Magazine, July 1929.*

Hundley, Norris, Jr.
Dividing the Waters. *Berkeley and Los Angeles: University of California Press, 1966.*

Hunt, Rockwell D.
Fifteen Decisive Events of California History. *Los Angeles Historical Society of California, 1959.*

Imperial Irrigation District
The Boulder Dam All-American Canal Project. *El Centro: 1924.*
Historic Salton Sea. *El Centro: 1965.*

Interviews
San Diego County Residents. *San Diego Historical Society, Special Collection, 1956-1962.*

Jackson, H. R.
Metropolitan Port Development. *San Diego Business, Jan. 1926.*

Jaeger, Hester Scott
Nolen Plan Enhances San Diego's Natural Setting. *San Diego Magazine, Oct. 1929.*

Jahns, Richard H.
The Gem Deposits of Southern California. *Engineering and Science Monthly, Vol. XI, No. 2, Feb. 1948.*

Jahns, Richard H., and Lauren A. Wright
Gem and Luthium-bearing Pegmatites of the Pala District, San Diego County. *San Francisco: California State Division of Mines, Special Report 7-A, 1951.*

James, George Wharton
Exposition Memories: Story of the San Diego Exposition, 1916. *Pasadena: The Radiant Life Press, 1917.*

Jensen, Joan M.
Irving Gill: San Diego's Progressive Architect. *San Diego County Historical Convention, address, 1965.*

Johnson, Hiram
Correspondence and Papers. *Bancroft Library, University of California, Special Collection.*

Johnson, W. Templeton
The Architecture of the Serra Museum. *San Diego Magazine, July 1929.*

Jones, O. J.
Rancho Santa Margarita Y Las Flores. *San Diego State College, thesis, 1957.*

Larsen, Charles
The EPIC Movement in California Politics, 1933-1934. *University of California, Berkeley, thesis, 1945.*

Lindbergh, Charles A.
We. *New York: G. P. Putnam's Sons, 1927.*

Literary Digest
San Diego Ready to Greet World Again (California Pacific International Exposition). *May 18, 1935.*

Long, Baron
Charm of Old Mexico Idealized at New Agua Caliente Hotel. *San Diego Magazine, March 1928.*

Los Angeles County Museum
Irving Gill: Los Angeles County Museum and La Jolla Art Center. *Los Angeles: 1958.*

Los Angeles Times
General Files, 1920-1940.

Lutz, Carl Lewis
The San Diego County Citrus Industry. *San Diego State College, thesis, 1964.*

McCoy, Esther
Five California Architects. *New York: Reinhold Publishing Corporation, 1960.*

McGrew, Clarence Alan
San Diego and San Diego County. *Chicago and New York: The American Historical Society, 2 Vols., 1922.*

McIntosh, Clarence
Upton Sinclair and the EPIC Movement, 1933-1936. *Stanford University, thesis, 1955.*

McLean, Robert R.
Avocados Race Citrus Over San Diego County. *San Diego Magazine, Jan. 1930.*

McMullen, James
The City Plan for San Diego. *San Diego Business, July 1926.*

McMullen, Jerry
Elegy on the Waterfront: Panama Pacific Arrivals Were Wet and Welcome. *San Diego Union, Dec. 15, 1963.*

McPherson, Orville
San Diego—Air Capital of the West. *San Diego Business, Sept. 1926.*
Southern California Proving Ideal Center for Aircraft Manufacturing. *San Diego Magazine, Aug. 1928.*

McWilliams, Carey
Factories in the Field. *Boston: Little, Brown and Company, 1939.*
Brothers Under the Skin. *Boston: Little, Brown and Company, 1943.*
Southern California Country. *New York: Duell, Sloan and Pearce, 1946.*

Macaulay, T. C.
Capitalizing on the Air Capital. *San Diego Magazine, Feb. 1928.*
North Island—Cradle of Army Aviation. *San Diego Magazine, Aug. 1928.*

Macay, Bruce
Daily Air Service Inaugurated Between San Diego, Imperial Valley and Los Angeles. *San Diego Magazine, Jan. 1929.*

Marquis, A. N. (ed.)
Who's Who in the West. *Chicago: A. N. Marquis Company, 1958.*

Marston, Mary Gilman
George White Marston: A Family Chronicle. *Los Angeles: Ward Ritchie Press, 2 Vols., 1956.*

Mattoon Settlement Campaign Committee
Mattoon Statisical Comparative Data—All Districts. *James B.*

Abbey Collection, San Diego, chart and map, June 30, 1934.

Mayo, Dwight E.
Arizona and the Colorado River Compact. *Arizona State University, thesis, 1964.*

Meadows, Don
Baja California, 1553-1950. *Los Angeles; The Plantin Press, 1951.*

Meixner, G. Donald
Historical Development of Water Utilization. *Prepared for the California State Water Resources Board, typescript, 1952.*

Melendy, H. Brett, and Benjamin F. Gilbert
The Governors of California: From Peter H. Burnett to Edmund G. Brown. *Georgetown, Calif: The Talisman Press, 1965.*

Metropolitan Water District of Southern California
History and First Annual Report. *Los Angeles: June 30, 1938.*
The Colorado Aqueduct. *Los Angeles: 1939.*
The Great Aqueduct. *Los Angeles: 1941.*
Water for the People: An Outline of the Metropolitan Water District Aqueduct from the Colorado River. *Los Angeles: 1962.*

Miller, H. L.
San Diego Boats Play Hide and Seek with Tuna. *The West Coast Fisheries, Dec. 1929.*

Millikan, Frank M.
Commercial Banking in San Diego County. *San Diego State College, thesis, 1960.*

Mills, John P.
Life Story of John P. Mills. *Writers Guild of American West, Inc., typescript, n.d.*

Mitchell, Fred B.
Safely Flying Over a Million Miles. *San Diego Magazine, Oct. 1929.*

Moore, Floyd Roscoe
San Diego Airport Development. *San Diego State College, thesis, 1960.*

Moore, J. M. (ed.)
Moore's Who is Who in Cali-

fornia. *Los Angeles: John M. Moore, 1958.*

Moore, Winston and Marian
Out of the Frying Pan (Ham and Eggs Campaign). *Los Angeles: DeVorss & Co., 1939.*

Mowry, George Edwin
The California Progressives. *Berkeley and Los Angeles: University of California Press, 1951.*

Mury, Maude (ed.)
The Tuna Industry of San Diego. *San Diego: Works Progress Administration, 1936.*

Nadeau, Remi A.
The Water Seekers. *Garden City: Doubleday & Co., 1950.*
Los Angeles from Mission to Modern City. *New York: Longmans, Green and Company, 1960.*

Nelson, Herbert J.
The Port of San Diego. *San Diego State College, thesis, 1956.*

Neuhaus, Eugen
San Diego Garden Fair: The Art of the Exposition. *San Francisco: Paul Elder, 1916.*

Nolen, John
City Plan for San Diego, California. *San Diego: City Planning Commission, 1926.*

Pacific Fisherman
Decade of Drama and Development, 1923-1932. *Aug. 1952.*

Parker, Horace
Anza-Borrego Desert Guide Book. *Palm Desert: Desert Magazine Press, 1957.*

Parker, Zelma
History of the Destitute Migrant in California, 1939-1940. *University of California, Berkeley, thesis, 1940.*

Parmalee, E. F.
Private Record: Chronicle of Interesting Events, 1899-1936. *San Diego Historical Society, typescript.*

Pettitt, George A.
So Boulder Dam Was Built. *Berkeley: University of California Press, 1935.*

Porter, Sam
San Diego Gets Support of Other Cities in State Highway Fight. *San Diego Magazine, Sept. 1926.*
Seeing San Diego by Automobile. *San Diego Magazine, June 1928.*
The Mathematics of San Diego County Fifty Mile Highway Building Program. *San Diego Magazine, March 1929.*

Pourade, Richard F.
The History of San Diego: The Explorers, Time of the Bells, The Silver Dons, The Glory Years, Gold in the Sun. *San Diego: The Union-Tribune Publishing Co., 5 Vols., 1960, 1961, 1963, 1964 and 1965, respectively.*

Price, Edmund T.
Solar Aircraft Scrapbooks, 1927-1942. *E. T. Price Collection, San Diego.*

Raber, W. F.
San Diego's Vacation Attractions Broadcast by Four'Fold Advertising Campaign. *San Diego Magazine, June 1929.*

Rae, John B.
The American Automobile: A Brief History. *University of Chicago Press, 1965.*

Raitt, Helen
Give Us Room: History of Scripps Institution of Oceanography. *San Diego, Radio KGB, broadcast, Dec. 17, 1961 and Jan. 28, 1962.*

Rathbun, Morris M.
Lower California Awakens. *Touring Topics, Oct. 1927.*

Read, Eddie
Bing's Baby. *San Diego & Point Magazine, July 1967.*

Ready, Lester S., Louis C. Hill and J. P. Buwalda
Report on Program of Water Development, the City of San Diego and the San Diego Metropolitan Area. *San Diego: Municipal Employees' Association, 1937.*

Requa, Richard S.
The Architectural Style for Southern California. *San Diego Business, Oct. 1926.*

Inside Lights on the Building of San Diego's Exposition: 1935. *San Diego: Frye & Smith, Ltd., 1937.*

Rhodes, Fred A.
San Diego's Plan of Water Development. *San Diego Business, Oct. 1926.*

Rider, A. F.
Rider's California, a Guidebook for Travelers. *New York: The Macmillan Co., 1925.*

Roesti, Robert M.
An Economic Analysis of the Tuna Canning Industry. *Journal of the West, Vol. IV, No. 4, Oct. 1965.*

Rick, Glenn A. and Charles W. Eliot
Old San Diego: Plans for Development. *San Diego City Planning Commission, 1946.*

Ridgely, Roberta
The Zoo Story. *San Diego & Point Magazine, April 1966.*
When Caliente Was Queen of Spas. *San Diego & Point Magazine, July 1966.*
Tijuana, 1920: Prohibition Pops the Cork. *San Diego & Point Magazine, May 1967.*

Rohr Magazine
Special Anniversary Issue. *Chula Vista: Summer, 1965.*

Rolle, Andrew F.
California: A History. *New York: Thomas Y. Crowell Co., 1963.*

Romer, Margaret
The Story of Los Angeles. *Journal of the West, Part I through Part VIII, Oct. 1962-Oct. 1964.*

Rush, Philip S.
History of the Californias. *San Diego: Philip S. Rush, 1958.*

Ryan Aeronautical Company
Thirtieth Anniversary Issue. *Ryan Reporter, 1952.*
Background of Manufacture of "Spirit of St. Louis." *San Diego, typescript, 1953.*

Ryan, Frederick L.
A History of the San Diego Labor Movement. *San Diego State College Press, 1959.*

Ryan, T. Antoinette
An Analysis of the Relation Between Old Age Assistance and Organized Pension Plans in California, 1931-1951. *Sacramento State College, thesis, 1951.*

Safley, J. C. (ed.)
The Copley Press. *San Diego: The Copley Press, Inc., 1953.*

Salmons, Frank
San Diego County: The Gem County of California. *San Diego Magazine, May 1928.*

San Diego Board of Education
100 Years of Public Education in San Diego, 1854-1954. *San Diego Unified School District, 1954.*

San Diego Business
General Files, 1925-1926; 1932-1945. *San Diego Chamber of Commerce.*

San Diego, California
Charter of the City of San Diego California, as Amended. *Adopted, 1931.*

San Diego California Club
Where Life Means Most. *San Diego Chamber of Commerce, 1919.*
Pertinent Facts Concerning San Diego, California: City and County. *San Diego County Board of Supervisors, 1923.*
Community Advertising Pays. *San Diego Business, May 1926.*

San Diego Chamber of Commerce
San Diego: A Base for the Light Forces of the United States Fleet. *San Diego: 1933.*
The Aviation Industry Looks to San Diego. *San Diego: 1940.*
City of San Diego Building Permits, 1916-1961. *Building Inspector's Office, report, 1961.*
Minute Books, 1920-1945. *San Diego Public Library.*
San Diego 1966 Business Survey. *San Diego: 1966.*

San Diego County Tax Collector's Office
Financial Statement of San Diego County, Fiscal Year Ended June 30, 1949 (comparative statement of tax delinquency, 1935-1949). *San Diego: 1949.*

San Diego Department of Motor Vehicles
San Diego County Motor Vehicle Registrations, 1920-1959. *San Diego Chamber of Commerce Research Department, report.*

San Diego Directory Company
San Diego City Directory. *Yearly editions, 1920-1945.*

San Diego Magazine
General Files, 1926-1932. *San Diego Chamber of Commerce.*

San Diego Sun
General Files, 1920-1939.

San Diego Tax Assessor's Office
Analysis of Credit Position of San Diego. *Report, 1934.*

San Diego Tourist and Convention Bureau
Visitor, Industry Report. *Typescript, 1965.*

San Diego Union
General Files, 1920-1945.

Sanders, Eric
San Diego Electric Railway Company's No. 2 Line Has Long History. *Dispatcher, June 1962.*
Santa Fe's Surf Line. *Dispatcher, Oct. 1965.*

Scofield, W. L.
History of Kelp Harvesting in California. *Sacramento: California State Printing Office, reprint from California Fish and Game, Vol. 45, No. 2, July, 1959.*

Scripps College Bulletin
Ellen Browning Scripps: Woman of Vision. *Claremont: Scripps College, 1959.*

Scripps, E. W.
Damned Old Crank: A Self-Portrait of E. W. Scripps from His Unpublished Writings. *New York: Harper & Brothers Publishers, edited by Charles R. McCabe, 1951.*

Sears, George W.
Financing the Tuna Fleet. *New Brunswick: Graduate School of Banking, American Bankers Association at Rutgers University, thesis, 1950.*

Seifert, Frank W.
Aviation Scrapbook. *F. W. Seifert Collection, San Diego.*

Serra, Junipero, O.F.M.
Letter from Viceroy Antonio Bucarelli Y Ursua (concerning the rights and use of San Diego River water and relocation of San Diego Mission). *Bancroft Library, Special Collection.*

Simmons, Ralph B.
Boulder Dam and the Great Southwest. *Los Angeles: Pacific Publishers, 1936.*

Simpich, Frederick
San Diego Can't Believe It (World War II boom, 1943-1945). *National Geographic Magazine, Jan. 1942.*

Sinclair, Upton
I, Governor of California, and How I Ended Poverty: A True Story of the Future. *Los Angeles: 1933.*
I, Candidate for Governor, and How I Got Licked. *New York: 1934.*

Smythe, William E.
The Conquest of Arid America. *New York: The Macmillan Company, 1905.*

Solar Blast
Solar: 30th Anniversary Issue, 1927-1952. *San Diego: Solar, 1952.*

Sorenson, Ethelyn
John D. Spreckels and San Diego. *University of California, Berkeley, thesis, 1948.*

Southern California Writer's Project
Balboa Park, San Diego, California. *San Diego: The Association of Balboa Park Institutions, 1941.*

Standard Oil Bulletin
Spanning Four Hundred Years: The San Diego "Garden Fair." *The Standard Oil Company of California, Oct. 1934.*

Steere, Collis H.
Imperial and Coachella Valleys: An Illustrated Guide. *Stanford University Press, 1952.*

Steinbeck, John
In Dubious Battle. *New York: 1936.*

The Grapes of Wrath. *New York: 1939.*

Stewart, Don M.
Frontier Port. *Los Angeles: Ward Ritchie, 1966.*

Swanson, Walter S.
The Thin Gold Watch: A Personal History of the Newspaper Copleys. *New York: The Macmillan Company, 1964.*

Swing, Phil D.
Correspondence and Papers. *University of California Los Angeles Library, Special Collection.*
Memoirs. *Edited by Robert R. Hind and Margaret Carry (see: Hind), Stanford University, typescript, 1965.*

Terrell, John Upton
War for the Colorado River. *Glendale: Arthur H. Clark Co., 1965.*

Title Topics
The Story of Del Mar, *Jul.-Aug. 1948;* Rancho Santa Fe, *Jan.-Feb. 1949;* San Diego's Beach Communities, *Jul.-Aug. 1950;* Gliders to Rockets . . . San Diego Leads the Way, *Jan.-Feb. 1951;* Tuna . . . San Diego's Most Important Crop, *Sept.-Oct. 1951;* Buried Treasure . . . San Diego County's Mining Industry, *Nov.-Dec. 1951;* San Diego Society of Natural History, *Nov.-Dec. 1951;* Aviation in San Diego, 1883-1952, *March-Apr. 1952;* Chula Vista, *Jan.-Feb. 1953;* Balboa Park: San Diego's All-Year Playground, *May-Jun. 1954;* Palomar: Highway to the Stars, *Jan.-Feb. 1956;* Highways and Freeways, *July-Aug. 1959. San Diego: Title Insurance & Trust Co.*

Tout, Otis B.
The First Thirty Years in Imperial Valley, California, 1901-1931. *San Diego: Arts & Crafts Press, 1931.*

Travis, Donald
A Study of Technocracy: The Theory and the Movement. *Sacramento State College, thesis, 1957.*

Tuna Fishing
Special Collection. *San Diego Public Library, California Room.*

United Air Lines
Report on Air Service in San Diego, 1927-1967. *San Diego United Air Lines Office, typescript, 1967.*

United States Department of Commerce, Census Bureau
Real Property Inventory. *San Diego: Civil Works Administration, Special Census, 1934.*

United States Department of Interior, Bureau of Reclamation
Boulder Canyon Project. *Washington: U.S. Government Printing Office, Final Reports, 1938.* The Contribution of the All-American Canal System, Boulder Canyon Project, to the Economic Development of the Imperial and Coachella Valleys, California, and to the Nation. *Washington: U.S. Government Printing Office, 1956.*
The Story of Hoover Dam. *Washington: U.S. Government Printing Office, Conservation Bulletin No. 9, 1961.*

United States Department of Interior, Fish and Wildlife Service
The California Tuna Fishery. *Washington: U.S. Government Printing Office, Special Scientific Report No. 104, 1952.*

United States Senate
Problems of Imperial Valley and Vicinity. *Washington: U.S. Government Printing Office, Document 142, 1922.*

Vincenz, Jean Lacey
San Diego Metropolitan Government. *San Diego State College, thesis, 1958.*

Wales, R. Ellis
The Why of the San Diego-California Club. *San Diego Business, Aug. 1926.*

Wangenheim, Julius
The Story of Presidio Hill. *San Diego Magazine, July 1929.*
An Autobiography, 1941. *California Historical Society Quarterly, 5 parts, June 1956 through June 1957.*

Waters, Frank
The Colorado. *New York: Rinehart & Company, 1946.*

Webber, Lane D.
The Case Against the Park Site for State College. *San Diego Business, Oct. 1926.*

Weber, F. Harold, Jr.
Mines and Mineral Resources of San Diego County, California. *Sacramento: California Division of Mines and Geology, County Report III, 1964.*

Wector, Dixon
The Age of the Great Depression, 1929-1941. *New York: The Macmillan Company, 1948.*

Wegeforth, Harry Milton, and Neil Morgan
It Began With a Roar: Story of the San Diego Zoo. *San Diego: Pioneer Printers, 1953.*

West Coast Fisheries, The
A Fisherman's Dream of a Tuna Clipper, *June 1929;* Another Stride in Tuna Boat Building is Taken as California Crafts Are Launched, *July 1929;* The Fishing and Boat-Building Industries of San Diego, *Sept. 1929;* Albacore: Its Range and Season in Domestic Waters of the Western American Coast, *Jan. 1930;* Great Tuna Fleet at San Diego, *Jan. 1931;* Tuna Fishing in Southern Seas, *De Luxe Reference Number, 1931.*

Whitaker, Thomas W. (ed.)
Torrey Pines State Reserve. *La Jolla: The Torrey Pines Association, 1964.*

Wilbur, Ray Lyman and Elwood Mead
Construction of Hoover Dam. *Washington: U.S. Government Printing Office, 1935.*

Wilbur, Ray Lyman and Northcutt Ely
Hoover Dam Documents. *Washington: U.S. Government Printing Office, 1948.*

Women's Regional Planning Club
Historical Series. *San Diego: KGB Radio Station Broadcast, 1961-1963.*

Woodbury, David O.
The Glass Giant of Palomar. *New York: Dodd, Mead & Co., 1939.*
The Colorado Conquest. *New York: Dodd, Mead & Co., 1941.*

Works Progress Administration, Division of Social Research
Urban Workers on Relief. *Washington: Gov. Printing Office, 1936.*

ACKNOWLEDGEMENTS

James B. Abbey, Walter Ames, Philip L. Gildred, Fred Heilbron, Arnold Klaus, Edmund T. Price, T. Claude Ryan, William Sharp, and William Wagner; Henry Huntington Library and Art Gallery and Robert Dougan, Librarian; Imperial Irrigation District and William J. Stadler, Public Information Officer; Junipero Serra Museum and San Diego Historical Society; Metropolitan Water District; San Diego Public Library, Mrs. Zelma Locker, former Librarian California Room, and Mrs. Marion Buckner, present Librarian; San Diego State College Library and Mrs. Mildred LeCompte, Library Assistant; San Diego Tuna Boat Association and Edward P. Silva, Executive Vice President.

ART SOURCES AND CREDITS

Acknowledgement for providing pictorial materials is made to the following institutions and individual collections, which are indicated in the Index to Illustrations by key initials:

Specially commissioned paintings by Arthur Beaumont, Los Angeles (AB); Alfred Mitchell, San Diego (AM); Bancroft Library, University of California, Los Angeles (B); Bureau of Reclamation, Department of Interior, Washington, D.C. (BofR); C. Arnholt Smith, San Diego (CAS); Edmund T. Price, San Diego (ETP); Fine Arts Society of San Diego (FAS); General Dynamics, Convair Division, San Diego (GD); Huntington Library and Art Gallery, San Marino (H); Harry Crosby, San Diego (HC); Image, Art Division of Frye & Smith Ltd., San Diego (I); Imperial Irrigation District, El Centro (IID); Joe B. Marques, San Diego (JBM); Los Angeles *Times* (LAT); Los Angeles Department of Water and Power (LAWP); Metropolitan Water District, Los Angeles (MWD); Old Town Gallery, San Diego (OTG); Ryan Aeronautical Company, San Diego (R); San Diego Chamber of Commerce (SDCC); San Diego Public Library (SDPL); Samuel W. Hamill, San Diego (SWH); Title Insurance & Trust Company, San Diego (T); Tuna Boat Association, San Diego (TBA); United Air Lines, San Diego (UAL); University of Southern California, Los Angeles (UofSC); Union-Tribune Publishing Company Library, San Diego (U-T); Vernon Brown, San Diego (VB); Ward Ritchie, Los Angeles (WR); Wilmer Shields, San Diego (WS); Mrs. William Templeton Johnson, San Diego (WTJ).

INDEX TO ILLUSTRATIONS

INDEX

This sixth volume of the History of San Diego was designed by Cas Duchow, Art Director for Anderson, Ritchie & Simon. Lithography by Anderson, Ritchie & Simon, on Hamilton Louvain 80 pound text. Typography by Computer Typesetting. The text used in this book is Century Schoolbook. Binding is by Pacific Library Binding Co.